Istanbul
day BY day
3rd Edition

First & Second Editions by
Emma Levine
Updated by Terry Richardson
& Rhiannon Davies

FrommerMedia LLC

Contents

Published by:

Frommer Media LLC

Copyright © 2015 FrommerMedia LLC, New York, NY. All rights reserved. No part of this publication may be reproduced, stored in a retrieval system or transmitted in any form or by any means, electronic, mechanical, photocopying, recording, scanning or otherwise, except as permitted under Sections 107 or 108 of the 1976 United States Copyright Act, without the prior written permission of the Publisher. Requests to the Publisher for permission should be addressed to Support@FrommerMedia.com.

Frommer's is a trademark or registered trademark of Arthur Frommer.

ISBN: 978-1-628-87136-4 (paper); 978-1-628-87137-1 (ebk)

Editorial Director: Pauline Frommer
Editor: Michael Kelly
Production Editor: Donna Wright
Photo Editor: Ellen Herbert
Cartographer: Elizabeth Puhl
Compositor: Heather Pope
Indexer: Maro Riofrancos

Front cover photos, left to right: Glass of Turkish tea, Istanbul © Saida Shigapova/Shutterstock.com; Interior of Süleymaniye Mosque, Istanbul © Mesut Dogan/Shutterstock.com; Fisherman along the coast of the Bosphorus, Istanbul © guroldinneden/Shutterstock.com.

Back cover photo: Rug fabric at Istanbul bazaar © CREATISTA/Shutterstock.com.

For information on our other products and services, please go to Frommers.com.

Frommer's also publishes its books in a variety of electronic formats. Some content that appears in print may not be available in electronic formats.

Manufactured in China

5 4 3 2 1

About This Book

Organizing your time. That's what this guide is all about.

Other guides give you long lists of things to see and do and then expect you to fit the pieces together. The Day by Day guides are different. These guides tell you the best of everything, and then they show you how to see it in the smartest, most time-efficient way. Our authors have designed detailed itineraries organized by time, neighborhood, or special interest. And each tour comes with a bulleted map that takes you from stop to stop.

Hoping to gaze up at the domed ceiling at the Süleymaniye Mosque, check out Istanbul's contemporary art scene, or watch fishermen where the Marmara Sea meets the Bosphorus? Planning to lose yourself in the music emanating from Galip Dede Caddesi, savor Turkish delicacies at one of Istanbul's many markets, or take a dramatic cable car ride up to Pierre Loti Kahvesi? Whatever your interest or schedule, the Day by Days give you the smartest routes to follow. Not only do we take you to the top attractions, hotels, and restaurants, but we also help you access those special moments that locals get to experience—those "finds" that turn tourists into travelers.

The Day by Days are also your top choice if you're looking for one complete guide for all your travel needs. The best hotels and restaurants for every budget, the greatest shopping values, the wildest nightlife—it's all here.

Why should you trust our judgment? Because our authors personally visit each place they write about. They're an independent lot who say what they think and would never include places they wouldn't recommend to their best friends. They're also open to suggestions from readers. If you'd like to contact them, please send your comments our way at feedback@frommers.com, and we'll pass them on.

Enjoy your Day by Day guide—the most helpful travel companion you can buy. And have the trip of a lifetime.

About the Authors

Emma Levine was born in Yorkshire, England, and fell in love with Istanbul on her first visit in 1989, and since then has been a regular visitor. After graduating in graphic design, she lived and worked as a writer and photographer in Mumbai, Hong Kong, and Istanbul, and has enjoyed many happy years having adventures around the world. For much of her working life, Emma has specialized in documenting the sporting culture of Asia, especially cricket culture in the Indian subcontinent, and traditional sports in countries such as Iran, Pakistan, and Kyrgyzstan in her book *A Game of Polo with a Headless Goat*. This book was later turned into a series of documentaries on the National Geographic Channel, which she wrote and presented. Emma is now based in North London, but still travels where and when possible.

Terry Richardson has been exploring Turkey since the early 1980s. He writes and updates several guidebooks to both the country and its leading city, and contributes regular travel features to a number of international and Turkish newspapers and magazines. He also leads groups of history and archaeology enthusiasts through Istanbul's incredible past. Terry divides his time between his native UK and the country that has become his obsession.

Rhiannon Davies fell for Turkey after a cycling trip across the country's remote Anatolian plateau. Lured to cosmopolitan Istanbul, she worked as the arts and culture editor for the travel and lifestyle magazine, *The Guide Istanbul*. She lives in the heart of Istanbul's vibrant entertainment quarter and spends her free time exploring the city's restaurant, art, and nightlife scenes. Rhiannon speaks Turkish and is always seeking out regional recipes to add to her collection.

An Additional Note

Please be advised that travel information is subject to change at any time—and this is especially true of prices. We therefore suggest that you write or call ahead for confirmation when making your travel plans. The authors, editors, and publisher cannot be held responsible for the experiences of readers while traveling. Your safety is important to us, however, so we encourage you to stay alert and be aware of your surroundings.

Star Ratings, Icons & Abbreviations

Every hotel, restaurant, and attraction listing in this guide has been ranked for quality, value, service, amenities, and special features using a **star-rating system.** Hotels, restaurants, attractions, shopping, and nightlife are rated on a scale of zero stars (recommended) to three stars (exceptional). In addition to the star-rating system, we also use a **kids** **icon** to point out the best bets for families. Within each tour, we recommend cafes, bars, or restaurants where you can take a break. Each of these stops appears in a shaded box marked with a coffee-cup-shaped bullet ☕.

The following **abbreviations** are used for credit cards:

AE	American Express	DISC	Discover	V	Visa
DC	Diners Club	MC	MasterCard		

Frommers.com

Now that you have this guidebook to help you plan a great trip, visit our website at **www.frommers.com** for additional travel information on more than 4,000 destinations. We update features regularly to give you instant access to the most current trip-planning information available. At Frommers.com, you'll find scoops on the best airfares, lodging rates, and car rental bargains. You can even book your travel online through our reliable travel booking partners. Other popular features include:

- Online updates of our most popular guidebooks
- Vacation sweepstakes and contest giveaways
- Newsletters highlighting the hottest travel trends
- Online travel message boards with featured travel discussions

A Note on Prices

In the "Take a Break" and "Best Bets" sections of this book, we have used a system of dollar signs to show a range of costs for 1 night in a hotel (the price of a double-occupancy room) or the cost of an entree at a restaurant. Use the following table to decipher the dollar signs:

Cost	Hotels	Restaurants
$	under $100	under $10
$$	$100–$200	$10–$20
$$$	$200–$300	$20–$30
$$$$	$300–$400	$30–$40
$$$$$	over $400	over $40

An Invitation to the Reader

In researching this book, we discovered many wonderful places—hotels, restaurants, shops, and more. We're sure you'll find others. Please tell us about them, so we can share the information with your fellow travelers in upcoming editions. If you were disappointed with a recommendation, we'd love to know that, too. Please write to: Support@FrommerMedia.com.

18 Favorite **Moments**

18 Favorite Moments

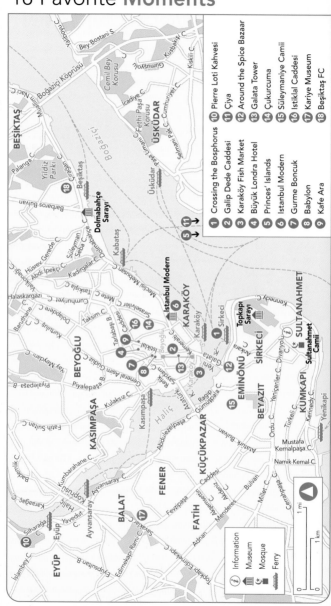

1 Crossing the Bosphorus
2 Galip Dede Caddesi
3 Karaköy Fish Market
4 Büyük Londra Hotel
5 Princes' Islands
6 Istanbul Modern
7 Gurme Boncuk
8 Babylon
9 Kafe Ara
10 Pierre Loti Kahvesi
11 Çiya
12 Around the Spice Bazaar
13 Galata Tower
14 Çukurcuma
15 Süleymaniye Camii
16 Istiklal Caddesi
17 Kariye Museum
18 Beşiktaş FC

ⓘ Information
🏛 Museum
☪ Mosque
⛴■ Ferry

0 ___ 1 mi
0 ___ 1 km

Previous page: Galata Tower at dusk.

Every visitor to this continent-spanning city of over 15 million inhabitants, once home to two of the world's greatest empires, will take away their own favorite moments. From Byzantine churches to Ottoman mosques, hip clubs and art galleries and thick black Turkish coffee to waterfront fish restaurants, there's something for everyone in this great world city.

❶ Head out of the Golden Horn and across the Bosphorus to Asia on a vintage ferry. Istanbul is a city both by and of the sea, and there's no better way to view it than from a boat taking you from Europe to Asia. *See p 17.*

❷ Wandering down Galip Dede Caddesi and listening to the sounds emerge from music stores—everything from electric guitars and keyboards to cymbals hand-crafted in Istanbul, the lute-like *saz* to the *ney*, the long Anatolian pipe. *See p 85.*

❸ Eating fresh grilled fish by Karaköy Fish Market. It's a bit rough and ready, but on a warm summer's evening, with the Old City skyline ahead, it can't be beaten for price and pure enjoyment. *See p 59.*

❹ Watching the sunset over the Golden Horn and Old City from the roof terrace bar of the Büyük Londra Hotel. If it was good enough for Hemingway, it's good enough for the rest of us. *See p 136.*

❺ The traffic-free, pine-clad Princes' Islands are just an hour's ferry ride away. What a great contrast to the vibrant mayhem of the city, especially when explored on foot or bike. *See p 144.*

❻ Perusing contemporary art at Istanbul Modern. For a beguiling overview of contemporary Turkish art and the chance to see a cracking temporary exhibition, try the city's leading modern art gallery, set right on the Bosphorus waterfront. *See p 30.*

❼ Try the full-on *meyhane* **experience at Gurme Boncuk in Beyoğlu.** Plates of meze, grilled fish, unlimited local drinks, and an Armenian accordion player all in a place jampacked with Istanbullus Friday and Saturday evenings. *See p 103.*

❽ It's hard to classify Istanbul's hippest club, Babylon. But whatever is on, whether live bands or DJ sets, it's the place to see and be seen. *See p 127.*

❾ Sipping Turkish coffee at Kafe Ara, surrounded by scenes of the city on the walls by Istanbul's photographer Ara Güler (b. 1928). A real "cafe society" feel. *See p 104.*

Fresh grilled fish at Karaköy fish market.

The colors of Istanbul's Spice Bazaar.

🔟 **Taking the teleferik to Pierre Loti Kahvesi on a warm summer evening.** After a fascinating morning people-watching around Eyüp Sultan Mosque and Meydanı, the short cable-car ride above the cemetery is a lovely, lazy way to reach the tea garden named after the romantic French author. *See p 54.*

⓫ **Taste your way around Turkey at Çiya,** on the Asian shores of the city. Three restaurants spread across a narrow alley dish up a cornucopia of delicious regional specialties hard to find elsewhere. *See p 102.*

⓬ **Check out the streets around the Spice Bazaar** for an arresting

selection of gourmet foodstuffs, from strings of sun-cured eggplants to dried mulberries, pistachios to plump Aegean olives. *See p 9.*

⓭ **Ascending Galata Tower** and circling the gallery a couple of times. The crowds may perturb, but the views never cease to amaze. *See p 10.*

⓮ **Getting lost on the winding backstreets around Çukurcuma,** browsing antique shops, jewelry makers, and tiny art galleries. *See p 85.*

⓯ **Looking up at the vast central dome and flanking semi-domes of the Süleymaniye Camii.** The interior of this mammoth but beautifully austere mosque is an architectural delight—no wonder its master architect Sinan had himself buried in its grounds. *See p 8.*

⓰ **Gallery hopping on Independence Street.** Istanbul has a thriving contemporary arts scene, best tasted by visiting the small galleries fronting Istiklal Caddesi (Independence Street). *See p 48.*

⓱ **Admiring the biblical scenes adorning the Byzantine church of St Savior** in Chora (Kariye Müzesi). The mosaics here are superbly crafted and tell familiar tales in the most charming manner. *See p 42.*

⓲ **Cheering on Beçiktaş soccer (football) club** at the spectacularly situated Inönü (Vodafone) stadium, with views of the Bosphorus and the Dolmabahçe Palace clock tower. *See p 129.* ●

The Best in **One Day**

1 Hagia Sophia
2 Sultanahmet Park
3 Süleymaniye Camii
4 Kurucu Ali Baba
5 Kapalı Çarşısı
6 Mısır Çarşısı
7 Bab-i Hayat
8 Rüstem Paşa Camii
9 Galata Köprüsü
10 Galata Kulesi
11 Galata Meydanı

(i) Information
🏛 Museum
(✸ Mosque
🖂 Post Office
P Police Station
⛴ Ferry
🚉 Train Station
—● Funicular
T Tram
M Metro

Previous page: Dazzling interior of the Blue Mosque.

Istanbul's history centers on Sultanahmet. Here, the ancient Greeks built the city's first incarnation; later, the district was the heart of both the Byzantine and Ottoman empires. This area is referred to as the Old City, or the Historic Peninsula of Istanbul's European side. Over the Golden Horn (an "arm" of the Bosphorus), and still in Europe, is the thoroughly modern Beyoğlu neighborhood. This busy tour gives you a taste of both. START: **Tram to Sultanahmet.**

① ★★★ 🧒 **Hagia Sophia (Ayasofya).** One of Istanbul's iconic landmarks, with a dusky red exterior and huge domes, there are usually long lines to enter what is today a museum. The first church built on this site dates to A.D. 360, but its present form dates back to the mid-6th century when it was rebuilt by Emperor Justinian I. Your first impression, on entering its dimly lit ground floor, is awe, as you stand beneath the magnificent 55m-high (184 ft.) dome, which measures 31.5m (103 ft.) in diameter. Also in the nave of the church are the omphalion, where Byzantine emperors were crowned, and the weeping column, so called because it is slightly damp to the touch. It supposedly cures all ills. Also at ground level, seen as you leave via the inner narthex (vestibule), is the best of the church's mosaic panels, depicting the Virgin Mary. On one side of her is the Emperor Constantine, offering her a model of Constantinople; on the other side, Justinian offers her a model of the Hagia Sophia. The upstairs gallery, reached via a long sloping ramp, houses beautiful 11th-century mosaics, including that of Christ flanked by Emperor Constantine IX and his wife, Empress Zoe. Close by you'll see Viking-era graffiti etched into the marble balcony and another stunning mosaic depicting Christ, the Virgin Mary, and John the Baptist. The church was converted into a mosque, the

Ayasofya, soon after the conquest of 1453 (p 171). In 1934, it became a museum. Additions from its time as a mosque include the *mihrab* (Mecca-facing niche) in the apse, a *minbar* (pulpit), a loge or raised platform where the sultan would pray, and below the dome, great circular plaques inscribed with the names of Allah, Mohammed, and the first four caliphs. ⏱ *90 min. Ayasofya Meydanı, Sultanahmet.* ☎ *0212/522-1750. www.ayasofya muzesi.gov.tr. Admission 30 TL adults, free for kids 12 and under; audio tours 10 TL. Tues–Sun Apr–Oct 9am–7pm, Nov–Mar 9am–5 pm. Tram: Sultanahmet.*

② ★ 🧒 **Sultanahmet Park.** Take a breather in this park area, its fountain lying between the striking

Take a break at Sultanahmet Park.

Sultanahmet Camii (Blue Mosque; p 15) and **Hagia Sophia.** Savor the precious location, and try barbecued or boiled corn-on-the-cob (*mısır*) from the push-carts. It's even better at night, when these two imposing buildings are spot-lit. It's popular for *iftar* (sunset "breaking the fast" meal during Ramazan), with picnicking locals. ⏱ *30 min. Open 24 hr. Tram: Sultanahmet.*

❸ ★★★ 🧒 **Süleymaniye Camii (Süleymaniye Mosque).** One of the masterpieces of Mimar Sinan (1489–1588), this architectural marvel is relatively quiet. With a huge central dome and four slender minarets it was, like many great mosques, part of a *külliye*, a mosque complex once housing a *caravanserai* (resting place for travelers), a hospital, several *medreses* (religious schools), a soup kitchen, and tombs. It was built in the mid-16th century under the order of Süleyman I, or Süleyman the Magnificent (p 171). The mosque's interior is breathtaking, its 47m-high (154 ft.) dome soaring above the subdued lighting from stained-glass windows made by Ibrahim "the Sot" (1615–48), so nicknamed because of his fondness for wine. Süleyman's tomb lies in the rose-clad graveyard; its marble

Intricate domes at Süleymaniye Camii.

pillars, hand-painted tiles from Iznik, and neat wooden alcoves are in sharp contrast to the modest tomb of his adored wife, Roxelana (p 15). ⏱ *1 hr. Prof Sıddık Sami Onar Cad.* ☎ *0212/513-3608. Free admission. Daily 9am–dusk. Tram: Laleli/Üniversite, then 15-min walk.*

❹ ★★ 🧒 **Kurucu Ali Baba.** The first tiny *lokanta* (simple restaurant) facing the mosque, this has served up tasty *kuru fasulye* (white beans) since 1939. Perfect for a no-frills lunch with the locals. *1/3 Prof Sıddık Sami Onar Cad, Süleymaniye.* ☎ *0212/520-7655. Fasulye beans and rice 7 TL.*

❺ ★★ 🧒 **Kapalı Çarşısı (Covered, or Grand, Bazaar).** You can easily spend half a day getting lost in the crowded market that comprises over 4,000 shops, 60 lanes, and 550 years of hearty trading. Built by Mehmet II shortly after the conquest of Constantinople in 1453 (p 171), its domed roofs and narrow streets now house colorful machine-made ceramics, with souvenirs replacing traditional trades like quilt- and fez-making. Previously, natural daylight from the ceiling illuminated the entire market; now most rely on electricity.

Sinan, Master Architect

You're likely to be awed by the work of one man: master architect of the Ottoman Empire, Mimar Sinan (1489–1588). He was "adopted" as the Ottoman Palace architect by Süleyman I, under whose reign arts and architecture flourished. Under him, Sinan built hundreds of mosques, *hamams*, bazaars, and hospitals throughout Turkey but most famously in Istanbul. Ironically, he chose the famous Byzantine Hagia Sophia basilica as inspiration for his mosques.

İç Bedesten is the oldest part of the bazaar; once a warehouse, it's now the hub of stylish cafes, although some trades are still booming, such as carpet dealers and gold and leather stores. There's a more peaceful ambience in the leafy courtyard **Zincirli Han.** Admire the sturdy entrance gates (over 20 of them) and cheap and cheerful outside stalls. Head north from the bazaar via **Valide Han** (p 78) to Eminönü, to Mısır Çarşısı, or take the tram. ① *1–3 hr. Mon–Sat 9:30am–7pm. Tram: Beyazit; or bus 61B from Taksim.*

⑥ ★★ kids **Mısır Çarşısı (Egyptian, or Spice, Market).** This L-shaped market, built in 1660 to finance Yeni Cami (p 65), was once filled with piles of fresh peppercorns, cilantro (coriander), henna, and dried herbs brought from Egypt. You can still find these goods today, though the market is very touristy. Inch your way past the crowds to see its delightful domed ceilings. If you want to hang out where the locals shop, concentrate on the stalls running around the outside wall of the market, where you can buy everything from fresh plaited cheeses to dried mulberries, pistachios to the walnut-stuffed, cured fruit-molasses treat *sucuk.* ① *1 hr. Daily 9:30am–7pm. Tram/bus: Eminönü.*

⑦ ★★★ kids **Bab-i Hayat.** Opened in 2007 and converted from a warehouse, this gorgeous domed restaurant looks out onto Mısır Çarşısı selling everything from *pide* to kebabs. *39/47 Mısır Çarşısı, Eminönü.* ☎ *0212/520-7878. Entrees from 15 TL.*

⑧ ★★ **Rüstem Paşa Camii (Rüstem Paşa Mosque).** Barely visible from street level, this

Vendors outside Mısır Çarşısı (Spice Market).

Sightseeing—the Basics

Most major attractions are open Tuesday to Sunday, 9am to 5pm, some opening later in summer. Getting around the Old City is best done by tram or on foot. Most mosques are open to visitors from dawn to nightfall, excluding prayer times; dress modestly, covering arms and legs, and women should cover their hair. To beat queues and save money on the major sights, try the **Museum Pass Istanbul** (www.muze.gov.tr). Costing 85 TL and valid for 72 hours, the pass gives fast-track entry to 10 museums, including Topkapı Palace and Hagia Sophia. A more comprehensive 5-day pass is also available for 115 TL.

mosque really is a hidden gem, reached by a flight of stone steps from the busy street below. One of Mimar Sinan's smallest creations, it was built in 1560 and originally funded out of proceeds from nearby tradesmen. It's one of the best places to see the famous blue Iznik tiles, here liberally covering both the interior and parts of the exterior. ⏱ *20 min. Hasırcılar Cad.* ☎ *0212/526-7350. Open daily dawn–dusk. Tram/bus: Eminönü.*

Climb Galata Tower for the best views.

❾ ★★ **Galata Köprüsü (Galata Bridge).** For centuries, the only way to cross the Golden Horn from the Old City to the "new," largely non-Muslim neighborhoods of Galata and Beyoğlu was by boat. This despite the fact that Leonardo da Vinci, no less, had mid-16th-century designs for a bridge rejected, and Michelangelo turned down an offer to design a new bridge. The first bridge was completed in 1845, though today's structure dates back only to 1994. It's almost 500m (1,640 ft.) long, with fishermen on the upper level and cafes and restaurants on the lower. No restaurants stand out, despite the efforts of front-of-housers to persuade you otherwise, but it's a good place to sit with a cool beer and watch the ships ply up, down, and across the Golden Horn. ⏱ *Varies. Tram: Eminönü or Karaköy.*

❿ ★★ **Galata Kulesi (Galata Tower).** This 62m-high (203 ft.) conical tower was built by the Genoese in 1348, a period when the Galata district was, in effect, an autonomous trading colony. Take the elevator to the top to walk around the narrow viewing gallery, overlooking disheveled rooftops, minarets, the Bosphorus, and even

Fishing off of Galata Bridge.

the Princes' Islands (p 144). If you don't fancy walking uphill to the tower, take the Tünel (the 19th-century underground funicular) from Karaköy to the Tünel terminus at the southern end of Istiklal Caddesi and walk down (p 48). ⊘ *1 hr. Büyük Hendek Sok, Galata. ☎ 0212/293-8180. Daily 9am–8pm. Admission 6.50€, or equivalent in TL, free for kids 5 and under. Tunnel to Tünel or tram to Karaköy.*

11 ★★★ kids **Galata Meydanı.** Right beneath the tower is a pleasant cobbled square lined to the north with several restaurants. Try Güney, a long-established, traditional place with good *pide* (Turkish pizza) and stews and some outside tables. *Kuledibi Sah Kapısı, Galata. ☎ 0212/249-0393. Pides from 11 TL.*

The Best in Two Days

1. Topkapı Sarayı
2. Arkeoloji Müzesi
3. Pudding Shop (Lale)
4. Sultanahmet Camii
5. Yerebatan Sarnıcı
6. Istanbul Modern
7. Bosphorus Cruise
8. Anadolu Kavağı ferry pier

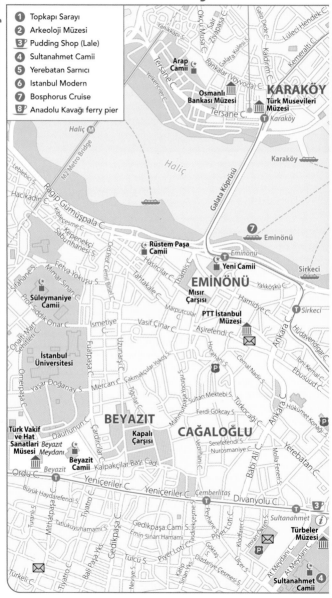

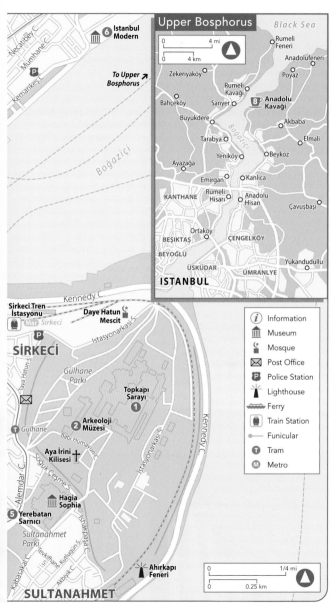

Upper Bosphorus

Black Sea

Rumeli Feneri
Anadolufeneri
Zekeriyaköy
Poyaz
Rumeli
Kavaği
Sanyer
8 **Anadolu Kavaği**
Bahçeköy
Buyukdere
Akbaba
Tarabya
Elmali
Ayazağa
Yeniköy
Beykoz
Emirgan
Kanlica
KANTHANE
Rumeli
Hisari
Anadolu
Hisari
Çavuşbaşı
Ortaköy
BEŞIKTAŞ
ÇENGELKÖY
BEYOĞLU
Yukandudullu
ÜSKÜDAR
ÜMRANLYE
ISTANBUL

6 Istanbul Modern

To Upper Bosphorus ↗

Necatibey C.
Mumhane C.
Kemankeş C.

Boğaziçi

Sirkeci Tren İstasyonu
Sirkeci
Daye Hatun Mescit
Kennedy C.
Istasyonarkasi S.

SIRKECI

Gülhane Parkı

Tava Hatun C.

Gülhane

2 Arkeoloji Müzesi

Babı Humayun

Topkapı Sarayı **1**

Aya İrini Kilisesi

Soğuk Çeşme S.

Istasyonarkasi S.

Kennedy C.

Alemdar C.

Hagia Sophia

5 Yerebatan Sarnıcı

Sultanahmet Parkı

Kabasakal C.
Nevşhane Kutluğun S.
Akbıyık S.

Ahırkapı Feneri

SULTANAHMET

ⓘ	Information
🏛	Museum
☪	Mosque
✉	Post Office
🅿	Police Station
🗼	Lighthouse
🚢	Ferry
🚉	Train Station
━	Funicular
Ⓣ	Tram
Ⓜ	Metro

0 — 4 mi
0 — 4 km

0 — 1/4 mi
0 — 0.25 km

On your second day, dip back into Sultanahmet for more history, including Topkapı Palace, centerpiece of the Ottoman Empire, and then hop across the Golden Horn to Istanbul Modern's collection of contemporary Turkish art. If you have more time, try to visit the palace and Archaeological Museum on separate days. A Bosphorus Cruise is a perfect way to end the day. START: **Tram to Gülhane or Sultanahmet.**

① ★★ Topkapı Sarayı (Topkapı Palace).

Built by Mehmet II in 1478 and center of the Ottoman Empire until 1853, it's no wonder that it's usually a struggle to catch sight of the famous 86-carat, tear-shaped Spoonmaker's Diamond and the Topkapı Dagger inside the crowded **Treasury.** Other highlights include the **Harem** (well worth the extra ticket), with its series of tiled chambers and pleasant terraces. Don't miss the religious artifacts, including those belonging to the Prophet Mohammed. ⏲ *2–4 hr. Bab-ı Hümayun Cad, Gülhane.* ☎ *0212/512-0480. www. topkapisarayi.gov.tr. Admission Museum 30 TL adults, free for kids 12 and under; Harem 15 TL adults, free for kids 6 and under. Wed–Mon Apr–Oct 9am–7pm, Nov–Mar 9am–5pm. Tram: Gülhane or Sultanahmet.*

② ★★★ kids Arkeoloji Müzesi (Archaeological Museum).

Situated in the grounds of the Topkapı Palace complex, this museum is world class. It was established to prevent classical antiquities from disappearing to Europe by curator and artist Osman Hamdi Bey (1842–1910), best known for his painting *The Tortoise Trainer,* now in the Pera Museum (p 30). With around a million relics spread over three buildings, be selective. The main building contains the most astounding exhibits; don't miss the beautiful Alexander Sarcophagus (4th-century B.C.) with carved marble scenes of battle, the Lycian Sarcophagus, and the mummy of Sidonian King Tabrit (500 B.C.). Across the courtyard, the **Ancient Orient Museum** has fabulous Babylonian tiled friezes and

Historic courtyard of the Archaeological Museum.

The Blue Mosque's distinctive minarets.

the Treaty of Kadesh tablet (1269 B.C.), the world's earliest surviving peace treaty, a copy of which adorns the United Nations headquarters in New York. The **Çinili Köşk (Tiled Pavilion)** has an outstanding collection of Seljuk and Ottoman tiles. Take a breather in the charming garden cafe. ⏱ *90 min–2 hr. Osman Hamdi Bey Yokoşu Sok, Gülhane.* ☎ *0212/520-7740. www.istanbularkeoloji.gov.tr. Admission 15 TL adults, free for kids 11 and under. Tues–Sun Apr–Oct 9am–7pm, Nov–Mar 9am–5pm, Tram: Gülhane.*

3 ★ **kids Pudding Shop (Lale).** This long-established cafe-diner became the staging post for India-bound travelers back in the hippy 1960s. The same brothers run it now as then, as a self-service joint with a range of basic but tasty traditional Turkish fare and, rarely for Sultanahmet, alcohol on the menu. Its English name comes from the rice puddings favored by hungry hippies—they remain a specialty. *Divan Youu Cad 6.* ☎ *0212/522-2970. Entrees from 12 TL.*

4 ★ **Sultanahmet Camii (Blue Mosque).** To emphasize the superiority of Islam over Christian Byzantium, the Blue Mosque was deliberately built right opposite the smaller Hagia Sophia. The approach to the mosque's courtyard from the Hippodrome (p 67) is delightful as the full impact of cascading domes and six soaring minarets unfolds in front of you. The number of slender minarets created consternation when it was built, as the only other mosque with six minarets is in Mecca. Built in 1617 by Mehmet Ağa, a student of Sinan, this was the last of the Imperial mosques, commissioned by the 19-year-old Sultan Ahmet I (hence,

Wooden roof ornaments at Topkapı Palace.

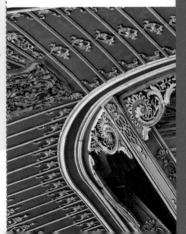

The mysterious Medusa's head at Yerebatan Sarnıçı.

its Turkish name). The courtyard, made from Marmara marble, is actually the same size as the interior of the prayer hall. Its most famous feature is the predominantly blue Iznik tiles that give the mosque its name. They cover much of the interior—over 20,000 tiles in total—and are beautifully illuminated by 260 windows. Astoundingly, each tile took 72 days to paint. Non-Muslim visitors will be ushered around the side of the courtyard and, unfortunately, allowed only at the back of the prayer hall, which tends to get very crowded' It's difficult to see the tiles' detail, or the carved white *minbar* (pulpit) and *mihrab* (niche pointing to Mecca) at the front. ⏱ 30 min. Sultanahmet Meydanı. Daily 9am–dusk, except during prayers. Tram: Sultanahmet.

⑤ ★★ kids Yerebatan Sarnıcı (Basilica Cistern). A great feat of Byzantine engineering, this is one of the city's most unusual and memorable sights, dating back to the 6th century. Back then, water came from the Belgrade Forest, some 19km (12 miles) away, through the 4th-century **Valens**

aqueduct (p 43) constructed by Emperor Valens. It's atmospherically lit and silent, except for the drip of water from the vaulted ceilings, but it gets very, very crowded—try to visit as early in the day as possible. Make your way to the northwest corner for the two Medusa-head columns, thought to be late Roman, one upside-down and the other tilted 45 degrees, both clearly reused from earlier buildings. Supporting the roof are 336 columns, some topped by ornate Corinthian capitals. Scenes in the 1963 James Bond film *From Russia with Love* were filmed here. ⏱ 45 min. 13 Yerebatan Cad, Sultanahmet. ☎ 0212/522-1259. www. yerebatan.com. Admission 10 TL adults, free for kids 7 and under. Daily Apr–Oct 9am–6:30pm, Nov–Mar 9am–5pm. Tram: Sultanahmet.

⑥ ★★★ kids Istanbul Modern. When you whizz over the Golden Horn by tram to Tophane, northeast of Karaköy, you leave behind centuries of history. Enter this converted customs house, opened in 2004, to see one of the country's finest modern art collections, from 20th-century Ottoman art to today, spread over its two floors. The huge gallery (it still looks like a warehouse from the outside) has a sublime waterfront location; admire it as you peruse the galleries of 20th- and 21st-century Turkish art, with paintings, sculpture, videos, and installations. There are always exciting temporary exhibitions to keep an eye out for, as well as art-house movies screened at the in-house cinema. There's a gift shop and decent cafe-restaurant here too, though prices are high. ⏱ 90 min. Meclis-i Mebusan Cad, Liman Işletmeleri, 4 Sahası Antrepo, Karaköy. ☎ 0212/334-7300. www. istanbulmodern.org. Admission 17 TL adults, 9 TL students and seniors,

Cruising the Bosphorus River.

free for kids 11 and under. *Tues–Sun 10am–6pm (Thurs till 8pm). Tram: Tophane.*

⑦ ★★★ kids Bosphorus Cruise. Locals and visitors adore cruising this famous waterway, strategically important for centuries. Trips begin at Eminönü pier, with stops including Beşiktaş and Yeniköy on the European side, Çengelköy on the Asian side, before terminating at **Anadolu Kavağı.** During summer, weekday trips leave at 7pm from Eminönü and make a wonderful evening, with enough time for the steep climb to the 14th-century Genoese **Yoros Castle** for incredible views of where the Bosphorus meets the Black Sea. En route you'll pass a number of magnificent *yalı* (waterfront mansions) and the Ottoman fortresses of Rumeli Hisarı and Anadolu Hisarı, as well as pass under two giant suspension bridges. Enjoy dinner on the pier and then return by ferry. If you're traveling during winter, you'll have to make the trip in the daytime, starting at 10:35am, and perhaps visit one of the museums the following day. From Eminönü, there are also hourly 90-minute round-trip cruises going as far as the second suspension bridge, with no stops, operated by both Sehir Hatları (see below) and the fast,

modern **TurYol** (www.turyol.com/en) for 12 TL. ⏱ *Varies. Check www.sehirhatlari.com.tr for timetables and prices. Ferries from Eminönü pier. Tram: Eminönü.*

⑧ ★ kids Anadolu Kavağı Ferry Pier. Passengers leaving the ferry may be bombarded with restaurants vying for business. Don't feel pressured; look around. There are also simple stalls cooking fresh *balık ekmek* (fried fish in bread). *Snacks from 6 TL; entrees (in restaurants) from 12 TL.*

Yoros Castle at Anadolu Kavağı.

The Best in **Three Days**

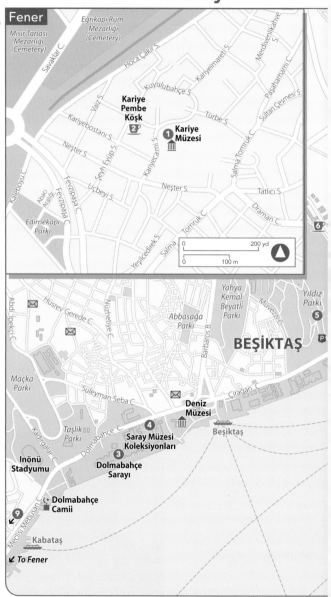

Fener

Mısır Tarlası Mezarlığı (Cemetery)

Eğrikapı Rum Mezarlığı (Cemetery)

Sayaklar C.

Hoca Çakır S.

Kariyeimareti S.

Medivenlikahve S.

Kuyulubahçe S.

Vaiz S.

Kariye Pembe Köşk

Kariyebostanı S.

Kariyecami S.

Kariye Müzesi

Türbe S.

Pașahamamı C.

Sultan Çeşmesi S.

Salma Tomruk C.

Neşter S.

Şeyh Eyüp S.

Üçbeyi S.

Kaleboyu C.

Abacı Atolığ

Fevzipaşa C.

Edirnekapı Parkı

Yeşilcedirek S.

Salma

Neşter S.

Tomruk C.

Tatlıcı S.

Draman C.

0 — 200 yd
0 — 100 m

6

Abdi İpekçi C.

Hüsrev Gerede C.

Nüzhetiye C.

Abbasağa Parkı

Yahya Kemal Beyatli Parkı

Yıldız Parkı

5

Müvezzi C.

Barbaros B.

BEŞİKTAŞ

P

Maçka Parkı

Süleyman Seba C.

Deniz Müzesi

Çirağan C.

Taşlik Parkı

Dolmabahçe C.

Saray Müzesi Koleksiyonları **4**

Beşiktaş

Kadırgalar C.

İnönü Stadyumu

3 **Dolmabahçe Sarayı**

Dolmabahçe Camii

Meclisi Mebusan C.

9

Kabataş

↙ **To Fener**

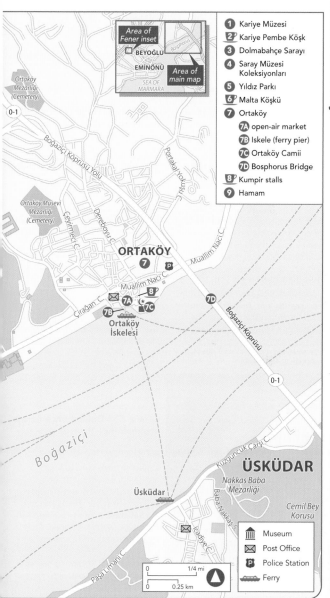

1 Kariye Müzesi
2 Kariye Pembe Köşk
3 Dolmabahçe Sarayı
4 Saray Müzesi Koleksiyonları
5 Yıldız Parkı
6 Malta Köşkü
7 Ortaköy
　7A open-air market
　7B İskele (ferry pier)
　7C Ortaköy Camii
　7D Bosphorus Bridge
8 Kumpir stalls
9 Hamam

Area of Fener inset
BEYOĞLU
EMİNÖNÜ
Area of main map
SEA OF MARMARA
Bosphorus

Ortaköy Mezarlığı (Cemetery)

O-1

Boğaziçi Köprüsü Yolu

Portakal Yokuşu C.

Ortaköy Musevi Mezarlığı (Cemetery)

Çevirmeci C.

Dereboyu C.

ORTAKÖY
7
P
Muallim Naci C.

Muallim Naci C.
8
7A
7C
7D
Boğaziçi Köprüsü
Çırağan C.
7B
Ortaköy İskelesi

O-1

Boğaziçi

Kuzguncuk Çarşı C.

ÜSKÜDAR
Nakkaş Baba Mezarlığı

Cemil Bey Korusu

Üsküdar

Baba Nakkaş S.

İcadiye C.

Paşa Limanı C.

	Museum
	Post Office
	Police Station
	Ferry

0　　1/4 mi
0　　0.25 km

Experience Istanbul's finest Byzantine art, and then indulge in Ottoman excess at Dolmabahçe Palace. You can walk from the palace to Yıldız Park and then along the Bosphorus to Ortaköy, a charming waterfront neighborhood with plenty of dining options. START: **Bus 86 from Eminönü or 87 from Taksim to Edirnekapı, and then a 5-minute walk.**

❶ ★★★ Kariye Müzesi (Kariye Museum/Chora Church).

Dating back as early as the 6th century, the Church of St. Savior in Chora was largely rebuilt in the early 12th century. The frescoes and mosaics, which are its glory, were added between 1316 and 1321 and are some of the world's finest examples of Byzantine art (p 172). When the church was converted to a mosque in 1511, they were plastered over, as representation of the human form is forbidden in Islam. In the restored church, now a museum, most of the beautiful mosaics are found in the inner and outer narthexes, illustrating scenes from the life of Christ and the Virgin Mary. Above the entrance to the nave, the figure of

Baroque and rococo luxury in the interior of Dolmabahçe Palace.

Theodore Metochites (1270–1332), the theologian who facilitated the church's redecoration, "presents" the church to Christ. The nave itself has a few more wonderful mosaic panels, and in the adjoining funerary chapel are frescoes that rival those of the Italian Renaissance. No flash photography or tripods. 🕐 *90 min. Kariye Camii Sok, Edirnekapı.* ☎ *0212/522-1750. Admission 15 TL adults, free for kids 11 and under. Thurs–Tues Apr–Oct 9am–7pm, Nov–Mar 9am–4.30pm. Bus 86 from Eminönü or 87 from Taksim, then 5-min walk; or tram to Pazartekke and 1.5km (1 mile) walk along land walls.*

❷ kids Kariye Pembe Köşk.

Rest in a peaceful courtyard opposite the museum with tea, toasted sandwiches, kebabs, or lentil soup. *27 Kariye Camii Sok, Edirnekapı.* ☎ *0212/635-8586. Lentil soup 7 TL, tea 2 TL.*

❸ ★★ kids Dolmabahçe Sarayı (Dolmabahçe Palace).

After lavish Topkapı Palace was built (p 24), the declining Ottoman Empire ended its days here. Its highly ornate appearance is an eclectic mix of mid-19th-century baroque and rococo styles. The highlight is the **Selamlık,** home to the head of the house, with an ostentatious marble exterior and entrance hall with a superb gilded ceiling. The Ambassadorial Reception hall was created to host guests; you can't miss one of the world's largest chandeliers, a 4-ton gift from

Queen Victoria. Tours of the **Harem**—the private, far-less-ornate women's quarters—and Selamlık are by guided tour only. You don't need a ticket to see the **Mehter band** (p 38) at 11am every Tuesday by the **Imperial Gate.** ⏱ 2 hr. Dolmabahçe Cad, Beşiktaş. ☎ 0212/236-9000. www.dolma bahce.gov.tr. Admission Selamlık 30 TL adults, Harem 20 TL adults, tour of both 40 TL; free for kids 11 and under. Tues–Wed and Fri–Sun Apr– Oct 9am–5pm, Nov–Mar 9am–4pm; closed Mon and Thurs. Tram/funicular: Kabataş.

④ ★★ **Saray Müzesi Koleksiyonları (Palace Museum Collection).** The former palace kitchen opened as a museum in 2005 with over 40,000 pieces salvaged from Dolmabahçe Palace. Few visitors make it here, so it's easy to discover the Sultan's monograms on intricate glass flasks, 4m-high (13 ft.) cabinets with gold leaf, gilded birdcages, and much, much more. ⏱ 1 hr. Dolmabahçe Cad, Beşiktaş. ☎ 0212/227-6671. www.millisaraylar.gov.tr. Admission 5 TL adults, free for kids 11 and under. Tues–Sun 9am–5pm. Tram/funicular: Kabataş.

⑤ ★ **kids Yıldız Parkı.** The sultans once strolled and hunted here while living at Çırağan Palace—which later burnt down, and is now a deluxe hotel (p 136)—and Yıldız Palace. The steep road up from the main entrance leads to **Yıldız Porcelain Factory & Museum**, built by Abdülhamit II in 1896 to produce porcelain to rival Iznik's that is still used today by artists. **Yıldız Sarayı Palace** has fascinating household items that belonged to later sultans who lived here, including Abdülhamit (1876–1909). Check out the 19th-century **Malta Köşkü** (⑥), with neo-classical, Islamic, and Ottoman styles; rococo arches; and

Fourteen-century wall mosaics of the ancient Chora Church.

baroque oval windows. Murat V (1840–1904) probably didn't notice, as he was imprisoned here by his brother Abdülhamit II for 27 years. **Çadır Köşkü** has a charming duck pond and cafe. ⏱ 1–2 hr. Yıldız Parkı. Çırağan Cad, Beşiktaş. ☎ 0212/261-8460. Open daily dawn–dusk.

⑥ **Malta Köşkü.** This imperial chalet turned cafe has a terrace commanding great Bosphorus views. Yıldız Korusu, Beşiktaş. ☎ 0212/444-6644. Tea and pastries from TL12.

⑦ ★★★ **kids Ortaköy.** Once a fishing village, Ortaköy today is a busy neighborhood, especially during weekends. On summer weekends, the ⑦A **open-air market** (p 90) has hats, handmade jewelry, and old books. From the ⑦B **Iskele (ferry pier),** ferries ply the Bosphorus. Perching by the Bosphorus is ornate ⑦C **Ortaköy Camii** (mosque; open dawn until nightfall), built in neo-baroque style in 1853 for

Ortaköy Camii, picturesque neo-baroque mosque.

Sultan Abdülmecit. At night, the lights on the mighty ⑦ **Bosphorus Bridge** change color engagingly. ⏱ *Varies. Bus to Ortaköy.*

⑧ ★★ kids **Kumpir stalls.** An alternative to Ortaköy's trendy restaurants, these simple stalls sell filled baked potatoes *(kumpir)*. Dine on the wall while watching the boats. *Mecidiye Köprüsü Sok, Ortaköy. Kumpir from 6 TL.*

⑨ ★★ **Hamam.** Substitute Ortaköy for a soak and scrub in a *hamam* (Turkish bath). **Çemberlitaş**

Hamamı, built in 1584 by Sinan, is foreigner-friendly. The huge marble slab and domes of the *sıcaklık* (hot room) are unchanged from Ottoman times, as are the attendants' energetic scrubs and massages. Men and women bathe separately. Visitors are given wooden shoes, soap, and a *peştamel* (wrap). Extra treatments range from a basic scrub to a luxurious oil massage. ⏱ *1–2 hr. 8 Vezirhan Cad.* ☎ *0212/522-7974. www.cemberlitas hamami.com.tr. Prices from 60 TL. Daily 6am–midnight. Tram: Çemberlitaş.* ●

2 The Best Special-Interest Tours

The Best Special-Interest Tours

Topkapı Palace

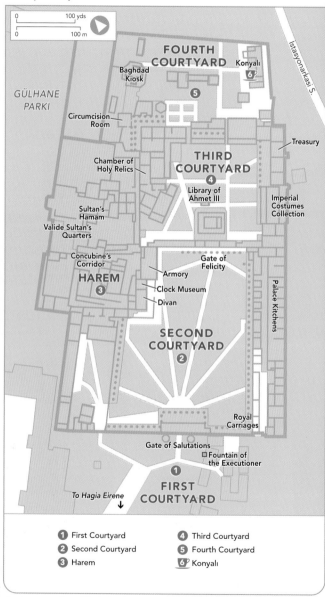

| 0 | 100 yds |
| 0 | 100 m |

FOURTH COURTYARD

Konyalı **⑥**

Baghdad Kiosk

⑤

İstasyonarkası S.

GÜLHANE PARKI

Circumcision Room

Treasury

Chamber of Holy Relics

THIRD COURTYARD ④

Library of Ahmet III

Sultan's Hamam

Imperial Costumes Collection

Valide Sultan's Quarters

Concubine's Corridor

HAREM ③

Gate of Felicity

Armory

Clock Museum

Divan

SECOND COURTYARD ②

Palace Kitchens

Royal Carriages

Gate of Salutations

□ Fountain of the Executioner

① FIRST COURTYARD

To Hagia Eirene
↓

① First Courtyard	**④** Third Courtyard
② Second Courtyard	**⑤** Fourth Courtyard
③ Harem	**⑥** Konyalı

Previous page: Scramble the battlements at Rumeli Hisarı Müzesi.

With the Hagia Sophia, this palace complex is considered one of Istanbul's two most famous attractions. Sprawling over some 80,000 sq. m (861,000 sq. ft.), Topkapı was built by Mehmet II in 1478 at Sarayburnu, at the tip of the historic peninsula overlooking the confluence of the Sea of Marmara, the Bosphorus, and the Golden Horn. It was both the seat of government of the Ottoman Empire and home to the Ottoman sultan and his wives for almost 400 years. Spend several hours enjoying its treasures.
START: **Tram to Sultanahmet.**

① ★ First Courtyard. Entered through the Bab-ı Hümayun gate, the first courtyard of the palace complex is today freely open to the public, as it was in Ottoman times, On your left as you enter is the **Hagia Eirene** (Church of the Holy Peace; admission 20 TL; Wed–Mon 9am–4pm). Most of what you see today dates back to the 6th century, when it was rebuilt, along with its much larger neighbor the **Hagia Sophia** (Church of the Holy Wisdom; p 7), after the Nika riots of 532. The most impressive part of the interior is the apse, the semi-dome decorated with a simple black cross against a gold mosaic background. Below it is a semi-circular tier of seating used by clergy in the Byzantine period. Unusually, it was never converted into a mosque, though it served as an armory in the Ottoman period.

On the opposite side of the courtyard is the **Cellat Çeşmesi (Fountain of the Executioner).** Although it resembles a disused water fountain, its use was far more macabre. In the 16th century, this is where the executioner washed the blood off his sword and hands after a public execution before re-entering the palace. Close to it is the ticket office where you buy your ticket before heading to the **Bab-üs Selam (Gate of Salutations),** which leads into the second courtyard. This gate is notable for its twin octagonal towers topped by conical roofs, which in Ottoman times only the sultan could ride through on horseback. Look up at the superbly extravagant gold-painted ceiling. Just inside, a couple of scale models of the palace and its surrounds might help your navigation. ⏱ *20 min.*

Bab-üs Selam, where traitors were strangled.

The cobbled Corridor of Concubines.

② ★★★ **kids** **Second Courtyard.** The domed, colonnaded series of buildings lining the southeast of the courtyard were once the palace kitchens, from which meals could be prepared for up to 5,000 Ottoman troops on special occasions. On the opposite, northwest side of the courtyard is the **Divan,** or council chamber, where the leading ministers (*viziers*) discussed matters of state before getting the final approval of the sultan. Next to it are a couple of interesting museums: the **Armoury,** with some fine European and Ottoman swords and other weaponry, and the **Clock Museum.** Cut diagonally across the courtyard to the **Bab-üs Saadet**

(Gate of Felicity), which leads to the third courtyard. In Ottoman times, the sultan sat here to review his crack troops before setting off on campaign. A small domed rock marks the spot where the imperial banner was raised. ① *30 min.*

③ ★★★ **kids** **Harem.** Next to the Divan in the Second Courtyard is the entrance to the Harem. Your journey into the "forbidden" quarter begins at the colonnaded, black-and-white cobbled **Corridor of Concubines,** where plates of food were laid out on marble counters. Worth admiring is the **Imperial Hall,** complete with crystal chandelier and sultan's sofa, where he entertained his best buddies. The sultan's **apartments** and marble *hamam* (Turkish bath), enclosed behind a golden door—allegedly for his own safety—contrast sharply with the more modest living quarters of the concubines and eunuchs. But the prize woman, the **valide sultan** (the sultan's mom), enjoyed five-star living quarters, where her devoted son visited her every morning. Note that the exit from the Harem is in the Third Courtyard. ① *45 min. Admission 15 TL.*

It's a Concubine's Life

Although "harem" perhaps conjures up images of Oriental debauchery, it literally means "forbidden" and refers to the palace's private women's quarters. Life in this 300-room, enclosed complex was no picnic; girls and young women were brought from all corners of the Ottoman Empire to live a mundane existence, working as servants, sleeping in dormitories, and learning the palace ways. The only other people allowed in the harem were the sultan and his sons, plus hundreds of eunuch slaves (castrated boys), who guarded the women. Favored girls were "trained" as wives or concubines for the sultans by the valide sultan (sultan's mother, who really ruled the roost), and ideally, they would bear him sons.

Topkapı Palace: Practical Matters

Topkapı Palace is perennially busy, especially in summer and on weekends, so beat the crowds by getting there at opening time or, in summer, late afternoons (Bab-ı Hümayun Cad; ☎ **0212/512-0480;** www.topkapisarayi.gov.tr; tram: Gülhane/Sultanahmet). Admission is 30 TL for adults, free for kids 12 and under. April through October, it's open Wednesday to Monday 9am to 7pm (till 5pm Nov–Mar). Buy separate tickets for the **Harem** (for 15 TL) and the **Hagia Eirene** (for 20 TL) at their respective entrances, as well as separate **audio guides** for the palace and harem, available in many languages.

❹ ★★★ **Third Courtyard.** Passing through the Gate of Felicity, you come first to the **Throne Room,** where the sultan gave his yea or nay to decisions taken in the Divan. Beyond it is the austere **Library of Ahmet III.** Housed in rooms to the northeast of the courtyard is the **Imperial Treasury.** Most visitors line up for a glimpse of the famous curved **Topkapı Dagger,** encrusted with diamonds and huge emeralds. If the eye-popping emeralds aren't enough, take a look at the 84-carat **Spoonmaker's Diamond,** named after the scrap merchant who found it and received three spoons in return.

In the northern corner of the courtyard is the **Chamber of the Holy Relics.** Religious items, plus holy objects found in Medina, were sent to sultans between the 16th and 19th centuries. The prized possession exhibited here is the Holy Mantle of the Prophet Mohammed. Look out also for the hair from the Prophet's beard and the sword of David. ⏲ *30 min.*

❺ ★★ **Fourth Courtyard.** Usually less busy than the rest of the complex, and aptly so as this courtyard was the sultan's pleasure gardens, of interest here are the beautifully decorated pavilions,

including the **Baghdad Pavilion,** with its ornate mother-of-pearl inlaid doors and lovely Iznik tilework. Even better is the **Circumcision Pavilion,** adorned with a splendid mix of Iznik tiles from several periods. The terrace between these two pavilions has great views out over Gülhane Park and the confluence of the Bosphorus and the Golden Horn. ⏲ *20 min.*

❻ **kids Konyalı.** The palace's only restaurant is pricey, although the traditional Turkish dishes are good. The adjacent terrace cafe is slightly cheaper, with the same superb Bosphorus view. ☎ *0212/513-9696. Entrees from 30 TL.*

The harem at Topkapı Palace.

Arty Istanbul

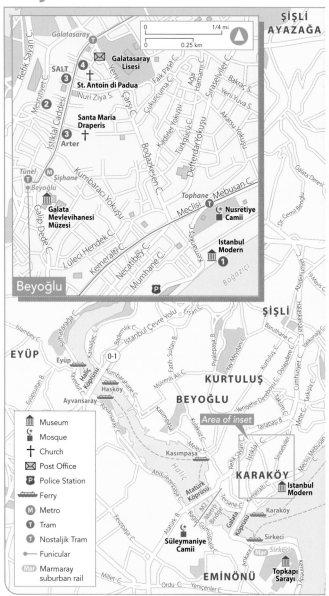

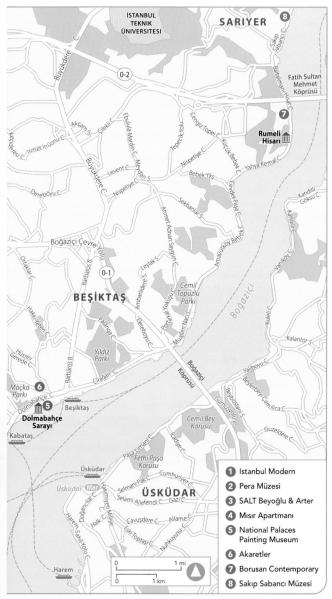

İSTANBUL TEKNIK ÜNIVERSITESI

SARIYER

Fatih Sultan Mehmet Köprüsü

Rumeli Hisarı

BEŞİKTAŞ

Boğaziçi

Yıldız Parkı

Cemil Topuzlu Parkı

Maçka Parkı

Dolmabahçe Sarayı

Beşiktaş

Kabataş

Üsküdar

Cemil Bey Korusu

ÜSKÜDAR

Fethi Paşa Korusu

Harem

0   1 mi
0   1 km

1 Istanbul Modern
2 Pera Müzesi
3 SALT Beyoğlu & Arter
4 Mısır Apartmanı
5 National Palaces Painting Museum
6 Akaretler
7 Borusan Contemporary
8 Sakıp Sabancı Müzesi

Historic treasures cram the city, but to understand Istanbul's full breadth, experience its artistic side. Over the last decade, new bijoux galleries have sprung up, mainly showcasing local artists. It's certainly been one of Istanbul's most exciting developments and has given the city a new cachet. START: **Tram: Fınıklı.**

❶ ★★★ Istanbul Modern.
When this contemporary art gallery opened in 2004 in a converted customs warehouse (p 16), it gave a huge boost to the local art scene. The first floor's permanent exhibition, Past and Future, is a good introduction to modern Turkish art. It takes visitors on a journey through Turkish art, beginning at the start of the 20th century with the documentary-style works of the last Ottoman Court painters. It then takes you through the modernization that occurred with the establishment of the republic; reflects the social concerns of the '60s, the rise of female artists in the '70s, and the urbanization of the '80s; and then finishes with some excellent examples of the more conceptual contemporary art of Turkey today.

Downstairs is a research area and diverse temporary and photography exhibitions. The shop has an eclectic collection of prints, mugs, and even kits to paint

reproductions of paintings on T-shirts. Tickets include entry to the cinema, often showing international art-house movies. ⏱ *90 min. Meclis-i Mebusan Cad, Liman Işletmeleri, 4 Sahası Antrepo, Karaköy.* ☎ *0212/334-7300. www.istanbul modern.org. Admission 17 TL adults, 9 TL students and seniors, free for kids 11 and under. Tues–Sun 10am–6pm (Thurs till 8pm). Tram: Tophane.*

❷ ★★ Pera Müzesi (Pera Museum). Open since 2005 in the beautifully restored Bristol Hotel, this jewel of a museum contains the private collection of Suna and Inan Kıraç. After the permanent displays of delicate Ottoman ceramics, head to the second floor for the Ottoman painting exhibition, including Osman Hamdi Bey's serene *Tortoise Trainer* (1906), Turkey's most valuable painting that sold for $3.5m in 2004, depicting himself as a dervish "training" the tortoises with music. The third and fourth

Turkey's first modern art gallery, Istanbul Modern.

floors house ever-changing exhibitions, often by prestigious international artists such as Picasso and Frida Kahlo. ⓘ *90 min. Meşrutiyet Cad, Tepebaşı.* ☎ *0212/334-9900. www.pm.org.tr. Admission 15 TL adults, 8 TL kids 12 and under. Tues–Sat 10am–7pm, Sun noon–6pm. Metro: Şişhane.*

③ ★★★ Contemporary Galleries on Istiklal Caddesi. With the boom in Istanbul's contemporary art scene, there has been a gallery explosion in central Istanbul. You can stumble upon these mostly privately funded galleries in any of Istiklal Caddesi's adjacent neighborhoods. All are free to visit and many are well worth a look. However, there are two notable art spaces on Istiklal itself. **ARTER** (no. 211; ☎ 0212/243-3767; www.arter. org.tr) opened in 2010. Spread over three floors it has hosted some notable international artists (such as Marc Quinn and Patricia Piccinini) along with a wide range of local talent. **SALT Beyoğlu** (no. 136; ☎ 0212/377-4200; www.saltonline. org) is a research institute, museum, gallery, and library all rolled into one that has an incredibly diverse range of exhibitions, often with a social-political focus; it has a second branch in Galata. ⓘ *45 min. Free admission. Mon–Sat noon–7pm. Bus/Metro: Taksim.*

④ ★★ Mısır Apartmanı. On the top floor of this early-20th-century building, the über-stylish rooftop bar and restaurant **360Istanbul** (p 119) opened in 2004, tempting more commercial art galleries here. Take the elevator to the top and then work your way down, looking out for new galleries opening up. Highlights include: **Galeri Nev** (4/F; ☎ 0212/252-1525; www.galerinev istanbul.com), which represents prominent contemporary Turkish artists such as Ali Kazma, Hale

An installation at Pi Artworks.

Tenger, and Serdar Arat. **Pi Artworks** (4/F; ☎ 0212/293-7103; www.piartworks.com) was founded in 1998 and in 2013 opened its second gallery in London. Directed by Yeşim Turanlı, it showcases both Turkish and international artworks by the likes of Nancy Atakan, Osman Dinç, and Volkan Aslan. **Galeri Zilberman** (3/F; ☎ 0212/251-1214; www.galeri zilberman.com) merged with its sister gallery CDA Projects in 2014 and now operates at Galeri I and Galeri II with more of a focus on established contemporary Turkish artists and a strong presence on the international fairs scene. ⓘ *1 hr. 163 Istiklal Cad.*

⑤ ★ National Palaces Painting Gallery. After a 7-year restoration period, this gallery opened in 2014 in the former Crown Prince residence located within the gardens of the ornate Dolmabahçe Palace. Spread throughout ten rooms and three ballrooms, 202 paintings are on display. They are divided into 11 sections that include themes such as Istanbul Views, Orientalist Painters, and

A roof sculpture at Borusan Contemporary overlooks the Bosphorus and second suspension bridge.

Westernization in the Ottoman Empire. Aside from Turkish painters, there are works by celebrated foreign artists such as Ivan Aivazovsky, Fausto Zonaro, and Stanislaw Chlebowski. The palace itself was home to six sultans and is an over-the-top show of baroque, neo-classical, and rococo styles blended with more traditional Ottoman architecture. It makes an appropriately elaborate setting to peruse the impressive paintings that depict various aspects of one of the world's most important empires. ⏲ *1 hr. Dolmabahçe Palace, Dolmabahçe Caddesi.* ☎ *0212/236-3577. www.millisaray lar.gov.tr. Free admission. Tue–Wed and Fri–Sun 9am–4pm. Tram: Kabataş.*

6 ★ Akaretler. Officially named Şair Nedim Caddesi, this sloping street was once the neoclassical accommodation built in 1875 for Dolmabahçe Palace staff; after renovation, it's an über-stylish row of commercial galleries and high-end designer brands, centering on the

W Hotel (p 142). **Rampa** (no. 21a; ☎ 0212/327-0800; www.rampa istanbul.com) is one of the biggest, with a huge space for large-scale works of its small stable of local contemporary artists, plus foreign artists including David LaChapelle. **C.A.M. Galeri** (no. 25; ☎ 0212/ 245-7975; www.camgaleri.com) has a strong focus on supporting young artists to produce innovative works. The second branch of **Art350** (no. 16; ☎ 0212/369-8050; www.art350. com) opened in May 2013 with a focus on international contemporary art in a variety of mediums. **Art ON** (no. 4; ☎ 0212/259-1543; www. artonistanbul.com) is another small gallery to open in this new art hub, focusing on emerging artists under the direction of Sinem Yılmaz. ⏲ *1 hr. Şair Nedim Cad, Beşiktaş. Tram: Kabataş.*

7 ★★★ Borusan Contemporary. An unusual gallery that during the week functions as the offices of the logistics company, Borusan Holding. On weekends, however, desks are (mostly) cleared and visitors are free to roam this

Modern art at Rampa.

Calligraphy at Sakıp Sabancı Müzesi.

distinctive, early-20th-century, 10-story redbrick building known locally as the "haunted mansion." The walls are hung with innovative contemporary art from local and international artists. Make sure to go all the way to the top to see the sculptures on the roof and take in the staggering Bosphorus views. ⏱ *30 min. Perili Köşçk, 5 Hisar Cad.* ☎ *0212/393-5200. www.borusan contemporary.com. Admission 10 TL adults, free for kids 12 and under. Sat–Sun 10am–8pm. Bus 22 or 42T: Rumelhisarı.*

❽ ★★ Sakıp Sabancı Müzesi (Sakıp Sabancı Museum). In an Italianate 1920s villa overlooking the Bosphorus, this world-class museum houses the private collection of the Sabancı family, a prestigious dynasty of Turkish industrialists. The permanent collection of Ottoman calligraphy in the elegant Atlı Köşk mansion (their former home) covers 500 years of works, including rare manuscripts of the Qur'an, exquisitely displayed. The annex holds temporary exhibits, often of modern European artists. Recent years have seen major retrospectives of Monet and Anish Kapoor. From the museum, take a stroll in nearby pleasant Emirgan Park. ⏱ *90 min. 42 Sakıp Sabancı Cad, Emirgan.* ☎ *0212/277-2200. http://muze.sabanciuniv.edu. Admission 15 TL adults, free for kids 14 and under; free on Wed. Tues–Sun 10am–6pm (Wed till 8pm). Bus: 22 or 42T.*

Istanbul with Kids

Legend:
- (i) Information
- 🏛 Museum
- ☪ Mosque
- 🚢 Ferry
- **Mar** Marmaray suburban rail

KAĞITHANE

ŞİŞLİ

Miniatürk 2

EYÜP

Eyüp 🚢

Haliç Köprüsü

Hasköy 🚢

Ayvansaray

KURTULUŞ

BEYOĞLU 3

KARAKÖY

Kasımpaşa 🚢

Atatürk Köprüsü

🏛 Istanbul Modern

Karaköy 🚢

10 Galata Köprüsü

11 🚢

Sirkeci

Süleymaniye Camii ☪

FATİH

8

Sirkeci Mar

9 🏛 **Topkapı Sarayı**

EMİNÖNÜ

(i) 🏛 ☪ **Hagia Sophia**

Sultanahmet Camii ☪

🚢 Yenikapi

Marmara Denizi

Rumeli Hisarı Müzesi ➐

O-1

BEŞİKTAŞ

Bogaziçi

Yıldız Parkı

Boğaziçi Köprüsü

Maçka Parkı

Dolmabahçe

Dolmabahçe Sarayı

Beşiktaş

Kâbataş

Cemil Bey Korusu

Üsküdar

Paşa Limanı C.

Fethi Paşa Korusu

Üsküdar Mah

ÜSKÜDAR

Şile Otoyolu

Harem

Karacaahmet Mezarlığı

D100 E5 Ankara İstanbul Devletyolu

Haydarpaşa

➊ santralistanbul
➋ Miniatürk
➌ Rahmi Koç Müzesi
➍ Istiklal Nostaljik Tram
➎ Dondurma stalls
➏ Askeri Müzesi
➐ Rumeli Hisarı Müzesi
➑ Panorama 1453
➒ Gülhane Park
➓ Galata Köprüsü
⓫ Eminönü fishing boats

0   1 mi
0   1 km

Much of everyday Istanbul life is a kids' paradise, although the crowds of the metropolis can be daunting in some areas. Locals adore children, so don't be surprised when grown men coo over your baby. The list below, ranging from world-class museums to Ottoman forts, is too much in one day, so pick and choose to suit ages and interests. START: **Bus from Taksim or Eminönü.**

❶ ★★★ santralistanbul.
Housed inside this refurbished Ottoman power station, the **Museum of Energy** has a Play Zone with 22 interactive machines, buttons, and games galore designed for ages 4 to 14. Create magnetic sculptures and even your own electricity, and then take a closer look at huge turbine generators dating back to 1911. Kids can mess around in the Switch Gear Room, where the original connecting cables distributed electricity to the whole city. ⏱ *1 hr. Eski Silahtarağa Elektrik Santralı, Kazım Karabekir Cad, Eyüp.* ☎ *0212/311-7809. www.santralistanbul.org. Admission 10 TL adults, 5 TL kids 6–17. Tues–Fri 10am–6pm, Sat–Sun 10am–8pm. Free shuttle from Atatürk Kültür Merkez (Taksim) every 20 min (Tues–Sat), every hour Sun; boat from Eminönü to Eyüp; bus 44B or 47 from Eminönü, 36T from Taksim.*

❷ ★★ Miniatürk. If you want to see Istanbul's best landmarks close up, this outdoor exhibition of 1.25-scale models is the place to do it. A few strides take you from Galata Tower to the Blue Mosque via Dolmabahçe Palace. There are 45 models of Istanbul's best-loved monuments, plus 15 from the Ottoman Empire, including the Egyptian pyramids, and a toy train ideal for small passengers to weave their way around the park. An indoor exhibition re-creates the World War I battlefields of the Dardanelles Campaign, complete with machine-gun fire and bombs, while the playground, giant chess set, and lovely cafe make it a great family trip. ⏱ *1–2 hr. Imrahor Cad, Sütlüce.* ☎ *0212/222-2882. www.miniaturk. com.tr. Admission 10 TL adults, free for kids 7 and under. Daily 9am–6pm. Boat from Eminönü or Eyüp to Sütlüce; bus 47 from Eminönü or 54HT from Taksim.*

Tiny world wonders at Miniatürk.

One of the many cars at the Rahmi Koç Museum.

❸ ★★ Rahmi Koç Museum.

Kids can jump aboard a Douglas DC-3 (1942) plane, gaze at huge anchors, and explore a plethora of cars ranging from Formula 1 and a 1908 Model T Ford to a 1958 German Amphicar. You can even enter their U.S.A.-produced submarine. Built in 1944 for service in World War II against the Japanese, it then saw 30 years service with the Turkish Naval Forces. You'll love pressing the buttons on the "How Does it Work?" exhibits to watch the mechanism in a cutaway car or domestic washing machine. On weekends, ride the 1960s diesel train along the Golden Horn, between Hasköy and Sütlüce.
🕐 *90 min. 5 Hasköy Cad, Hasköy.* ☎ *0212/369-6600. www.rmk-museum.org.tr. Admission 12.50 TL adults, 6 TL kids 7–17. Submarine 7 TL adults, 6 TL kids 7–17. Tues–Fri 10am–5pm, Sat–Sun 10am–8pm (till 6pm Oct–Mar). Boat from Eminönü or Eyüp to Hasköy. Bus: 54HT from Taksim, 47 from Eminönü.*

❹ ★ Istiklal Nostaljik Tram.

The tram that ran along this street (known as the Grand Rue de Pera) in the 19th and early 20th centuries was taken out of service in 1961. A restored version was re-introduced in 1990, by which time the street had changed its name to the current Istiklal Caddesi (Independence Street). Grab a window seat for a street-level view on the 1.6-km (1-mile) journey, taking about 10 minutes, with a stop halfway at Galatasaray Lisesi (p 49). Use your *Istanbulkart* (transport card; p 164)

Nostaljik tram running down Istiklal Caddesi.

Mehter—Band of the Ottoman Army

The world's oldest military band, the Mehter, accompanied Ottoman armies into battle to instill confidence and, ideally, strike terror into the enemy. These days, various bands perform marches and recitals at the **Military Museum** (daily) and **Dolmabahçe Palace** (p 20), plus at various special events. In full Ottoman costume, the band uses traditional Turkish instruments including *zurna* (reed instrument) and *davul* (large drum). Its stirring style and beat are thought to have influenced European classical composers such as Mozart, Beethoven, and Haydn—though their music did not have to evoke such terror as their Ottoman counterparts' did.

or pay the driver. ⏱ *10 min. Ticket 4 TL, 1.95 TL Istanbulkart. Trams run from Atatürk Monument (Taksim Meydanı) to Tünel Meydanı, every 5–8 min, 9am–11pm.*

5️⃣ ★ **Dondurma Stalls.** You can't miss the traditional *dondurma* (ice cream) stalls dotted along Istiklal—originally from the city of Kahramanmaraş. *Dondurma* (4 TL) is thicker, stickier, and stretchier than normal ice cream thanks to extra ingredients like mastic and *sahlep* (starch from orchids), and is served up by sellers clad in traditional Ottoman costume garb. *Istiklal Cad.*

A street vendor sells dondurma, *a chewy, sticky ice cream made from the root of a wild orchid.*

6️⃣ ★ **Askeri Müzesi (Military Museum).** The army played a huge role in Istanbul's history—modern Turkey's founder Mustafa Kemal Atatürk (p 171) was previously an army general—and this well-laid-out museum celebrates military history from the Ottoman Empire to the present day. Highlights include the Hall of the Conquest of Istanbul, recreating the battle scene, and from the same era, the mammoth chains placed at the entrance of the Golden Horn. Kids will love the dazzling Ottoman gold-plated armor and Yemeni daggers. People gather for the afternoon Mehter performances (above), the uniformed, pompous Janissary band (outdoor in summer, indoor in winter) that led the army into battle. ⏱ *90 min (including Mehter). Harbiye.* ☎ *0212/233-2720. Admission 3 TL adults, 1.30 TL kids 6–12; extra for camera, video. Wed–Sun 9am–4:30pm, Mehter band 3–4pm. M2 Metro Osmanbey/bus: Harbiye.*

7️⃣ ★★★ **Rumeli Hisarı Müzesi (Fortress of Europe).** This 30,000 sq. m (323,000 sq. ft.) landmark fortress overlooking the Bosphorus, with its sturdy walls and watchtowers, was built by Mehmet

the Conqueror in 1452 in just 4 months. It lies opposite his Anadolu Hisarı (Fortress of Asia) on the narrowest part of the strait, and was part of the sultan's plans for his siege of Constantinople in 1453. Its three sturdy towers, 12-sided flag tower, and rows of cannons dating back to Süleyman the Magnificent (p 171) make great exploring, though take great care as there are no guardrails. ⏱ *90 min. Yahya Kemal Cad, Sariyer.* ☎ *0212/263-5305. Admission 3 TL. Thurs–Tues 9am–4:30pm. Bus: 25 or 40E from Beşiktaş.*

⑧ ★★★ Panorama 1453 Museum. Just west of the Byzantine land walls of Theodosius and an easy tram ride from the Old City, this is a great place to help kids (and adults) envisage the great Ottoman siege of Byzantine Constantinople in 1453. Painted around the inside of a giant dome is a vivid re-creation of the siege, complete with Greek fire being hurled from catapults, collapsing walls, battered siege engines, and giant cannons. There are over 10,000 figures painted in the scene, realistic sound effects, and some lovingly recreated models for the diorama. ⏱ *45 min. Topkapı Kültür Merkezi, Topkapı.* ☎ *0212/415-1453. www. panoramikmuze.com. Admission 10TL. Daily 9am–6pm. T1 tram: Topkapı.*

⑨ ★ Gülhane Park. This clean, well-laid-out park (p 92), with broad avenues lined with ancient plane trees, provides some breathing space. Great for the kids to run around, it also houses a museum, historic artifacts, and a good hilltop cafe. ⏱ *Varies. Tram: Gülhane.*

⑩ ★★ Galata Köprüsü (Galata Bridge). An Istanbul landmark (p 10), this makes a lovely end to the day. From the bridge, watch

Hub of fishing on Galata Bridge.

the row of fishermen cast lines, peering optimistically into the murky waters below. Kids can check out their pots of bait (usually maggots) and buckets of tiny fish. Breathtaking views take in ferries cruising up the Haliç (Golden Horn), the mélée of people crowding into Eminönü's markets, and spot-lit mosques at night. *Bridge joining Eminönü to Karaköy. Bus/tram: Eminönü or Karaköy.*

⑪ ★★ Eminönü Fishing Boats. Bobbing on Eminönü's waterfront are huge ornamental fishing boats, offering fresh fish cooked by elaborately dressed attendants in matching Ottoman costume. Feast on cheap *balık ekmek* (fresh fish in bread) with salad, or a corn-on-the-cob with a cool drink. *Eminönü pier, west of Galata Bridge. Balık ekmek 5 TL.*

Byzantine Constantinople

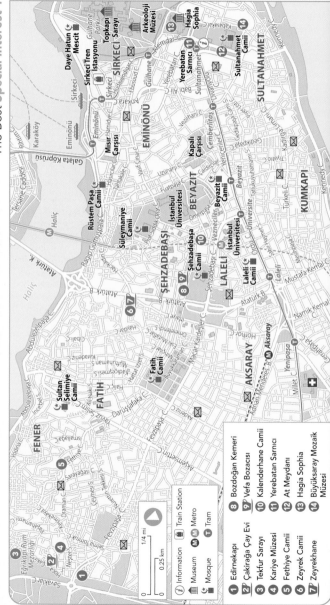

ⓘ Information	🚆 Train Station
🏛 Museum	Ⓜ Ⓜ Metro
☪ Mosque	Ⓣ Tram

0 — 1/4 mi
0 — 0.25 km

1 Edirnekapı
2 Çakırağa Çay Evi
3 Tekfur Sarayı
4 Kariye Müzesi
5 Fethiye Camii
6 Zeyrek Camii
7 Zeyrekhane
8 Bozdoğan Kemeri
9 Vefa Bozacısı
10 Kalenderhane Camii
11 Yerebatan Sarnıcı
12 At Meydanı
13 Hagia Sophia
14 Büyüksaray Mozaik Müzesi

After Istanbul's mosques, it's time for pre-Ottoman monuments. The city founded as Byzantium in the 7th century B.C. was re-founded in A.D. 330 by the Roman emperor Constantine and soon became known as Constantinople (city of Constantine). The capital of the Byzantine Empire (the Christianized inheritor of the wealthy eastern half of the Roman Empire), it was adorned with everything from cisterns to churches, city walls to grandiose columns. START: **Bus to Edirnekapı.**

---

❶ ★ Edirnekapı (Charisius Gate). This gate piercing the 6.5km-long (4 miles) 5th-century city land walls, built by Emperor Theodosius II (408–450), makes a good point to contemplate arguably the greatest and most important fortifications ever built. The inner and outer walls and ditch in front of them still survive remarkably intact and can be followed between the Sea of Marmara and the Golden Horn. For over a thousand years, they defied all foreign foes. Had they fallen to the invading Arab armies of Islam in either the 7th or early 8th centuries, Western Europe may well have become entirely Muslim and the course of world history changed. The Ottoman Turkish Sultan Mehmet the Conqueror rode triumphantly through these gates into the city after the siege of 1453, finally bringing the city into the fold of Islam. ⏱ *30 min. Bus: 87 to Edirnekapı.*

❷ ★ Çakirağa Çay Evi. This traditional teahouse is in keeping with the historic, earthy neighborhood. Sip tea inside or take a table under the canopy opposite. *Hoca Çakır Cad. Bus: 87 to Edirnekapı.*

❸ ★ kids Tekfur Sarayı (Palace of Constantine Porphyrogenitus). Under major restoration at the time of writing (completion date unknown), this former Byzantine palace, built into the city land walls, will be restored to its former glory. Completed in the early 14th century, it later served as a zoo, brothel, pottery workshop, and poorhouse before being abandoned in the late 18th century. Adjacent is the weekend **Pigeon Market** where birds cost up to $500. ⏱ *15–30 min. Corner of Şişhane Cad and Hoca Çakır Cad. Bus: 87 to Edirnekapı.*

The beautiful exterior of the Church of St. Savior in Chora.

Christ adorns the dome at Fethiye Camii.

4 ★★★ Kariye Müzesi (Kariye Museum, or Church of St. Savior in Chora). Inside this modest-looking 11th-century church are world-class frescoes and mosaics, endowed by Theodore Metochites (1270–1332), writer and senior member of the Byzantine administration who died here in 1332. Among these stunning works, look out for his portrait in the inner narthex, offering a model of the church to a seated Christ. Spread over the two narthexes and side chapel are three cycles of biblical stories told in charming figurative mosaic form, starting with the birth of the Virgin Mary, continuing with Christ's birth, and ending with Jesus' miracles. The side chapel is also home to some superb frescoes including, in the apse, Christ breaking down the gates of Hell on resurrection day. It was converted to a mosque soon after the Conquest, then into a museum in the 1950s. ⏱ *60–90 min. Kariye Camii Sok, Edirnekapı.* ☎ *0212/522-1750. Admission 15 TL adults, free for kids 11 and under. Thurs–Tues Apr–Oct 9am–7pm, Nov–Mar 9am–4:30pm. Bus 86 from Eminönü or 87 from*

Taksim, then 5-min. walk; or tram to Pazartekke and 1.5km (1 mile) walk along land walls.

5 ★★ Fethiye Camii (Church of the Pammakaristos). From **4**, walk down to Draman Caddesi and then Fethiye Caddesi (10 min). The church was built in 1292 and served as a nunnery and seat of the Patriarchate (1456–1568) until it was converted into a mosque in 1573 by Murat III who renamed it Fethiye (victory) to celebrate his conquests over Georgia and Azerbaijan. Part of the former church still operates as a mosque, but the funerary chapel was turned into a museum when amazingly well-preserved Byzantine mosaics were discovered beneath the whitewash. ⏱ *40 min. Fethiye Kapısı, off Fethiye Cad.* ☎ *0212/635-1273. Admission 5 TL. Thurs–Tues 9am–4:30pm Bus: 90 Eminönü to Draman.*

6 ★ kids Zeyrek Camii (Monastery of the Pantocrator). Set in a rapidly gentrifying area of traditional wooden houses, this monastery church turned mosque was under major restoration at the time of writing. The original church of the monastery was built between 1118 and 1124 by Empress Eirene Komnena. Mehmet II turned the monastery into a *medrese* (religious school) and the church into a mosque. ⏱ *20 min. Ibadethane Sok. Bus: Taksim or Eminönü to Atatürk Bulvarı.*

7 ★ Zeyrekhane. Opposite the monastery, sip coffee or taste Turkish dishes on the restaurant's terrace, a restored building within the old monastery complex. A perfect stop on a Byzantine tour. *10 Ibadethane Arkası Sok, Zeyrek.* ☎ *0212/532-2778. Bus: Taksim or Eminönü to Atatürk Bulvarı. Entrees from 25 TL.*

The 4th-century two-tiered Aqueduct of Valens.

⑧ ★ kids Bozdoğan Kemeri (Aqueduct of Valens). This 4th-century, 18m-high (59 ft.) two-tiered aqueduct was completed under Emperor Valens to carry water from Belgrade Forest to the palace, and was still in use in the 19th century. 🕐 20 min. *Aqueduct parallel to Mustafa Kemalpaşa Cad, crossing Atatürk Bulvarı.*

⑨ ★★ kids Vefa Bozacısı. A favorite since 1876, with an original intricately tiled interior. Try *boza*, made from fermented millet, or the fruity *şıra* drink. *104 Katıp Çelebi Cad. Bus: 87 to Edirnekapı. Boza 3 TL.*

⑩ ★★ Kalenderhane Camii (Church of Theotokus Kyriotissa). This early-Byzantine cross-in-square, domed church was much rebuilt in the late 12th century. It was converted to a mosque following the 1453 conquest and renamed when Mehmet II assigned it to the Kalenderi Dervish order. Inside this working mosque, look for the fresco fragments above the main doorway, although most of the frescoes discovered during its 1966 restoration are now in the Archaeological Museum (p 14). From here, you can walk to the tram for Sultanahmet. 🕐 20 min.

16 Mart Şehitleri Cad. Open prayer times only. Tram: Üniversite.

⑪ ★★★ kids Yerebatan Sarnıcı (Basilica Cistern). The Byzantines used engineering know-how to bring water to the city, despite droughts and sieges. Founded in A.D. 532 by Emperor Justinian (487–565), this vast underground cistern held around 100,000 tons of water, with 336 9m-high (30 ft.) columns holding up the roof. Once traversed by rowing boat, today by walkway, this is the most magnificent of the many cisterns beneath the city. Opposite the entrance, the **Milion Stone** is all that remains of a monumental triumphal arch, which once marked distances from Constantinople to other prominent cities in the Byzantine Empire. 🕐 45 min. *13 Yerebatan Cad, Sultanahmet.* ☎ *0212/522-1259. www.yerebatan.com. Admission 10 TL adults, free for kids 7 and under. Daily Apr–Oct 9am–6:30pm, Nov–Mar 9am–5pm. Tram: Sultanahmet.*

⑫ ★★ kids At Meydanı (Hippodrome). Standing in this rectangular open square, repaved in 2013, try to imagine thousands of fans cheering on chariot racing, or perhaps macabre jeering at public executions, in one of the Empire's

The vast underground 5th-century water cistern at Yerebatan Sarnıcı held 100,000 tons of water.

largest hippodromes (p 67). Built in the 3rd century and enlarged by Constantine I, this was the site of 30,000 deaths during the A.D. 532 Nika Riots. ⏱ *30 min. At Meydanı. Tram: Sultanahmet.*

⑬ ★★★ kids **Hagia Sophia.** Rebuilt by Emperor Justinian in A.D. 537, its hulking exterior contrasts with its ornate interior and breathtaking dome. It followed a basic rule of Byzantine architecture: A modest exterior to save your attention for inside. ⏱ *90 min. Ayasofya Meydanı, Sultanahmet.* ☎ *0212/522-1750. www.ayasofyamuzesi.gov.tr. Admission 30 TL adults, free for kids 12 and under; audio tours 10 TL. Tues–Sun Apr–Oct 9am–7pm, Nov–Mar 9am–5 pm. Tram: Sultanahmet.*

⑭ ★ **Büyüksaray Mozaik Müzesi (Mosaic Museum).** Nestled behind **Arasta Bazaar and Blue Mosque,** the stone walls are the only remains of Emperor Justinian's 6th-century Byzantine Great Palace, in ruins since 1206. The incredible mosaics you see today— huntsmen spearing gazelles and tussling elephants and lions—are among the few remaining Byzantine non-religious mosaics left in the city. ⏱ *40 min. Arasta Çarşısı, Torun Sok.* ☎ *0212/518-1205. Admission 8 TL adults, free for kids 11 and under. Tues–Sun 9am–4pm. Tram: Sultanahmet.* ●

The Egyptian obelisk at the Hippodrome.

Istiklal Caddesi

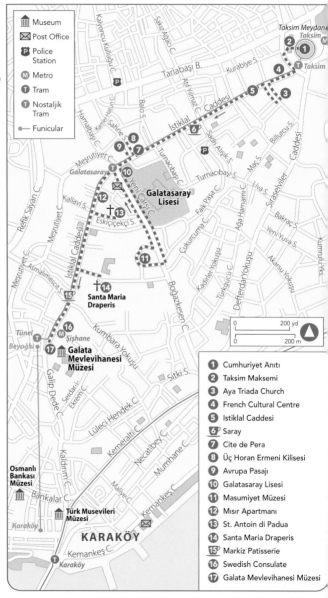

Legend:
- 🏛 Museum
- ✉ Post Office
- 🅿 Police Station
- Ⓜ Metro
- 🚋 Tram
- 🚋 Nostaljik Tram
- Funicular

Taksim Meydanı
Taksim
Taksim

Galatasaray Lisesi

Santa Maria Draperis

Tünel
Beyoğlu

Galata Mevlevihanesi Müzesi

Osmanlı Bankası Müzesi

Türk Musevileri Müzesi

Karaköy

KARAKÖY

Karaköy

0   200 yd
0   200 m

1. Cumhuriyet Anıtı
2. Taksim Maksemi
3. Aya Triada Church
4. French Cultural Centre
5. Istiklal Caddesi
6. Saray
7. Cite de Pera
8. Üç Horan Ermeni Kilisesi
9. Avrupa Pasajı
10. Galatasaray Lisesi
11. Masumiyet Müzesi
12. Mısır Apartmanı
13. St. Antoin di Padua
14. Santa Maria Draperis
15. Markiz Patisserie
16. Swedish Consulate
17. Galata Mevlevihanesi Müzesi

Previous page: From Yeni Camii to Galata Tower, walk among Istanbul's many sights.

This 3km-long (2-mile) pedestrianized boulevard (Independence Street), known in the 19th century as the Grande Rue de Pera, remains modern Istanbul's main artery. It's the city's shopping hub and home to myriad bars, restaurants, and clubs; a plethora of churches; cinemas; a few mosques; and numerous Art Nouveau–style buildings. START: **Bus, Metro, or tram/funicular to Taksim.**

❶ ★ Cumhuriyet Anıtı (Republic Memorial). This striking arch-shaped monument was commissioned by Mustafa Kemal Atatürk to commemorate the founding of the Turkish Republic and made by Italian sculptor Pietro Canonica in 1928. At last, the post-Ottoman era meant figurative expressions could now be used (previously forbidden in Islam). So one shows Atatürk the leader, with Ismet İnönü (the Republic's first president) and Fevzi Çakmak (soldier and ex-prime minister) marking the foundation of the young Turkish Republic. Around the other side, Atatürk stands with soldiers, representing the War of Independence. ⏱ *10 min. Taksim Meydanı.*

❷ ★ Taksim Maksemi (Water Distribution Center). This white, low, octagonal building, the first

Cumhuriyet Anıtı in Taksim Square.

structure in Taksim Square, was the water distribution center ordered by Sultan Mahmut I in 1732. Today it is the municipality-run Taksim Art Gallery. The square itself, a symbol of the secular Turkish republic, is the hub of most political demonstrations. These are best avoided, especially on May Day. The spring of 2013 saw major confrontations between police and protestors attempting to save one of the square's few patches of green, Gezi Park, from being lost to a government-sponsored redevelopment. *Taksim Meydanı.*

❸ ★ Aya Triada Church. A short walk from Taksim Maksemi is Istanbul's largest Greek Orthodox Church, on the left at the junction of Istiklal and Sıraselviler Caddesis. This majestic white church was built in 1880 by Greek architect Kampanaki. It's officially only open for Sunday services, although you may be able to peek inside if the caretaker is around. It has impressive frescoes above the gallery, a painted dome, and mosaics of the Virgin Mary and Christ that dominate the entrance hall. This monumental church is a reminder of the former wealth and power of the city's Greek Orthodox population, shrunk from around 300,000 at the birth of the Turkish Republic in 1923 to just a couple of thousand today. ⏱ *15 min. Entrance off Meşelik Sok, off Istiklal Cad. Services Sun 9–11am. Bus/tram/funicular to Taksim.*

❹ ★ French Cultural Center. Opposite the church on the west side of Istiklal Caddesi, this fine

Aya Triada, Istanbul's largest Greek Orthodox church.

19th-century building houses the pleasant Café Francais, where in decent weather you can sit in the peaceful courtyard and enjoy a latte, full breakfast, or sandwich. The center is home to many temporary art exhibitions, screens movies, and acts as an occasional concert venue. *4 Istiklal Cad.* ☎ *0212/393-8111. Sandwiches 10 TL and up; latte 7 TL.*

⑤ ★ Istiklal Caddesi. As you walk down bustling Istiklal Caddesi, look out for **Rumeli Han** on the right, one of the most adorned doorways with inscriptions in Arabic. A little further down on the same side is the Ağa Camii, a pretty mosque with a typically Ottoman domed roof and cylindrical minaret, dating to 1594. Just past it is the modern Demirören mall, which blends in quite well with the 19th-century buildings around it. ⓘ *10 min. Istiklal Cad.*

⑥ ★ kids Saray. Traditional Turkish pudding shop dating back to 1935, with several floors to sit and partake of baklava, milk puddings, and other goodies—and a choice of entrees and snacks. *105 Istiklal Cad.* ☎ *0212/236-1617. Coffee and baklava 15 TL.*

⑦ ★★ Cite de Pera. A fine reminder of the Grande Rue de Pera's glory years. Originally it was the Naum Theater and hosted Italian operas. After it burned down during the great Pera fire of 1870, Greek-Turkish banker Hristaki Zografos Efendi bought the land and rebuilt it as Cite de Pera. In the 1940s, florists traded from the first-floor stores, and it was known as **Çiçek Pasajı (Flower Passage),** a name still used today. After a major renovation of the building in 1978, it was filled with noisy *meyhanes* (taverns). It lacks the character of former days but has been beautifully restored and it is worth a look inside. ⓘ *10 min. 172 Istiklal Cad.*

⑧ ★ Üç Horan Ermeni Kilisesi (Armenian Church of Three Altars). A hidden gem on **Balık Pasajı,** this church behind heavy wooden doors (usually open to the public) celebrated its 200th anniversary in 2008. With a plain exterior and graceful interior, the story goes that an unknown sick man prayed to be cured, promising to build a church with three altars if his prayers were answered. Peek inside to see the famed altars. ⓘ *15 min.*

Historic Cite de Pera, now Çiçek Pasajı.

Small black angel statues line Avrupa Pasajı.

24 Sahane Sok, Balık Pasajı. Services Sun 9am–noon. Open daily 8am–5pm.

⑨ ★ Avrupa Pasajı (Europe Arcade). This cute 19th-century arcade is lined on either side by neo-classical statues, perched several meters above ground level. It's a reasonable place to browse for interesting ephemera. ⏱ *15 min. Off Sahne Sok. Most stores open daily 10am–7pm.*

⑩ ★★ Galatasaray Lisesi. A major landmark, this school was established in the 15th century, when Sultan Beyazit II (1447–1513) responded to an old man's wish to build a school for educating "promising young men." Fast forward to the late 19th century when Sultan Abdülaziz acquired the help of Napoleon III in transforming the school to the contemporary French *lycée* system, a huge influence on modernizing Ottoman Turkey. Since 1992, it's been part of Galatasaray University, and is co-educational with entrance exams required, even at primary level. Visitors are allowed to enter the grounds (9am–5pm) or just peer through the ornate gilded gates. ⏱ *15 min. Istiklal Cad.*

⑪ ★★ Masumiyet Müzesi (Museum of Innocence). Take a 10-minute detour down Yeniçarşı

Caddesi to a curious museum opened in 2008 at the behest of the Istanbul-born, Nobel Prize–winning author Orhan Pamuk. It's best to have read the novel of the same name first, otherwise the 4,000 cigarette butts on display, along with a plethora of other mundane objects, will mean little to you. ⏱ *30 min. Çukurcuma Caddesi, Dalgıç Çıkmazı.* ☎ *0212/252-9738. www.masumiyetmuzesi.org. Admission 25 TL adults, 10 TL students. Open Tues–Sun 10am–6pm (Thurs till 9pm).*

⑫ ★★ Mısır Apartmanı. This white six-story apartment block was built in 1920 by Hovzep Aznavur, a

The top floor of stylish 360Istanbul.

prominent Armenian architect who also built St. Stephen of the Bulgars (p 73). Take the lift to the top floor and walk down, popping into the small private art galleries inside or lunch in the stylish **360Istanbul** on the top floor (p 119). This building was the winter residence for 19th-century Abbas Halim Pasha, son of an Egyptian prince; *Mısır* is Turkish for Egypt. ⏱ *30–60 min. 163 Istiklal Cad.*

⓭ ★ **St. Antoin di Padua.** This one is easy to miss: It's set back from the main drag behind a triple-arched gateway. The huge neo-Gothic Catholic church, built in 1913 by Giulio Mongeri, replaces the original one here from 1725. The interior is dominated by a statue of Christ on the cross suspended from the ceiling. The leafy courtyard is delightful, with circular stained-glass windows and flowerpots up on the ledges of the entrance archway, originally part of apartments built as a source of income for the church. The statue of Pope John XXIII, who served Istanbul's Catholic community (1935–44), was unveiled by Pope Benedict XVI on his 2006 visit. ⏱ *15 min. Istiklal Cad. Daily 8am–7:30pm.*

⓮ ★ **Santa Maria Draperis.** Even easier to pass by than St. Antoin di Padua, the church is reached via a steep flight of steps running down from the street. This unusual location dates from the days when it was forbidden for churches to have visible spires. This Franciscan church, dating back to 1789, has a gorgeous bell tower, visible from the courtyard. ⏱ *15 min. 215 Istiklal Cad. Daily 10am–noon and 2–6pm.*

⓯ ★ **kids** **Markiz Patisserie.** Now called Yemek Külübü, this was loved by Pera's bohemian elite, including young author Orhan Pamuk. The huge Art Nouveau tile panels by French artist J.A. Arnoux once depicted all four seasons, although only spring and fall remain. *172A Istiklal Cad.* ☎ *0212/252-2701. Sandwiches from 6 TL.*

St. Antoin di Padua.

Santa Maria Draperis, hidden from view.

⓰ ★ Swedish Consulate.

Among the street's many consulates, mainly European, this is one of the most attractive. Resembling a summer palace, it was built on land bought in 1757, and was Sweden's first state-owned property overseas. Its chapel, built in 1858, is still used by the Protestant congregation. ◷ *15 min. 247 Istiklal Cad, Tünel.*

⓱ ★★ kids Galata Mevlevihanesi Müzesi (Galata Dervish Lodge Museum).

Reopened in 2011 after a major restoration, the museum housed in the 1491 *tekke* (lodge) built for the Mevlevi (Whirling Dervishes) contains traditional musical instruments, illuminated Qur'ans, and costumes. Many of the lodge's Sufis are buried in the serene graveyard, including the tomb of Galip Dede, the revered 17th-century Sufi poet, and the ornate fountain of Hasan Ağa (1649). This is the venue of the famous *sema* ceremony, where white-clad Dervishes perform their trancelike "whirling" meditation that brings them closer to God. Check the time of performances at the gate. ◷ *30 min. 15 Galip Dede Cad.* ☎ *0212/245-4141. www. galatamevlevihanesimuzesi.gov.tr. Admission 10 TL adults, free for kids 7 and under. Wed–Mon 9:30am– 4:30pm. Bus/funicular: Taksim, then walk. Tunnel: Tünel.*

Eyüp's Sacred Sites

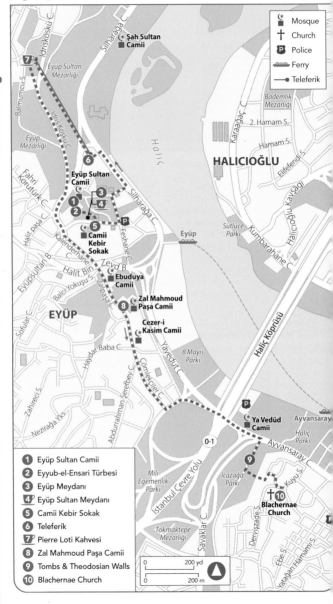

Legend:
- (★ Mosque
- † Church
- **P** Police
- Ferry
- Teleferik

Map labels:

Şah Sultan Camii

Eyüp Sultan Mezarlığı

İdrisköşkü C.

Silharaǧa C.

Balmumcu c.

İdris Köşkü C.

Eyüp Mezarlığı

Fahri Korutürk C.

Haliç

Bademlik Mezarlığı

HALICIOĞLU

2. Hamam S.

Hamam S.

Karaağaç C.

Elifefendi S.

Kumbarahane C.

Haliçlioğlu Kayğaǧı

Eyüp Sultan Camii

Silharaǧa C.

Kalenderhane

Camii Kebir Sokak

Meşhane C.

Eyüp

Sütlüce Parkı

Halit paşa C.

Eyüpsultan B.

Balcı Yokuşu S.

Halit Bin Zeyd B.

Zalpaşa

Ebuduya Camii

Zal Mahmoud Paşa Camii

Cezer-i Kasim Camii

Haliç Köprüsü

EYÜP

Sofular C.

Haydar Baba C.

Zahire C.

Neziraǧa Yks.

Abdurrahman Şeretbey C.

Çömlekçiler C.

Yavedut C.

8 Mayıs Parkı

P

Ya Vedüd Camii

Ayvansaray

Haliç Parkı

0-1

Ayvansaray C.

Mili Egemenlik Parkı

İstanbul Çevre Yolu

Savaklar C.

Tokmáktepe Mezarlığı

İcazaǧa Parkı

Dervişzade C.

† Blachernae Church

Ebe S.

Yatağan Hamamı S.

Kuyu C.

Numbered list:

1. Eyüp Sultan Camii
2. Eyyub-el-Ensari Türbesi
3. Eyüp Meydanı
4. Eyüp Sultan Meydanı
5. Camii Kebir Sokak
6. Teleferik
7. Pierre Loti Kahvesi
8. Zal Mahmoud Paşa Camii
9. Tombs & Theodosian Walls
10. Blachernae Church

0   200 yd
0   200 m

Join religious pilgrims in Eyüp, located beyond the 5th-century land walls of Theodosius. It's best known for the sacred Eyyub-el-Ensari tomb, and on weekends, small boys in white satin costumes fill the square for their circumcision ceremony (*sünnet*). You could reverse this tour to end at the Pierre Loti cafe at sundown. START: **Bus 55T from Taksim or 99A from Eminönü to Eyüp.**

❶ ★★ kids Eyüp Sultan Camii. The mosque you see today, completed in 1880, replaces the first imperial mosque, built by Mehmet II in 1458, a few years after the fall of Constantinople. Its vast courtyard was the site of the Ottoman Girding of the Sword of Osman, the enthronement rite where the sword of 13th-century leader Osman Gazi was passed on. Local people watched the ceremony and, in so doing, accepted that the ruler had possession of the city. ⏱ *20 min. Eyüp Meydanı. Open daily dawn–dusk.*

❷ ★★ Eyyub-el-Ensari Türbesi (Tomb). Adjacent to the mosque, this shrine is one of Islam's holiest sites. Standard-bearer and companion of the Prophet Mohammed, Eyüp Sultan (as he was later known) was killed in the 7th century during the Arab siege of Constantinople and buried outside the city. Before conquering Constantinople in 1453, Mehmet II rediscovered Eyüp's grave and built a shrine and mosque. The tomb attracts many worshippers, especially on Fridays; non-Muslims wearing modest clothing are welcome (p 166). Inside, vivid blue Iznik tiles contrast with the silver sarcophagus. Look out for the footprint of Mohammed in marble framed and embedded in the tomb's left-hand wall. ⏱ *15 min. Eyüp Meydanı. Free admission. Daily 9am–5pm.*

❸ ★★ kids Eyüp Meydanı (Eyüp Square). Take a breather to people-watch in this enthralling

Dazzling tiles outside the tomb.

public square, adjacent to the tomb. During weekends, family groups gather for photographs along with their small sons, aged between 4 and 8, decked out in white satin *sünnet* (circumcision) suits. ⏱ *15–30 min.*

❹ ★ kids Eyüp Meydanı. Plenty of busy food options in the main square. A safe bet is Karadeniz Pide—or choose ice cream and waffles if you need a sugary snack. *Pide 8 TL.*

❺ ★★ kids Cami Kebir Sokak (Cami Kebir Bazaar). This lively bazaar lines both sides of the

What's in a Name?

In 2007, a dispute over a name opened a can of worms: The hillside topped by Pierre Loti Kahvesi was known as Pierre Loti Heights, but the mayor of Eyüp wanted it changed to Eyüp Sultan Heights, after the sacred man (**2**), so he put up a new sign at the *teleferik*. Local opinion in this conservative enclave divided along secular and religious lines, with some saying Pierre Loti was part of the city's cultural history, and others feeling that to name it Eyüp Sultan was more in keeping with Muslim Turkish history.

pedestrianized street in front of the mosque, catering to religious visitors. Multi-colored headscarves swirl in the breeze, copies of the Qur'an are piled up on the stalls, jewelry and trinkets add a touch of glamour, and a crackly CD player usually blasts out Qur'anic or musical recitals. ⏱ *30 min. Cami Kebir Sok. Daily 9am–6pm.*

6 ★★ kids **Teleferik (Cable Car).** From Cami Kebir Sokak, turn left past Sultan Mehmed Resad

Headscarves fill the Cami Kebir Bazaar.

Han Tomb, turn right at the end, and left onto the main road. You're now at the cable-car station for the 3-minute journey up Pierre Loti Hill above the huge Eyüp Sultan Cemetery. It's a good choice if you don't fancy the fascinating half-hour hike. If you walk down through the cemetery, take a closer look at the Ottoman-era gravestones. Expect long lines for the *teleferik* on weekends and late afternoons in summer. ⏱ *30–60 min. Ticket 3 TL, Istanbulkart 1.95 TL. Daily 8am–10:30pm.*

7 ★★★ kids **Pierre Loti Kahvesi.** Named after the pining Turkophile French novelist who penned Aziyade in 1879 about his lover, this cafe has Golden Horn views and a shady terrace, one of Istanbul's best. *Balmumcu Sok, Gümüşsuyu Cad.* ☎ *0212/581-2696. Tea 2 TL.*

8 ★★ kids **Zal Mahmoud Paşa Camii (Zal Mahmoud Paşa Mosque).** Walk through the cemetery and across the main square, down Kalenderhane Caddesi, then down Hz Halid Bulvarı, a street dotted with quaint wooden houses. On the left is this dark-stone mosque complex, built by Mimar Sinan (p 9) in 1571, which also contains the tomb of Zal Mahmoud Paşa, Süleyman I's teacher. ⓘ *15–30 min. 36 Feshane Cad.*

⑨ ★ **Tombs & Land Walls of Theodosius.** From the mosque, walk south down Çomlekçiler Caddesi, under the Haliç Bridge spanning the Golden Horn. This heads into the Ayvansaray neighborhood, marked by the land walls of Theodosius II, built in A.D. 413 to seal Constantinople against invasion. From the main road, turn left into the grounds of the tiny mosque, Hacı Husrev Mescidi, and take the main gates on the left. Walk through the gorgeous rose gardens, under the stone arch and past the tomb of Ebu Şeybetul el Hudri Hz. Turn left and downhill to follow the inside of the land walls through quaint old houses and cottage gardens. ⓘ *30 min.*

The Theodosian Walls, built in A.D. 412.

A view and a glass of tea at Pierre Loti Kahvesi.

⑩ ★ **Blachernae Church.** After descending the city walls, turn left down Toklu Ibrahim Sokak and follow Kafesci Yumni Sokaği. At the end, to the right you'll see the secluded Blachernae Church. Originally built in A.D. 451 and once a venerated Byzantine shrine, it was rebuilt several times. Today, its late-19th-century incarnation houses the Blachernae *ayazma* (sacred spring), thought to have healing powers. The waters dripped into a reservoir behind the building, accumulated in a large pool, and then through holes in the hands of a marble relief (replaced after breakage in 1960) of the Virgin Mary. Byzantine times saw emperors plunge three times into the pool. Now, the holy water is poured for Greek Orthodox worshippers to drink. Services are held every Friday at 9:30am. ⓘ *15 min. Ayvansaray Kuyusu Sokaği, off Mustafa Paşa Bostanı Sok. Daily 8am–5pm.*

Tünel to **Karaköy**

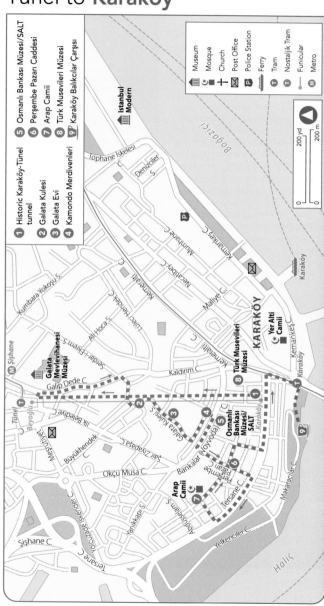

1 Historic Karaköy-Tünel tunnel
2 Galata Kulesi
3 Galata Evi
4 Kamondo Merdivenleri
5 Osmanlı Bankası Müzesi/SALT
6 Perşembe Pazarı Caddesi
7 Arap Camii
8 Türk Musevileri Müzesi
9 Karaköy Balıkçılar Çarşısı

Museum
Mosque
Church
Post Office
Police Station
Ferry
Tram
Nostaljik Tram
Funicular
Metro

200 yd
200 m

İstanbul Modern

Tophane İskelesi

Denizciler S.

Kemankeş C.

Mumhane C.

Necatibey C.

Kemeraltı C.

Maliye C.

KARAKÖY

Karaköy

Lüleci Hendek C.

Ali Hoca S.

Serdar-ı Ekrem S.

Kaldırım C.

Kemeraltı C.

Yer Altı Camii

Kemankeş C.

Karaköy

Galata Mevlevihanesi Müzesi

Galip Dede C.

Türk Musevileri Müzesi

M Şişhane

Beyoğlu

Tünel

İlk Belediye C.

Galata Kulesi S.

Kaldırım C.

Osmanlı Bankası Müzesi/SALT

Karaköy

Meşrutiyet C.

Büyükhendek C.

Şair Ziyapaşa C.

Bankalar (Voyvoda) C.

Perşembe Pazarı

Okçu Musa C.

Tersane C.

Makalacılar C.

Arap Camii

Abdüsselam S.

Yanıkkapı S.

Tersane C.

Yelkenciler C.

Sişhane C.

Tersane C.

Yüzücüzade İskender C.

Haliç

Boğazici

This neighborhood walk centers on Galata, part of Beyoğlu in today's bohemian Istanbul, and the epitome of 19th-century European culture. After decades of neglect, today it is gentrified, with affluent restored housing, its steep cobbled streets, and a mix of stylish coffee shops and traditional workshops. START: **Tunnel from Karaköy to Tünel.**

1 ★★ kids **Historic Karaköy–Tünel Tunnel.** Beginning at Karaköy, take a ride on the world's second-oldest subway system (after the London underground)—and the shortest. French engineer Eugene Henri Gavand built the 573m-long (1,880 ft.) funicular in 1874 with a steam engine and gas lamps, after seeing locals struggle between Galata and Pera. If you're staying in Beyoğlu, start your walk from Tünel. 🕐 15 min. Sebahattin Evren Cad. www.iett.gov.tr/en. Electronic ticket 4 TL, or Istanbulkart 1.95 TL. Mon–Sat 7am–10:45pm, Sun 7:30am–10.45 pm.

2 ★★★ kids **Galata Kulesi (Galata Tower).** Ascend the tower for Istanbul's best panoramic view. In the late 17th century,

Take a ride through the Karaköy–Tünel tunnel, the world's second-oldest subway system.

Hazerfan Ahmet Çelebi allegedly became one of the world's first aviators, using artificial wings to power his flight as he leapt off the tower over the Bosphorus. 🕐 1 hr. Büyük Hendek Sok, Galata. ☎ 0212/293-8180. Daily 9am–8pm. Admission 6.50€, or equivalent in TL, free for kids 5 and under. Tunnel to Tünel or tram to Karaköy.

3 ★ **Galata Evi (Galata House).** From the tower, head left down Galata Kulesi Sokak to this historic residence. Converted by architects Mete and Nadire Göktuğ in the 1990s into a restaurant, it was built in the early 20th century as a jail for British subjects. Have a drink and poke around its tiny dining areas and terrace, and try to spot the prisoners' graffiti. 🕐 15–30 min. 61 Galata Kulesi Sok. ☎ 0212/245-1861 (restaurant reservation). www. thegalatahouse.com.

4 ★★ **Kamondo Merdivenleri (Camondo Staircase).** From Galata Kulesi Sokak, turn left onto Kart Çınar Sokak and on the right you'll see a curvaceous double staircase. Built in 1860 by Avram Camondo, head of the Jewish banking family (see "The Camondo Dynasty" box, p 59), this led from Voyvoda Caddesi, today known as Bankalar Caddesi or Street of the Banks, to the family home on Felek Sokak. Built soon after his son Moise was born, its hexagonal design meant there wasn't far to fall if a child slipped. Camondo, a leading merchant in the city, was the first foreigner given the right to own real estate during the

Ottoman Empire, and this staircase was his gift to the city. ◷ *10 min. Off Voyvoda Cad.*

❺ ★★ kids Osmanlı Bankası Müzesi (Ottoman Banking Museum) and SALT Gallery. From the bottom of the steps, turn right and cross the road to this great little museum. Housed in the former Ottoman bank headquarters, this was Constantinople's first "modern" bank. There are plenty of explanatory boards giving the surprisingly interesting history of the bank and its cosmopolitan customers and employees—largely Jews, Armenians, and Greeks. Venture into the vaults storing banknotes from 1875. The remainder of this grandiose late-19th-century building, designed by French architect Vallaury, is now the SALT contemporary arts gallery, with an ever-changing series of exhibitions. ◷ *1 hr. 32 Mete Cad.* ☎ *0212/292-7605. www.obmuseum. com. Free admission. Tues–Sat noon–8pm, Sun noon–6pm. Tram: Karaköy.*

❻ ★ Perşembe Pazarı Caddesi. From the museum, turn left

The ethnographic section of the Jewish Museum of Turkey.

The hexagonal curves of the Camondo staircase.

and left again onto this historic trading street. One of the area's busiest (except on Sun) and most charming streets, this is chock-full of *hans*, sturdy 18th-century merchants' houses. ◷ *10 min.*

❼ ★ Arap Camii (Arab Mosque). Approach from Tersane Caddesi for a dramatic first glimpse. The mosque's deep-red minaret was once the bell tower of the church, built by the Genoese; later it was the original church for Black Friars. Mehmet II turned it into Galata Camii in the 1470s, known as Arap Camii when Beyazit II assigned it to Moors (Muslims from the Spanish region) fleeing the 15th-century Spanish Inquisition. The courtyard is an oasis of peace, the interior beautifully restored in 2012–13. ◷ *15 min. 15 Futuhat Sok. Open daily dawn–dusk.*

❽ ★★ Türk Musevileri Müzesi (Jewish Museum of Turkey). Hidden up an alleyway, the museum is housed in the former 17th-century Zulfaris Synagogue, rebuilt in neo-classıcal form in the

The Camondo Dynasty

Istanbul's Jewish community was largely established by those fleeing the 1497 Spanish Inquisition, when Jews were forced to convert to Christianity or face death. The Camondo family, well-known bankers, fled to Vienna, and then came to Istanbul following the Austrian takeover in 1798. Once again they soon flourished as merchants and philanthropists, respected by their adopted country despite being "minorities." Such was the esteem shown to Avram (**5**) that, after he moved to Paris in his 80s and died there in 1873, his body was flown back to Istanbul for a state funeral.

late 19th century. It gives a fascinating insight into local Jewish history, revealing how Jews living in Bursa considered the Ottomans as saviors when they captured the city from the Byzantines in 1326. Even more importantly, when the Jews were expelled from Spain and Portugal in 1492, Ottoman sultan Beyazit II (1448–1512) welcomed them with open arms. More recently, Atatürk invited Jewish scientists from Nazi Germany, and several Turkish diplomats saved Turkish Jews during the Holocaust. Look out for displays of silver used inside for synagogue services, and displays highlighting the historic cultural similarities between Muslims and Jews.

🕐 *1 hour. Selanik Pasajı, Perçemli Sok, Karaköy Meydanı.* ☎ *0212/292-6333. www.muze500.com. Admission 10 TL adults, 3 TL kids 12–17. Mon–Thurs 10am–4pm, Fri and Sun 10am–2pm. Closed Sat and Jewish holidays. Tram/tunnel: Karaköy.*

9 ★★ kids **Karaköy Balıkcılar Çarşısı (Karaköy Fish Market).** Enjoy simple, fresh grilled fish with salad and bread on wooden rickety tables next to the market. Stunning views of the Old City skyline. Open late in summer; cash only. *Fish sandwich with salad from 5 TL.*

Karaköy Fish Market is the most popular fish market in Istanbul.

Üsküdar

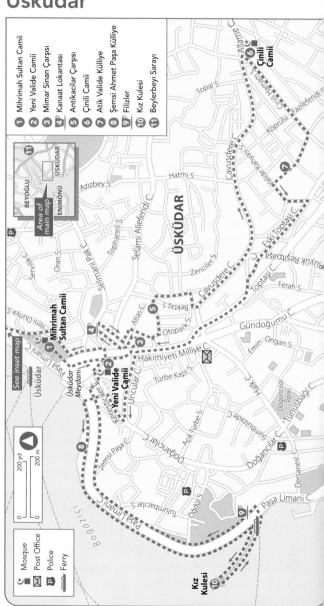

1. Mihrimah Sultan Camii
2. Yeni Valide Camii
3. Mimar Sinan Çarşısı
4. Kanaat Lokantası
5. Antikacılar Çarşısı
6. Çinili Camii
7. Atik Valide Külliye
8. Şemsi Ahmet Paşa Külliye
9. Filizler
10. Kız Kulesi
11. Beylerbeyi Sarayı

R ide the ferry from Europe to Asia to visit this charming, if conservative, neighborhood scattered with some lovely Ottoman-era mosques. You could return to Europe through the Bosphorus tunnel via the Marmaray Metro. START: **Ferry from Eminönü, Beşiktaş or Karaköy to Üsküdar.**

① ★★ **Mihrimah Sultan Camii (Mihrimah Sultan Mosque).** Dominating your first sight of Üsküdar from the ferry is this mosque built by Sinan in 1548. Also known as Iskele ("docks") Camii, it was built for Süleyman I in memory of his favorite daughter, Mihrimah, on a raised platform to protect it from the water. With no space for a central courtyard, Sinan used a protruding roof to cover the *Şadırvan* (ablutions fountain). ○ *20 min.*

② ★ **Yeni Valide Camii (Yeni Valide Mosque).** Walk to the south side of the former plaza, since 2013 the superstructure of the first station on the Asian side of the Marmaray Metro line linking the European and Asian sides of the city by the Bosphorus tunnel, to the mosque. It was completed in 1710

Mihrimah Sultan Camii, named after Süleyman the Magnificent's daughter.

for Gülnuş Emetullah Valide Sultan, mother of Sultans Mustafa II and Ahmet III. She was buried in 1716 in the simple adjacent tomb. An iron domed roof, rather like a birdcage, lies over the open stone tomb. ○ *20 min. Uncular Cad.*

③ ★ **Mimar Sinan Çarşısı.** From the tomb, cross the main road Hakımıyeti Milliye Caddesi to this pleasant fountain courtyard. The market isn't much of a shopping experience, but the building and location are charming. Sinan built this in 1583 as the *hamam* of the Mihrimah Sultan complex. It was restored as a covered bazaar in the 1960s. ○ *15 min. Hakımıyeti Milliye Cad. Daily 9am–6pm.*

④ ★★ kids **Kanaat Lokantası.** This has been a locals' favorite since 1933, with hearty traditional dishes like *tandir* (tandoori) lamb and döner kebab with tomatoes and butter. *25 Salmanipak Cad.* ☎ *0216-553-3791. Entrees from 14 TL.*

⑤ ★★ kids **Antikacılar Çarşısı (Antique Market).** Return to Mimar Sinan Çarşısı and continue up to the quaint three-domed **Karadavut Paşa Camii.** Turn left up the side street opposite, following it to the left then right to the **antique market,** housed in an unassuming two-story building. Browse its two levels of around 40 stores with dusty antiques, including Ottoman carved wooden doors, tables, brassware, and lighting. ○ *30 min. 32 Buyük Hamam Sok, Bulgurlu Mescit Sok. Daily 10am–7pm.*

⑥ ★★ Çinili Camii (Tiled Mosque). From the market, turn right onto Evliye Hoca Sokak and left onto Çavuşdere Caddesi. It's a pleasant 20-minute uphill walk along a residential street to this tiny neighborhood mosque. Closed between prayer times, the caretaker may open up to show you its interior adorned with Iznik tiles. Dated 1640, it was built under Mahpeyker Kösem, a wily woman with political ambitions, especially after the death of her husband, Sultan Ahmet I. ⏱ *20 min. Çinili Mescit Sok. Open prayer times only.*

⑦ ★ Atik Valide Külliye. From the main gate of Çinili Camii, turn left down Çinili Hamam Sokak (the *hamam* is on your right), then right down Kartalbaba Caddesi. You'll see the impressive *külliye* (mosque complex) ahead, Mimar Sinan's final major building, completed in 1583. Built for and funded by Valide Nur Banu, wife of Selim II, it's one of Istanbul's most impressive complexes. It contained the Ottoman Empire's first mental hospital, and became a tobacco warehouse in 1935. ⏱ *20 min. Kartalbaba Cad. Mosque closed outside prayer time.*

⑧ ★★ Şemsi Ahmet Paşa Külliye. Turn left out of Atik Valide Külliye, under the arch and down the steps ahead onto Eski Toptaşı Caddesi. Veer left, continue to Hakımıyeti Milliye Caddesi, and head to the waterfront around the construction work. This sympathetically restored gem of a mosque, with a single dome and minaret, was designed by Sinan for Şemsi Paşa in 1580, its *medrese* (religious school) turned into a public library in 1953. Local fishermen and promenaders gather along the pier admiring the view of Istanbul's European side. ⏱ *15 min. Sahil Yolu.*

⑨ ★ kids Filizler. This cavernous place specializes in delicious grilled meatballs and massive breakfast/brunch spreads. It's packed out with families on Sunday mornings . Great views across the Bosphorus to the Old City. *61 Harem Sahil Yolu.* ☎ *0216/342-0000. Turkish breakfast 17.5 TL.*

⑩ ★ kids Kız Kulesi (Maiden's, or Leander's, Tower). From the cafe, it's a pleasant waterfront walk to the shuttle boat to this iconic tower (10-min journey). Used as a lighthouse for centuries, legend has it that a sultan built the tower to

The iron-domed roof of Yeni Valide Camii.

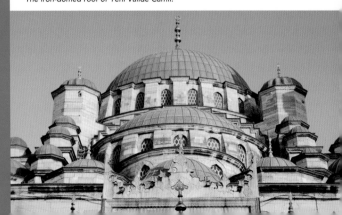

Kız Kulesi, wrapped in legend and movie kudos.

protect his daughter from a deadly serpent's bite, as predicted by a soothsayer. But to no avail, as the snake arrived in a basket of fruit and she died in her father's arms. The tower was featured in the 1999 James Bond movie *The World Is Not Enough*. There's a great viewing point on the upper gallery, but the restaurant is overpriced. ⏲ *1 hr. (exc journey). www.kizkulesi.com.tr. Return ticket 5 TL. Ferries depart daily 9am–6:45pm.*

⓫ ★ kids **Beylerbeyı Sarayı (Beylerbeyı Palace).** It's a 4km (2½ mile) walk or bus ride north to the waterfront palace, located just beyond the Bosphorus Bridge. This late-19th-century palace was built by Armenian architect Sarkis Balyan for Sultan Abdülaziz when the Ottoman Empire was in decline. The Blue Hall boasts one of the world's largest *Hereke* (luxurious silk) carpets, and Arabic poems inscribed on the ceilings. Look out also for chairs made by Sultan Abdulhamit, imprisoned here for 6 years until his death. The pretty gardens (entry 1 TL) have a decent cafe. ⏲ *1 hr. Abdullah Ağa Cad.* ☎ *0216/321-9320/21. www.millisaraylar.gov.tr. Admission (inc guided tour) 20 TL adult, 10 TL kids 12–17. Tues–Wed and Fri–Sun, Mar–Sept 9:30am–5pm, Oct–Feb 9:30am–4pm. Bus: 15 from Üsküdar pier.*

Eminönü to **Sultanahmet**

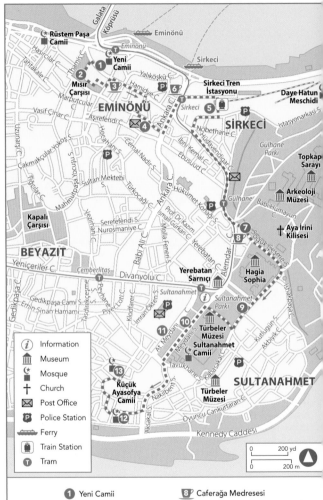

Legend:

- (i) Information
- 🏛 Museum
- ☪ Mosque
- † Church
- ✉ Post Office
- 🅿 Police Station
- ⛴ Ferry
- 🚉 Train Station
- Ⓣ Tram

1. Yeni Camii
2. Mısır Çarşısı
3. Yeni Camii Parkı
4. Sirkeci PTT & Müzesi
5. Sirkeci Garı & Müzesi
6. Konyalı
7. Soğukçeşme Sokak
8. Caferağa Medresesi
9. Haseki Hürrem Hamamı
10. At Meydanı
11. Türk ve Islam Eserleri Müzesi
12. Küçük Ayasofya Camii
13. Sokullu Mehmet Paşa Camii

Stroll from the chaotic waterfront of the Golden Horn and uphill, past the famous terminus of the Orient Express at Sirkeci station, into the heart of the Old City. En route, you'll view an eclectic mix of historic buildings, many ignored by the majority of visitors rushing from one big name sight to the next. START: **Tram or bus to Eminönü.**

A group of Muslim women walking outside Yeni Camii.

1 ★★ kids Yeni Camii (New Mosque). Although this mosque is a massive landmark, its domes and minarets dominating the waterfront by the Galata Bridge, it's off the main tourist trail. Ascend the broad steps, past swarms of pigeons, and enter the courtyard centered on a marble ablutions fountain. Blue and turquoise tiles and a multi-domed ceiling dominate its interior. Commissioned by Valide Safiye Sultan, mother of Mehmet III, work began in 1597, forcing out many residents from the Jewish neighborhood. Plagued with leaks, funding problems, embezzlement, and the death of the sultan, construction was not

completed until 1663. As with all mosques, avoid prayer time. ① *20 min. Eminönü Meydanı. Open daily dawn–dusk.*

2 ★★ kids Mısır Çarşısı (Egyptian, or Spice, Bazaar). The Spice Bazaar (p 9) remains a great place to buy the obvious spices, Turkish delight, and other goodies. But prices are better on narrow **Hasırcılar Caddesi,** running to the west, the best place to buy quality dried fruit, nuts, olives, and many more traditional Turkish food-stuffs. On the northeast side of the bazaar are outdoor stalls selling plant seeds (mainly vegetables and herbs), chickens, and even jars of medicinal leeches. ① *30–60 min. Eminönü. Mon–Sat 9am–7pm.*

3 ★ kids Yeni Camii Parkı. This outdoor tea garden covers a huge area between the mosque, tomb, and market. Find a spare seat for a glass of tea and wonderful people-watching. *Yeni Camii Parkı.*

4 ★ kids Sirkeci PTT & Müzesi (Sirkeci Central Post Office & Museum). Join Büyük Posthane Cad, and on the right you'll see the imposing **Sirkeci PTT,** the late-19th-century main post office. Next door, the **PTT Museum,** part of the original post office, has Morse code machines, Ottoman stamps, and vast leather mailbags used by mail-men making deliveries on horse-back. Unfortunately, there are few captions in English. As you exit, turn right and look across the road to **Vlora Han,** a beautiful example of

Sirkeci's historic station houses the Railway Museum.

Art Nouveau architecture, its facade a lively mass of stylized plaster roses and whiplash wrought iron–work balcony rails. ⏱ *30 min. PTT Müzesi, Büyük Posthane Cad. Free admission. Mon–Fri 9am–noon and 1:30–4pm. Tram: Sirkeci.*

⑤ ★★ kids **Sirkeci Garı & Müzesi (Sirkeci Station & Museum).** Now a stop on the Marmaray Metro line, the station was originally completed in 1890. Designed by the Prussian architect Jachmund as a kind of Orientalist

Mimar Sinan watches over visitors to Caferağa Medresesi.

fantasy, it was the final station for the fabled Orient Express between the Ottoman capital and Europe. For visitors arriving from Berlin, Vienna, and Paris, it was their first glimpse of Constantinople. Entering the station (now a stop on the Marmaray Metro line and last station before the Bosphorus tunnel) from the north, on your left is the nostalgia-driven, overpriced Orient Express restaurant; on the right is the small **Railway Museum,** with exhibits from the iconic train, including the front cab and silver cutlery. There are few English captions, but look out for the tile stove used to heat the waiting hall in 1890, and the original 1930 weighing machine. Exit today's main (west) entrance and walk across the tram tracks. ⏱ *30 min. Museum: Sirkeci Istasyon Cad. ☎ 0212/520-6575. www.tcdd.gov.tr. Free admission. Tues–Sat 9am–5pm.*

⑥ ★★ kids **Konyalı.** Istanbul's famous pastry house has syrupy cakes and *su böreği* (a pasta-type layered cheese snack). Its walls are lined with signed endorsements from luminaries such as Mohammed Ali and Queen Elizabeth II. *5 Mimar Kemalettin Cad. ☎ 0212/527-1935. Tea and su böreği 8 TL.*

7 ★★ **Soğukçeşme Sokak.**
Follow the tram track sweeping up
the hill, past the entrance to Gülhane
Park, and head straight up cobbled
Soğukçeşme Sokak. In 1984, the
Turkish Touring and Automobile
Foundation (TTOK) tore down the
dilapidated, 300-year-old houses lining this street running behind the
Hagia Sophia. They then recreated
them as accurately as possible,
although with more pastel blues and
pinks than the original. Many
became the **Ayasofya Konakları**
guesthouses (p 136). If you need a
break, try **Cafeağra Medresesi**
opposite (**8**). The ornate **Ahmet
Çeşme,** Sultan Ahmet III's fountain
by Topkapı Palace's Imperial Gate, is
at the top. On your right is **Hagia
Sophia.** Housed in the soup kitchens
built next to the Hagia Sophia after it
was turned into a mosque in 1453 is
the Carpet Museum (Halı Müzesi),
opened in 2013. Inside the three
beautifully restored domed structures of the soup kitchen complex is
a wonderful array of antique Turkish
carpets and flat-weave rugs, mostly
dating from the 14th and 15th centuries. ⏱ *30 min. Soğukçeşme Sokağı.*
☎ *0212/512-6993. www.halimuzesi.
com. Free admission, but call ahead as
charge likely to be introduced. Tues–
Sun 9am–4pm.*

8 ★★ kids **Cafeağra Medresesi.** Craft shops now fill the original medrese built by Sinan, plus
there's a tiny cafe in a gorgeous
courtyard cooking homely traditional dishes. Open Tues–Sun.
Caferiye Sok. ☎ *0212/513-3601.
Tea and soup 8 TL.*

9 ★★ kids **Haseki Hürrem
Hamamı (Baths of Roxelana).**
Built for Roxelana (Haseki Hürrem),
Süleyman I's cunning wife, architect
Sinan designed this elegant dou-
ble-domed *hamam* in 1556 for worshippers at the Ayasofya mosque
(the Ottoman name for Hagia
Sophia). It was not used as a
hamam between 1910 and 2011,
when it was re-opened as a luxury
bath house. It's a perfect chance to
see the original marble floors, hexagonal marble massage slabs, and
domed hall with tiny skylight. *2/4
Bab-ı Hümayun Cad.* ☎ *0212/517-
3535. www.ayasofyahurremsultan
hamami.com. Hamam open daily
7am–midnight. Tram: Sultanahmet.*

10 ★★ kids **At Meydanı (Hippodrome).** The late-Roman/
Byzantine-era chariot-racing track
(p 43) was turned into an exercise
area for horses in the Ottoman

Elegant baths built for Roxelana, wife of Süleyman I.

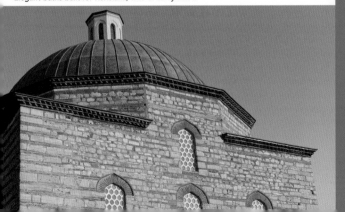

period, hence its current name, At Meydanı, or Square of Horses. Surviving from its time as the Hippodrome are three monuments lined up on what was the *spina* or central reservation area of the chariot-racing track. The granite **Egyptian Obelisk** dates back to 1500 B.C. and was taken from Luxor. Its base is relief carved with scenes of the Byzantine emperor Theodosius I watching the chariot racing from the imperial box, which stood where the Blue Mosque now rises imperiously. Intertwined bronze serpents form the 5th century B.C. **Serpentine Column,** the heads since knocked off (one is in the Archaeological Museum; p 14). The structure was originally the base of a cauldron that stood outside the Temple of Apollo at Delphi in Greece. The bronze covering the **Column of Porphyrogenitus** (named after a 10th-century emperor) was melted down by the Crusaders to make coins. Fast forward a few centuries to the **fountain,** presented by Kaiser Wilhelm II to Sultan Abdülhamit after his visit to the city in 1898. The gold-ceilinged, eight-columned covered

Cool down at Kaiser Wilhelm's fountain in the Hippodrome.

fountain still has cool water flowing from its taps. ⏱ *30 min. At Meydanı. Tram: Sultanahmet.*

⓫ ★★ **Türk ve Islam Eserleri Müzesı (Museum of Turkish and Islamic Arts).** Housed in the beautifully restored 16th-century house of Ibrahim Paşa, one-time grand vizier to Süleyman the Magnificent, this museum is an excellent introduction to the world of Islamic arts. Exhibits range from priceless Turkish rugs to miniature Qur'ans, the tents of Anatolian nomads to exquisite Seljuk Turkish tiles. The museum flanks the western side of the Hippodrome. ⏱ *45 min. At Meydanı Sokak.* ☎ *0212/518-1805. Admission 10 TL. Daily Nov–Mar 9am–5pm, Apr–Oct 9am–7pm. Admission 10TL. Tram: Sultanahmet.*

⓬ ★ **Küçük Ayasofya Camii (Küçük Ayasofya Mosque).** From the southern end of At Meydanı, walk down Tavukhane Sokak, and turn right onto Nakilbent Sokak; Küçük Ayasofya Caddesi then brings you to a surprisingly run-down area with a little-visited gem of a church cum mosque. The Küçük (little) Ayasofya mosque was originally the Church of SS Sergius and Bacchus, built by Emperor Justinian in the 6th century. Converted to a mosque in the late 15th century, its mosaics and frescoes are long gone, but the Greek inscription on the marble frieze inside names Justinian and his wife as founders. Walk up to the balcony to find the tiny section of original stone walls preserved behind glass, and an area of flooring on the first floor. Opposite the entrance is a tea-garden housed in a leafy courtyard, once part of the old *medrese,* today with minuscule artists' studios making traditional crafts, including calligraphy and ceramics. ⏱ *20–40 min. Mosque open dawn–dusk, tea gardens open daily 10:30am–6:30pm.*

The ornate interior of the Kücük Ayasofya Mosque.

⑬ ★★★ Sokullu Mehmet Paşa Camii. This beautiful mosque is reached in 5 minutes by following Bardakçı Sokak to Kadirga Liman Caddesi and turning left, then right onto Mehmet Paşa Yokuşu. It is one of the most attractive Ottoman mosques in the city, built at the behest of Sokullu Mehmet Paşa, grand vizier to Süleyman the Magnificent, and was completed in 1571. The *medrese* housed in the courtyard attached to the entrance to the mosque itself is still used for theological teaching and learning. Inside, the mosque is sparingly adorned with best-period Iznik tiles, and fragments of the Kaaba (the black stone sacred to all Muslims, which forms part of the ancient stone building in Mecca towards which all the faithful pray) are embedded in the *mihrab* and over the entrance. The complex, cleverly built into a steep hillside, is the work of master architect Sinan. It's just a few minute's walk east back to the Hippodrome. ⏱ *20 min. Mehmet Paşa Yokuşu.*

70

Fener & Balat

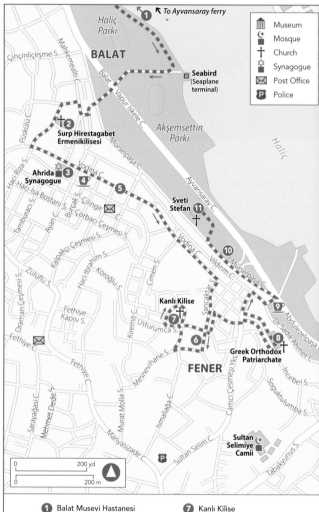

1 Balat Musevi Hastanesi
2 Surp Hirestagabet Ermenikilisesi
3 Ahrida Synagogue
4 Börekci
5 Vodina Caddesi
6 Özel Fener Rum Lisesi
7 Kanlı Kilise
8 Greek Orthodox Patriarchate
9 Tarihi Haliç Işkembecisi
10 Kadin Eserleri Kütüphanesi
11 Sveti Stefan

Hugging the Golden Horn, these neighborhoods were once home to sizable Jewish, Greek, and Armenian communities. Today, it's mainly migrants from eastern Anatolia and the Black Sea region. Discover tucked-away gems revealing the city's multicultural history. START: **Bus 99A to Balat, opposite Balat Iskele (pier); or walk along the waterfront.**

1 ★ **Balat Musevi Hastanesi (Balat Jewish Hospital).** From Ayvansaray ferry terminal, head diagonally south to join the main road, passing immediately in front of an attractive stone building signed BALAT HASTANESI. Completed in 1898, this neo-classical structure was originally the Or-Ahayim hospital, designed by Gabriel Tedeschi, that was built to serve the local Jewish community. The building (which has a Hebrew inscription on the facade) remains a noted hospital today. ○ *5 min.*

2 ★ **Surp Hirestagabet Ermenikilisesi (Holy Angels Armenian Church).** From the hospital, continue southeast down the waterfront to the Seabird sea plane terminal. Cross the road by the striped Yusuf Sucaadin Ambari Camii, and head into the backstreets via Balat Kapısı Sokak, once a gate in the Byzantine-era sea walls of the city. Turn left and then immediately right onto a road that forks to the left on either side of an estate agent's office. Take the right fork and first right onto Kamiş Sokak. In the 17th century, the Armenian community took over this sizable, stone-built church, which up until then had served the Greek Orthodox community. The sacred spring in the basement is still in full flow and draws many Armenian pilgrims. However, every year on September 16, worshippers from all faiths come from all over Turkey for all-night prayers, believing that the sacred waters have miraculous powers. ○ *20 min. 2 Kamiş Sokaği. Thurs and Sun 10am–2pm.*

Walk along the Golden Horn on Balat's waterfront.

3 ★★ **Ahrida Synagogue.** From the church, turn left down Hacı Isa Mektabi Sokak and onto Kurkcuçeşme Sok. You'll soon see the deep-red exterior of Turkey's oldest Sephardic synagogue, established in 1430 by Macedonians. Inside, the most eye-catching piece is the *tevah,* the central raised platform from where Torah readings take place. Some say it's shaped like a galley, to symbolize the Ottoman ships that brought the Sephardic Jews here after their expulsion from Spain in 1492. To visit, e-mail for permission at least 3 days in advance (see website below). Bring your passport for ID. *9 Kurkcuçeşme Sok, Balat. www. musevicemaati.com. By appointment only, Mon–Fri 9:30am–noon.*

Balat's ramshackle charm.

4 ★ **kids Börekci.** Join the locals and have a snack in one of the traditional teahouses and *börek* (savory pastries) parlors. *Vodina Cad. Tea and börek 5 TL.*

5 ★ **Vodina Caddesi.** Continue along atmospheric, photogenic Vodina Caddesi, which cuts through an area once home to Çifit Çarşısı, or Jewish Market. Newly restored houses stand beside untouched and decrepit buildings dating from the Byzantine through to the early 20th century. ⏱ *15min. Most shops open daily 9am–7pm.*

6 ★★ **Özel Fener Rum Lisesi (Fener Greek School for Boys).** Turn right up the steep, cobbled Sancaktar Sokak, and half-way up you'll see this immense neo-Gothic red-brick monolith. Founded in 1454 as the Ottoman capital's most important Greek educational institution, what you see today was built in 1881 with bricks brought from France. Pupil numbers have declined to around 50. Turn the corner, keeping the school on your right to reach **7**. ⏱ *10 min. Sancaktar Yokuşu.*

7 ★★ **Kanlı Kilise (St. Mary of the Mongols).** Turn right three times and you'll come to this little church tucked behind high walls. This is the only Byzantine church that was never converted to a mosque after the Ottoman conquest of 1453, thanks to a decree by Mehmet II. Maria (Mary), the illegitimate daughter of Byzantine emperor Michael VIII Palaeologus, married off to the Mongolian Khan Abaga in the 13th century to improve relations between the two nations. Widowed after 15 years, she returned to Constantinople and founded the monastery, where she spent her remaining years. A mosaic image of her can be seen beseeching Christ in the largest panel at the nearby Church of St Savior in Chora (p 42). Ring the bell for entry (tip for the caretaker appreciated). Retrace your steps and descend the hill, turning right at Baki Dede Sokak and onto Yıldırım Sokak. ⏱ *15 min. Tevkii Cafer Mektebi Sok.*

The famous Greek School in Balat.

The high-walled Greek Orthodox Patriarchate.

⑧ ★★ Greek Orthodox Patriarchate. Enter the high-walled courtyard of the Patriarchate, which has been here since it was moved down the hill from the Pammakaristos (p 42) in 1586. The Patriarchal church of **St. George,** built in 1720, has a neo-classical marble facade. Inside, in the right-hand aisle and close to the *iconstasis* (gilt altar screen), look out for two portative 11th-century mosaics, one of the Virgin Mary, the other of John the Baptist, as well as a holy relic, the Column of Flagellation, to which Christ was bound and flogged. Many of the treasures—including lecterns inlaid with mother-of-pearl—were brought from other regions. ⊙ *30 min. 35 Sadrazam Ali Paşa Cad. www.ec-patr.org. Daily 9am–4:30pm.*

⑨ ★★ kids Tarihi Haliç Işkembecisi. Famed for its *işkembe* (tripe soup) *kokorec,* this 24-hour restaurant is filled with *Atatürk* memorabilia, topped by a fabulous terrace. *117 Abdulezelpasa Cad.* ☎ *0212/534-9414. Işkembe 8 TL.*

⑩ ★ Kadin Eserleri Kütüphanesi (Women's Library and Information Center). This interesting late-Byzantine building has been converted into Turkey's only library devoted to books by and about women. In truth, there's little to be seen if you can't read Turkish, but the bare-brick, vaulted interior is attractive. ⊙ *15 min. Fener Vapur Iskelesi Karşısı.* ☎ *0212/523-7408. www.kadineserleri.org. Mon–Fri 10am–6pm.*

⑪ ★★ Sveti Stefan (St. Stephen of the Bulgars). It's hard to believe that this dazzling white church was created from iron panels, cast in Vienna and shipped down the Danube into the Black Sea, and then brought down the Bosphorus and up into the Golden Horn. Inside, the iron pillars and six majestic bells in the 40m-high (13 ft.) belfry were all made in Russia. Unfortunately, restoration work ongoing in 2014 is likely to stretch into 2015. From here, either catch a bus to Eminönü or Taksim, walk down the waterfront to the Galata Bridge, or up it to Ayvansaray pier for a ferry down the Golden Horn to Karaköy or Eminönü. ⊙ *20 min. Mürsel Paşa Cad. Daily 8am–5pm.*

Beyazit's **Bazaars & Mosques**

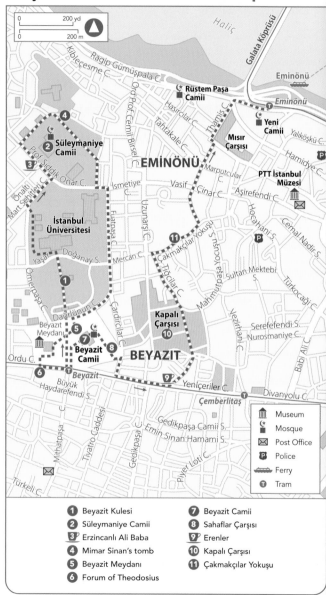

1 Beyazit Kulesi	**7** Beyazit Camii
2 Süleymaniye Camii	**8** Sahaflar Çarşısı
3 Erzincanlı Ali Baba	**9** Erenler
4 Mimar Sinan's tomb	**10** Kapalı Çarşısı
5 Beyazit Meydanı	**11** Çakmakçılar Yokuşu
6 Forum of Theodosius	

Dominated by two major landmarks, **Kapalı Çarşısı** (Grand Bazaar) and Süleymaniye Camii, historic Beyazit has been a center of commerce for centuries. From Eminönü, you pass a busy working area filled with *hans* (workshops) and the sounds of hammering and chiseling, contrasting to the ethereal mood of the vast Süleymaniye mosque complex. START: **Tram or walk to Beyazit.**

① ★ kids Beyazit Kulesi (Beyazit Tower). From the tram stop, enter the ornate gateway to the grounds of **Istanbul University.** The fire watch tower you see today is the work of architect Senekerim Balyan (p 173). It was constructed from stone in Ottoman baroque style in 1828; two earlier wooden watch towers, ironically enough, burned down in one of the fires that periodically swept the Old City. ① *10 min.*

② ★★★ Süleymaniye Camii. Walk through the university's grounds to Mimar Sinan's greatest creation in the city, perched atop the third of Istanbul's seven hills. Aside from the Hagia Sophia, this *külliye,* or mosque complex, is

Beyazit Kulesi.

arguably the most important historic site in the city. To the south of the mosque at the heart of the *külliye* are several multi-domed *medreses,* one of which is now the Süleymaniye Kütüphanesi, or library, and a hospital. Along the west side of the mosque are a soup kitchen and *caravanserai* (resting place for travelers); to the east is a beautifully restored *hamam* (www. suleymaniyehamami.com). Built into the underside of the terrace supporting the northern side of the walled mosque compound are shops, the rent from which helped with the upkeep of the complex. Today, they mainly sell items useful to pilgrims on the Haj (pilgrimage) to Mecca—from worry beads to prayer rugs and tea pots. Just east of the mosque are the tombs of the complex's benefactor, Süleyman the Magnificent, and his wife Roxelana. Between the mosque and the *medreses* on the south side of the complex is so-called "addicts alley," where opium and hashish were once sold from cafes. ① *1 hr. (See p 8 for details.)*

③ ★★ kids Erzincanlı Ali Baba. A good choice for creamy white beans in tomato sauce, mopped up with crusty white bread and washed down with the traditional yogurt drink *ayran.* In good weather, you can sit outside and admire the mosque and passers-by on "addicts alley." *11 Sıddık Sami Onar Cad, Süleymaniye Camii Yani. Beans 5 TL.*

④ ★ Mimar Sinan's Tomb. Sinan's modest tomb, which he designed, lies just outside the mosque's main walls and precisely where the architect wanted to be, close to his favorite Istanbul creation. From the street, you can catch a glimpse of the white tomb built from *kufeki* stone, with its marble sarcophagus. ⏱ *10 min. Corner of Mimar Sinan Cad and Fetva Yokuşu Sok.*

⑤ ★★ Beyazıt Meydanı (Beyazit Square). Walk down Mimar Sinan Caddesi, a lovely little street dotted with metalworking shops, hammering out copper and chrome household goods. Turn right onto Fuatpaşa Caddesi to rejoin the Hürriyet Meydanı, the Old City's largest public square, better known today as Beyazıt Meydanı but originally a late-Roman-era forum (public square). Usually the square is peaceful, lined with push-carts selling *simit* (sesame bread) and headscarved women selling grain to feed the massed pigeons. ⏱ *15 min.*

⑥ ★★ Forum of Theodosius. Nip across busy Ordu Caddesi to what's left of a triumphal arch, built by Theodosius the Great in 393. All that's left of this once grandiose, triple-gated triumphal arch is an untidy pile of shattered columns and broken capitals, discovered between 1948 and 1961. The columns are decorated with a striking tear-drop design. A couple of the decorated columns in the Yerebatan Cistern (p 16) were almost certainly pillaged from here. The arch once graced the largest square in Constantinople, the Forum of Theodosius (today, Beyazıt Meydanı covers only a part of the former forum), and straddled the main street that led from the Hagia Sophia to the land walls of Theodosius and, eventually,

Süleymaniye Camii, Mimar Sinan's favorite creation.

on into Thrace and thence the Adriatic. ⏱ *15 min. Ordu Cad.*

⑦ ★ Beyazit Camii (Beyazit Mosque). Built between 1501 and 1506, this is the city's oldest surviving, purpose-built imperial mosque. Inspired by the **Hagia Sophia** (p 7), it has a 17m-diameter (56 ft.) dome and galleries overlooking the central prayer area. Today, it's likely to be full at lunchtime with market traders. Like all imperial mosques, this was part of a *külliye* comprising *hamam*, *medrese*, and kitchen. Its serene courtyard houses the limestone tomb of Beyazit II (1447–1512) at the back of the gardens, plus that of his daughter and Grand Vezir Koca Reşit Paşa (1800–58), the distinguished leader of the 19th-century Tanzimat (reform) movement (p 171). Close by is the city's oldest-surviving primary school, restored and now the Hakki Tarik

Us Research Library, with a digitized archive of Ottoman periodicals. ⏱ *20 min. Hürriyet Meydanı. Open daily dawn–dusk. Tram: Beyazit.*

⑧ ★ Sahaflar Çarşısı (Booksellers Bazaar). Before the arrival of printing machines in 1729, the printed book was seen as a corrupting European influence, so only handwritten manuscripts were sold here. Today, the picturesque courtyard market specializes in textbooks for local students, with some stalls selling photographic books on Istanbul, calligraphy, and miniatures. At the center, look out for the bust of Ibrahim Muteferrika, who printed the first books in Turkish in 1732. Outside, you'll probably see sellers of *tespi* (prayer beads) and collectors' items, including foreign banknotes. If you need some respite before hitting the Grand Bazaar, turn left at the tram tracks and enter the grounds of Çorlulu Ali Paşa mosque. ⏱ *20 min. Sahaflar Çarsısı Sok. Daily 9am–8pm. Tram: Beyazit.*

⑨ ★★★ kids Erenler. If you need a sit-down with a glass of tea and fruity *nargile* (tobacco waterpipe), head to this laid-back cafe in the gorgeous leafy courtyard of the Çorlulu Alipaşa Medresesi, adjacent to the mosque. It is packed with backgammon-playing locals and—thankfully—charges local prices. *36 Çorlulu Alipaşa Medressesi, Yeniçeriler Cad.* ☎ *0212/511-8853. Tea 1 TL.*

⑩ ★★ kids Kapalı Çarşısı (Covered, or Grand, Bazaar). From Erenler, you can walk up Bileyciler Sokak, past wholesale silver shops, and enter the Grand Bazaar through Kurkculer Kapısı (gate 2). Keep your eye on the signs or enjoy getting lost! If you're shopping for anything specific, don't buy at the first place you see, especially if it's a big buy; take a business card and shop around. As long ago as the early 20th century, the British adventurer E.B. Soane remarked on the commercialism of the Grand Bazaar: "The effect was

Beyazit Camii, Istanbul's oldest-remaining imperial mosque.

The Grand Bazaar is one of the largest and oldest covered markets in the world, with 61 covered streets and over 3,000 shops.

so often spoiled by the interpreter of Mr. T. Cook and his amiable creatures, seeking out the secret of the mysterious east." The passage of time has made the bazaar more touristy than ever. So although it retains elements of its centuries-old trading practices, the TV screens suspended from the ceilings, cappuccinos in stylish cafes, and hordes of cruise ship passengers bring it firmly into the 21st century. If you need an escape from the inside, explore the surrounding streets, which still retain an air of authentic trading. ⏲ *1–3 hr. Mon–Sat 9:30am–7pm. Tram: Beyazit; or bus 61B from Taksim.*

⑪ ★★ kids **Çakmakçılar Yokuşu.** Exit from Mercan Kapısı (gate 16) and turn right down the busy Çakmakçılar Yokusu Sokak (look to the left to see Beyazit Tower). You're now on the street with two of the most famous old *hans*, usually three levels of tiny workshops built around a courtyard, also used for storage. Downhill on the left is the entrance of **Büyük Valide Han** built by Valide Sultan Kösem just before her death in 1651, with a vast courtyard surrounded by a double-tiered arcade housing a Cem Evi, a prayer hall for locals adhering to the Alevi faith, an offshoot of (but quite different from) Shia Islam. Further down the street on the opposite side is **Büyük Yeni Han,** built in 1764 by Mustafa III. At the bottom of the street, turn left and head down toward Yeni Camii and Eminönü's transport hub. ⏲ *40 min. Hans open Mon–Sat 9:30am–6:30pm. Tram: Beyazit.* ●

Shopping Best Bets

Best for **Obscure Turkish Records**
★★★ Lale Plak *1 Galip Dede Cad* (p 84)

Best for **Carpets for All Budgets**
★★★ Nakkaş *6 Nakilbent Sok* (p 86)

Best for **Kookie Kitchenware**
★ Karınca *2A Galip Dede Cad* (p 88)

Best for **Turkic Felt Designs**
★★★ Cocoon *19 Küçük Ayasofya Cad* (p 85)

Best **Arty Glassware**
★★ Paşabahçe *150A Istiklal Cad* (p 88)

Best **Luxury Ottomania**
★★ Sevan Bıçakcı *3/1A Şair Nedim Cad* (p 89)

Best for **Vintage Rummaging**
★★ By Retro *Suriye Pasajı, off Istiklal Cad* (p 86)

Best for **Tasty Turkish Coffee**
★★★ Kurukahveci Mehmet Efendi *66 Tahmis Sokak* (p 88)

Best for **Bargaining Enthusiasts**
★★★ Kapalı Çarşısı (Grand Bazaar) *Beyazit* (p 90)

Best for **Vintage Men's Fashion**
★★★ Civan *42 Çukurcuma Cad* (p 87)

Best for **Satisfying a Sweet Tooth**
★★ Hafız Mustafa *84–86 Hamidiye Cad* (p 87)

Best for **Wannabe Interior Designers**
★★★ A La Turca *4 Faikpaşa Yokuşu* (p 84)

Best for **Gaziantep Pistachios**
★★★ Mısır Çarşısı (Spice Market) *Eminönü* (p 90)

Best for **Local Handicrafts**
★★ Ortaköy Craft Market *Ortaköy Meydanı* (p 90)

Best **Hassle-Free Treasure Trove**
★★★ Dösim G.E.S. *2/1 Şeyhülislam Hayriefendi Cad* (p 85)

Best **Natural Produce Market**
★★★ Çarşşamba Pazarı *Fatih* (p 90)

Best **Postcards of Old Istanbul**
★★ Levant Koleksiyon *64B Meşrutiyet Cad* (p 84)

Best for **Luxury Souvenirs**
★★★ Armaggan *65 Nuruosmaniye Cad* (p 88)

Carpets from Adnan & Hasan. Previous page: Make the perfect Turkish coffee in a copper cezve from Mısır Çarşısı.

Old City Shopping

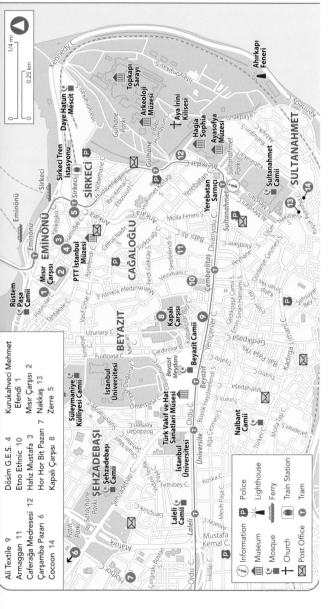

Ali Textile 9
Armagaan 11
Caferağa Medresesi 12
Çarşamba Pazarı 6
Cocoon 14

Dösim G.E.S. 4
Etno Ethnic 10
Hafız Mustafa 3
Hor Hor Bit Pazarı 7
Kapalı Çarşısı 8

Kurukahveci Mehmet Efendi 1
Mısır Çarşısı 2
Nakkaş 13
Zerre 5

(i) Information ☪ Police ✳ Lighthouse
(museum) Museum 🕌 Mosque ⚓ Ferry
✝ Church ▨ Post Office ⬛ Train Station Ⓣ Tram

Beyoğlu Shopping

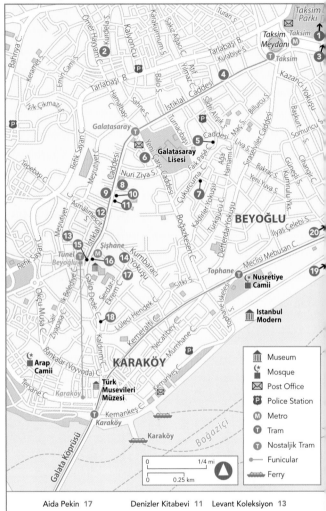

Aida Pekin 17	Denizler Kitabevi 11	Levant Koleksiyon 13
A La Turca 5	Haremlique 3	Ortaköy Craft Market 19
Aponia 18	Homer Kitabevi 6	Paşabahçe 9
Atelier 55 14	Kanyon 1	Robinson Crusoe 10
Beyoğlu İş Merkezi 8	Karınca 15	Sevan Bıçakcı 20
By Retro 12	Kiğılı 4	Tarlabaşı Market 2
Civan 7	Lale Plak 16	Zorlu Center 3

Grand Bazaar Shopping

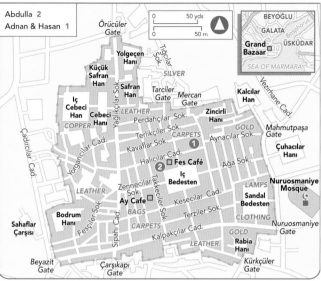

Abdulla 2
Adnan & Hasan 1

Örücüler Gate
BEYOĞLU
GALATA
Grand Bazaar
ÜSKÜDAR
SEA OF MARMARA
Bosphorus

Yolgeçen Hanı
Tığcılar Sok.
SILVER
Küçük Safran Han
Safran Han
Tarciler Gate
Mercan Gate
Kalcılar Han
Vezirhane Cad.
İç Cebeci Han
Cebeci Hanı
LEATHER
COPPER
Perdahçılar Sok.
Zincirli Hanı
GOLD
Mahmutpaşa Gate
Çadırcılar Cad.
Yağlıkçılar Sok.
Terlikçiler Sok.
CARPETS
Aynacılar Sok.
Çuhacılar Hanı
Yorgancılar Cad.
Kavaflar Sok.
Halıcılar Cad.
Fes Café
Ağa Sok.
Zennecilar Sok.
İç Bedesten
LAMPS
Nuruosmaniye Mosque
LEATHER
Ay Cafe
Kesecilar Cad.
Sandal Bedesten
Takkeciler Sok.
BAGS
Bodrum Hanı
Feşçiler Sok.
Sipahi Cad.
Terziler Sok.
CLOTHING
Nuruosmaniye Gate
Sahaflar Çarşısı
CARPETS
Kalpakçılar Cad.
GOLD
Rabia Hanı
LEATHER
Beyazıt Gate
Çarşıkapı Gate
Kürkçüler Gate

Nişantaşı Shopping

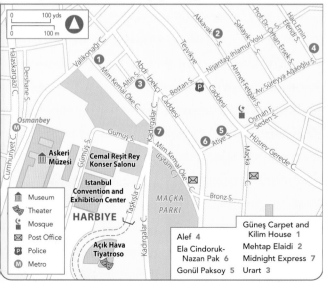

Halaskargazi C.
Valikonağı C.
Akkavak S.
Teşvikiye
Prof. Dr. Orhan Ersek S.
Hacı Emin Efendi S.
Dershane S.
Mim Kemal Altın S.
Abdi İpekçi Caddesi
Bostan S.
Nişantaşı Ihlamur Yolu
Şakayık S.
Ahmet Fetgari S.
Av. Süreyya Ağaoğlu S.
Osmanbey
Cumhuriyet C.
Gümüş S.
Kadırgalar C. (Eytam C.)
Caddesi
Osman F. Seden S.
Askeri Müzesi
Cemal Reşit Rey Konser Salonu
Atiye S.
Hüsrev Gerede C.
Gümüş S.
Mim Kemal Öke C.
Maçka
Istanbul Convention and Exhibition Center
Bronz S.
HARBIYE
Taşkışla C.
MAÇKA PARKI
Kadırgalar C.
Açık Hava Tiyatrosu

Museum
Theater
Mosque
Post Office
Police
Metro

Alef 4
Ela Cindoruk-Nazan Pak 6
Gonül Paksoy 5

Güneş Carpet and Kilim House 1
Mehtap Elaidi 2
Midnight Express 7
Urart 3

Istanbul **Shopping A to Z**

Antiques & Vintage

★★★ A La Turca ÇUKUR-CUMA   Chic showroom over four floors with European and Turkish treasures, from *kilims* (rugs) to early 1900s pottery, metal milk churns, and gilded mirrors. Oozing good taste. *4 Faikpaşa Yokuşu.* ☎ *0212/245-2933. www.alaturca house.com. AE, DC, MC, V. Bus/ Metro: Taksim. Map p 82.*

★★ Hor Hor Bit Pazarı AKSA-RAY   Tucked away in a working-class neighborhood, this six-floor arcade has over 200 stores specializing in early-20th-century French and Ottoman antiques. Look for furniture and chandeliers, or candlesticks for easier transportation. *13 Kiriktulumba Sok, off Horhor Cad. MC, V. Tram/Metro: Aksaray. Map p 81.*

★★ Levant Koleksiyon BEYOĞLU   Although a little tourist-oriented, this is still a treasure

Browse the four floors of chic showroom at A La Turca.

trove of old maps, engravings, and postcards of old Istanbul scenes. With the city's ever-changing face, this shop gives a real hint of its past. *64B Meşrutiyet Cad.* ☎ *0212/293-4394. www.levant koleksiyon.com/index.htm. MC, V. Metro: Şişhane. Map p 82.*

Books & Music

★ Denizler Kitabevi BEYOĞLU   Specializing in everything nautical, the books will delight old sailors, and 5 centuries of Istanbul maps, posters, and old prints will look good on anyone's wall. *199 Istiklal Cad.* ☎ *0212/249-8893. www.denizlerkitabevi.com. MC, V. Metro: Şişhane Map p 82.*

★★ kids Homer Kitabevi GALATASARAY   A charming bookstore full of English- and European-language books, specializing in international history, art, and architecture. There's a children's section on the lower level. *12A Yeni Çarşı Cad.* ☎ *0212/249-5902. www. homerbooks.com. MC, V. Bus/Metro: Taksim. Map p 82.*

★★★ Lale Plak TÜNEL   Located on "music street," where you can find every type of instrument, this store stocks an extensive selection of new vinyl records and CDs from a wide variety of Turkish and international genres. *1 Galip Dede Cad.* ☎ *0212/293-7739. AE, MC, V. Funicular: Tünel. Map p 82.*

★★★ Robinson Crusoe BEYOĞLU   This is probably Istanbul's best-loved English-language bookstore, with a charming wooden interior that is stacked floor to ceiling with page turners. *195 Istiklal Cad.* ☎ *0212/293-6968. www. rob389.com. AE, MC, V. Metro: Şişhane. Map p 82.*

Shopping Zones

The Grand Bazaar and Beyazit area has everything from carpets to glassware, plus cheap jeans and leather jackets. **Sultanahmet** caters to the tourists, with souvenirs galore, and earthy **Eminönü** has traditional shopping streets around the **Spice Market.** Trawl **Çukurcuma's** streets for antique furniture and quaint contemporary arts. In **Beyoğlu,** Turkish fashion stores and lively bookstores cram **Istiklal Caddesi,** and its continuation **Galip Dede Caddesi** is the place for musicians. *Fashionistas* flock to **Nişantaşı's** boutiques for Turkish and foreign designers.

Carpets, Kilims & Fabrics

★ **Adnan & Hasan** BEYAZIT A novelty in the bazaar's carpet shops: Prices are fixed and clearly displayed. Laid-back owners are knowledgeable about their selection of carpets and *kilims* from Turkey, the Caucasus, and Afghanistan, and they have a great international following. *89–92 Halıcılar Cad, Kapalı Çarşısı.* ☎ *0212/527-9887. www. adnanandhasan.com. AE, DC, MC, V. Tram/bus: Beyazit. Map p 83.*

★★★ **Ali Textile** BEYAZIT The affable Ali has doubled his shop size in this courtyard lined with carpet-repair workshops. Ali sells bags and cushion-covers made from carpets, plus *kilims* and traditional Central Asian coats, all very affordable. Fixed price and friendly. *32/4–5 Çorlulu Ali Paşa Medrese, Yeniçeriler Cad.* ☎ *0535/367-5333. MC, V. Tram: Beyazit. Map p 81.*

★★★ **kids Cocoon** SULTANAHMET Handmade felt accessories come in bright colors, all from traditional Central Asian designs, plus Turkish and Persian *kilims*. Their second store a few doors down also sells cushions, handbags, jewelry, and souvenirs. Great for gifts. *19 Küçük Ayasofya Cad.* ☎ *0212/638-6450. www.cocoonchic.com. AE, MC, V. Tram: Sultanahmet. Map p 81.*

★★★ **Dösim G.E.S.** EMINÖNÜ This immense government-run emporium has carpets, leather bags, painted ceramics, and glassware (all modern replicas of old designs), at very reasonable, fixed prices. What it lacks in atmosphere it more than compensates in choice and value. *2/1 Şeyhülislam Hayriefendi Cad.* ☎ *0212/526-6813. www. ges.gov.tr. MC, V. Tram/bus: Eminönü. Map p 81.*

★★ **Güneş Carpet & Kilim House** NIŞANTAŞI A woman in

Prints and maps at Denizler Kitabevi.

Clued Up on Carpets

How much do carpets cost? Anything between $100 and $10,000. If you know what you want and what it should cost, the Grand Bazaar is a good starting point, with many stores competing for business. Novices should visit fixed-price stores with no hard-sell, to better understand what your money can buy. Try the government-run **Dösim G.E.S.** (p 85) with prices of new carpets and kilims clearly marked, starting from $80. If local "friends," tour guides, or hotel staff take you to a store, their commission—anything from 20 to 50%—will be added to your price; best go alone.

this male-dominated business, Güneş Öztarakçı, has been selling carpets for 35 years, with an astounding collection in her "carpet museum." An expert, without the high-pressure sales pitch. *5 Mimar Kemal Öke Cad.* ☎ *0212/ 225-1954. AE, DC, MC, V. Metro: Osmanbey. Map p 82.*

★★★ **Nakkaş Oriental Rugs & Textiles** SULTANAHMET One of the city's most respected carpet dealers, the huge and varied collection has something to suit every budget, from the antique to the contemporary. The basement is a restored Byzantine cistern used as an exhibition space. *6 Nakilbent Sok.* ☎ *0212/516-5222. www. nakkasrug.com. AE, MC, V. Tram: Sultanahmet. Map p 81.*

Clothes & Accessories
★★ **Atelier 55** GALATA An elegant fashion boutique at the end of Galata's most chic and quirky street, Serdar-Iı Ekrem Sokak. Stocks clothing, accessories, jewelry, shoes, and housewares from a range of Turkish and international designers, along with its own brand. *55 Seraskerci Çk.* ☎ *0212/245-3255. www.atelier-55. com. MC, V. Metro: Şişhane. Map p 82.*

★★★ **Aponia** GALATA A friendly shop where you can find original gifts that won't break the bank or verge on the tacky. Bags, posters, and wearable T-shirts sport playful graphics, taking their inspiration from Istanbul, among other ideas. *101/A Galip Dede Cad. No phone. www.aponiastore.com. MC, V. Tram: Karaköy. Map p 82.*

★★ **By Retro** BEYOĞLU This treasure trove crams in second-hand clothes from the 1920s to the

Wander among the stacks at Robinson Crusoe.

present day, from Turkey and Europe. A number of the items were used on movie sets, so it's the place to browse for vintage 1950s wedding dresses, military costumes, and hippy hats. *Suriye Pasajı, off Istiklal Cad.* ☎ *0212/245-6420. MC, V. Bus/Metro: Şişhane/Tünel; funicular: Taksim. Map p 82.*

★★★ **Civan** ÇUKURCUMA   In this bohemian area of town made famous by Orhan Pamuk's *The Museum of Innocence,* there is an obvious love for anything nostalgic. In this "fashion house for men," you can find a variety of ultra-hip collections with a nod to the past, along with antique buttons and an in-house tailoring service. *42 Çukurcuma Cad.* ☎ *0212/243-3211. www. civanblogging.com. MC, V. Bus/ Metro: Taksim, then walk. Map p 82.*

★★★ **Gonül Paksoy** NIŞANTAŞI Using the very best fabrics, Paksoy's designs luxurious clothing and accessories. Made with silks, linen, and wool, naturally dyed in mulberry and brown tones, all her pieces are unique, from exquisite handmade shoes to simple, elegant jackets. *6A Atiye Sokak.* ☎ *0212/261-9081. AE, DC, MC, V. Metro: Osmanbey. Map p 83.*

★★ **Kiğılı** BEYOĞLU   A hard one to pronounce, Kiğılı *(keelu)* has top men's clothes over two floors, from fine cotton shirts to the best woolen suits and silk ties, using top European designs. *34 Istiklal Cad.* ☎ *0212/245-0011. www.kigili.com. tr. MC, V. Bus/funicular: Taksim. Map p 82.*

★ **Mehtap Elaidi** NIŞANTAŞI Local designer Mehtap Elaidi puts a twist on conventional styles, like crisp tailored shirts with balloon sleeves, or fitted skirts with a fish tail. Check out the small collection of striking, simple jewelry.

Turkish and Persian textiles at Cocoon.

Hacı Ömer Apt, 18 Akkavak Sok. ☎ *0212/236-3783. www.elaidi.net. MC, V. Metro: Osmanbey. Map p 83.*

★★★ **Midnight Express** NIŞANTAŞI   Tucked-away boutique from Istanbul's husband-and-wife team Banu Bora (fashion designer) and Tayfun Mumcu (architect), which is now a small chain. Includes ready-to-wear clothing and accessories from up-and-coming designers. The name is an ironic nod to the classic book/ movie. *8/3 Açık Hava Apt, Kadırgalar Cad.* ☎ *0212/231-2628. www.mid nightexpress.com.tr. MC, V. Metro: Osmanbey. Map p 83.*

Food

★★ **Hafız Mustafa** EMINÖNÜ Sample some of Turkey's best *lokum* (Turkish delight), here since 1864, or satisfy a sweet tooth with pastries and fruity boiled sweets. You can also escape to the simple cafe upstairs for a glass of tea. *84–86 Hamidiye Cad.* ☎ *0212/513-3610. www.hafizmustafa.com. MC, V. Tram: Eminönü. Map p 81.*

★★★ Kurukahveci Mehmet Efendi
EMINÖNÜ The grandfather of coffee, Mehmet Efendi has roasted beans since 1871. The perennially popular family store outside the Spice Market still roasts and grinds beans in all varieties; a good place for packs of Turkish coffee ("Turks gift to the world," as they point out). *66 Tahmis Sokak. ☎ 0212/511-4262. www.mehmet efendi.com. MC, V. Tram: Eminönü. Map p 81.*

Housewares & Handicrafts
★★ Abdulla
BEYAZIT Gorgeous handmade fragranced olive-oil soaps in wooden presentation boxes, natural loofahs, and hand-spun wool shawls make this a popular choice for quality gifts. *62 Halıcılar Cad, Kapalı Çarşısı. ☎ 0212/527-3684. www.abdulla.com. MC, V. Tram: Beyazit. Map p 83.*

★★★ Armaggan
NURUOSMANIYE This seven-floor store sells its own-label designer goodies with a strong Turkish slant. Look out for vases with Ottoman carvings and hand-woven silks printed with organic dyes. *65 Nuruosmaniye Cad. ☎ 0212/522-4433. www.armaggan. com. AE, MC, V. Metro: Beyazit. Map p 81.*

★★ Haremlique
ZINCIRLIKUYU Duvets designed with Ottoman scenes, colored organic bathrobes, and limited-edition fabrics will bring a touch of glamour to your bathroom or bedroom. Monogrammed towels make a lovely (if expensive) gift. *Zorlu Center, Zincirlikuyu. ☎ 0212/236-3843. www. haremlique.com. MC, V, AE. Metro: Gayrettepe. Map p 82.*

★ Karınca
TÜNEL These bold, original, and humorous items, including graters shaped like women's dresses, clocks created from kitchen utensils, and elephant-trunk funnels, will brighten up any home. Novel gift ideas. *2A Galip Dede Cad. ☎ 0212/252-8843. www. karincadesign.com. MC, V. Funicular: Tünel. Map p 82.*

★★ Paşabahçe
BEYOĞLU Creating household glassware since 1935, Paşabahçe's showroom is a few notches above the rest with exquisite tableware, ceramics, contemporary vases, and candlesticks. Check out their hand-painted coffee cups downstairs. *150A Istiklal Cad. ☎ 0212/244-0544. www. pasabahce.com.tr. AE, MC. V. Bus/ metro: Taksim. Map p 82.*

★★ Urart
NIŞANTAŞI A dazzling display of creations, some of them taking inspiration from the artifacts in the Archaeological Museum (p 14). Ancient pieces are recreated from silver, gold, or marble. Look out for a miniature version of a Topkapı Palace pillar and prehistoric Hittite relics, recreated as gold jewelry. *18 Abdi Ipekçi Cad. ☎ 0212/246-7194. AE, DC, MC, V. Minibus: Nişantaşı/ Teşvikiye. Map p 83.*

Jewelry
★ Aida Pekin
GALATA Open since 2009, this little boutique sells designs of its eponymous owner. She uses delicate lines to create whimsical pieces, with a touch of romance. Her Istanbul collection makes nice souvenirs. *44A Serdar-ı Ekrem Sok. ☎ 0212/243-1211. www.aidapekin.com. MC, V. Metro: Şişhane. Map p 82.*

★★★ Alef
TEŞVIKIYE A jewelry store, gallery, and workshop that showcases the work of goldsmith Yeşim Yüksek. Located in one of Istanbul's fanciest neighborhoods, here you can find stunning contemporary pieces made using traditional techniques. *4A Hacı Emin Efendi Sok. ☎ 0212/241-3558. www.alef.com.tr. AE, MC, V. Metro: Osmanbey. Map p 83.*

What Time?

Opening hours vary, depending on the neighborhood, but are usually 10am to 7pm, and many stores on Istiklal Caddesi—especially book and music stores—are open until 11pm on Friday and Saturday. Most stores city-wide open on Sunday, except for small, privately run places. The Grand Bazaar is closed Sunday. Istanbul's ever-increasing malls—adored by locals during the weekend—usually close at 10pm.

★★ Ela Cindoruk-Nazan Pak

NIŞANTAŞI Young designers Cindoruk and Pak showcase their exquisite jewelry in unusual forms and materials, including paper and resin. Also features collections from other young designers. *14 Atiye Sokak, off Abdi Ipekçi Cad.* ☎ *0212/232-2664. www.ela cindoruknazanpak.com. MC, V. Minibus: Nişantaşı/Teşvikiye. Map p 83.*

★★ Etno Ethnic

NURUOSMANIYE This long-standing fixture in the Grand Bazaar sells both Turkish and international designs. The jewelry, trinkets, and talismans on offer are created from a wide range of materials from around the world. *71 Verzihan Cad.* ☎ *0212/527-4683. www.etnoethnic.com. AE, MC, V. Tram: Cemberlitaş. Map p 81.*

★★ Sevan Bıçakcı

AKARETLER Superb one-off pieces by a master jewelry designer means sculpted Ottoman-inspired rings the size of golf balls, using traditional and unique techniques like micro-mosaics and miniature paintings. *3/1A Şair Nedim Cad.* ☎ *0212/236-9199. www.sevanbicakci.com. AE, DC, MC, V. Bus: Beşiktaş/Tram: Kabataş. Map p 82.*

★★ Zerre Design

SIRKECI Özlem Tuna is a world-renowned designer who specializes in contemporary jewelry and home accessories, such as chunky gold pendants, stylized tulips, and delicate ceramics. *23 Nemlizade Han, 65 Ankara Cad.* ☎ *0212/527-9285. www.ozlemtuna.com. AE, MC, V. Tram: Sirkeci. Map p 81.*

Markets & Malls

★★★ kids Beyoğlu Iş Merkezi

BEYOĞLU In a three-floor scruffy mall, trawl through stalls of 90% rubbish to find knock-off gems at a fraction of the original price. *Terzi* (tailors) downstairs make fast alterations for a couple of liras. Great for a cheap wardrobe revamp. *187 Istiklal Cad. Most stalls cash only. Bus: Taksim. Map p 82.*

★ Caferağa Medresesi

SULTANAHMET Located in an old *medrese* (religious school), artisans in tiny workshops surrounding the courtyard run courses including hand-painted ceramics and Ottoman calligraphy. They also sell their

Ela Cindoruk-Nazan Pak Jewelry Gallery's pioneering Turkish designs.

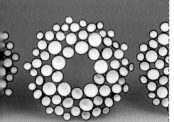

handicrafts. *Caferağa Sokak, 1 Soğukkuyu Çikmazi.* ☎ *0212/513-3601. Some stalls take credit cards. Tram: Sultanahmet. Map p 81.*

★★★ Çarşamba Pazarı (Wednesday Market) FATIH

This weekly market, held every Wednesday, is one of the city's largest, with over 4,000 stores selling just about every type of fresh and preserved produce you can imagine. Good for gift shopping for foodies. Conservative clothing is advised. *On the streets around Yusuf Ziya Paşa Sok. Cash only. Metro: Fatih. Map p 81.*

★ Kanyon LEVENT

One of Istanbul's most up-market malls houses boutiques, brasseries, and movie halls, curving around a clever use of courtyards and terraces. Look out for **Remzi Kitabevi** (books), **Harvey Nichols** (designer fashion), **Vakko** (fashion), and **Paşabahçe Bütik** (housewares). *Büyükdere Cad.* ☎ *0212/353-5300. www.kanyon. com.tr. AE, MC, V. Metro: Levent. Map p 82.*

★★★ Kapalı Carşısı (Grand Bazaar) BEYAZIT

The grande dame of markets, this is a great historical shopping destination. It has Istanbul's best selection of carpets, leather, painted ceramics, and gold, for a souvenir-rich shopping experience. (See p 8 for more details.) *Beyazit. www.kapalicarsi. org.tr. Some stores accept credit cards. Tram/bus: Beyazit. Map p 81.*

★★★ Mısır Carşısı (Spice, or Egyptian, Bazaar) EMINÖNÜ

An ancient Istanbul spice market, now veering toward souvenirs and jewelry stores. A good selection of spices, dried fruit, and *lokum* (Turkish delight), with more choices at the stalls outside where the locals shop. (See p 9 for more details.) *Eminönü. Some stores accept credit cards. Tram/ bus: Eminönü. Map p 81.*

A glassblower at Ortaköy Craft Market.

★★ Ortaköy Craft Market

ORTAKÖY   Fun weekend market on cobbled streets with jewelry and accessories, busy in summer. Browse the waterfront stalls with good-natured vendors. (See p 21 for more details.) *Ortaköy Meydanı. Some stores accept credit cards. Bus/ferry: Ortaköy. Map p 82.*

★ Tarlabaşı Pazarı TARLABAŞI

Colorful Sunday street market where locals shop for the best and cheapest fruit, vegetables, cheeses, and honey, plus headscarves, stripy socks, and bed linen. Forget souvenirs; this gypsy area is wonderful for people-watching. *Note:* Guard your valuables *very* well! *From Omer Hayyam Cad. Cash only. Bus: Tepebaşı (Tarlıbaşı Cad). Map p 82.*

★ Zorlu Center ZINCIRLI-KUYU

If you're searching for luxury brands, then this is the best option (after Nişantaşı). Here, international brands such as Stella McCartney rub shoulders with local favorites, Beymen and Vakko. There is also a selection of international chain restaurants such as Jamie's Italian and Tom's Kitchen. *Zorlu Center, Zincirlikuyu.* ☎ *0212/924-0124. www.zorlucenter.com. Metro: Gayrettepe. Map p 82.* ●

5 The Best of the **Outdoors**

Gülhane **Park**

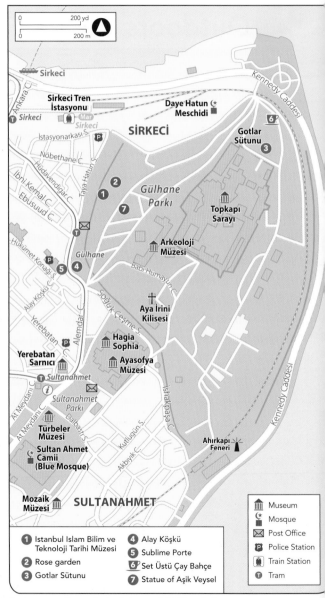

0 | 200 yd
0 | 200 m

🚉 Sirkeci

Sirkeci Tren İstasyonu

🚇 Sirkeci

İstasyonarkasi S.

Nöbethane C.

İbni Kemal C.
Ebusuud C.

Hükümet Konağı C.

Daye Hatun 🕌 Meschidi

SİRKECİ

Tava Hatun S.

Gotlar Sütunu ③

Gülhane Parkı

① ②
⑦

📮 Gülhane

Arkeoloji Müzesi 🏛

🏛 **Topkapı Sarayı**

Babı Hümayun C.

Soğuk Çeşme C.

⑤ ④

Alay Köşkü C.

Alemdar C.

✝ **Aya İrini Kilisesi**

🅿 **Yerebatan**

Yerebatan C.

🅿

🚇 Sultanahmet

ℹ

🏛 **Hagia Sophia**

🏛 **Ayasofya Müzesi**

İshakpaşa C.

Kennedy Caddesi

📮

Sultanahmet Parkı

At Meydanı C.

Dalbatı S.

🏛 **Türbeler Müzesi**

🕌 **Sultan Ahmet Camii (Blue Mosque)**

Kutlugün S.

Akbıyık C.

Ahırkapı 🔆 Feneri 🗼

🏛 **Mozaik Müzesi**

SULTANAHMET

❶ İstanbul İslam Bilim ve Teknoloji Tarihi Müzesi	❹ Alay Köşkü
❷ Rose garden	❺ Sublime Porte
❸ Gotlar Sütunu	❻ Set Üstü Çay Bahçe
	❼ Statue of Aşik Veysel

🏛	Museum
🕌	Mosque
📮	Post Office
🅿	Police Station
🏢	Train Station
🚇	Tram

Previous page: Escape city bustle in peaceful Gülhane Park.

Nestled in the original first courtyard of Topkapı Palace, Istanbul's oldest park is also, at 66 hectares (163 acres), the city center's largest. Used in Byzantine times as a barracks and a military warehouse, it became the sultans' imperial garden and an important public meeting place. Today it's a respite from the city, a locals' favorite for weekend strolls and picnics. START: **Tram to Gülhane.**

1 ★★ kids **Istanbul Islam Bilim ve Teknoloji Tarihi Müzesi (Istanbul Museum of the History of Science & Technology in Islam).** This fascinating museum is located in the northwest corner of the park, right up against the late-15th-century crenellated walls that ringed the Topkapı Palace complex. Housed in former Ottoman imperial stable buildings, it was opened in 2008 by Turkish historian Fuat Sezgin. The museum tells the story of Islamic scientists and astrologers from the 9th to 16th centuries. With instruments and other objects recreated by a German university, it demonstrates how these great men were at the forefront of early intellectual discoveries. Exhibits cover the first astrological instruments in the Islamic world, dating back to the 9th century, and include spherical astrolabes, the precursors to the sextants that were used to measure

celestial bodies and as navigation aids. At the main entrance, don't miss the re-creation of a globe made by 14th-century Caliph al-Ma'mun, with Baghdad at the center of the known world. Learn about the first pioneers of calculus (perhaps bringing back memories of school math exams) and even the math of music, where the 13th century saw divisions of the octave into 17 unequal degrees. There's even a 14th-century distillation apparatus for making rose-petal extract. ⏱ *1 hr. Gülhane Park.* ☎ *0212/528-8065. www.ibttm.org/ENG. Admission 10 TL, free for kids 6 and under. Wed–Mon, 9am–5pm. Tram: Gülhane.*

2 ★ **Rose Garden.** *Gülhane* is Persian for "house of roses," so it's no coincidence that recent improvements include a newly planted rose garden outside the museum. This historic park was originally made into a rose garden

One of the park's many waterfalls.

Tulip Mania

In April, Gülhane Park becomes a part of the Tulip Festival (p 160), a period when many thousands of this noble flower are in full, multi-color bloom. The tulip, known as *lale* in Turkish, is every bit as important to Turkish culture as the rose—if not more so. Tulip mania swept the Ottoman Empire in the 18th century; bulbs were highly prized, they changed hands for fortunes, and stylized tulips adorned everything from Iznik tiles to kaftans. So pervasive was the tulip's influence that this era became known as the *Lale Devri*, or Tulip Age, a period associated with the Baroque architecture that was displacing traditional Islamic/Turkish forms of architecture. *Lale* is a common name for Turkish girls today, and Turkish Airlines uses a tulip image on the fuselage of its planes.

to allow the flowers' scent to waft over to the palace, and now, thanks to the smartening-up or removal of several ugly buildings, the flowers stand out so much better. A new curved wooden sculpture, like a latticed dome, is a graceful addition outside the museum. Includes some plants from Northern Cyprus and a miniature of Galata Tower, a favorite photo point (p 10).

❸ ★ **Gotlar Sütunu (Goth's Column).** No, nothing to do with dressing in black. On the eastern edge of the park, look through the trees to this 15m-high (49 ft.) granite monolith, surmounted by a Corinthian capital, dating back to the 3rd century—one of Istanbul's oldest monuments. Although its history is uncertain, it probably derived its name from the Latin inscription at its base: "Fortune is restored to us because of victory over the Goths," commemorating a 3rd-century Roman victory. For such a historic landmark, it's a shame there's no sign to explain its history. Close by are more historic remains, probably belonging to an early Byzantine structure. A squat column of stones is topped with a

relief of a cross, and behind a fenced-off area lie the remains of a series of small rooms and an irregular colonnade.

❹ ★ **Alay Köşkü.** Translated as Procession Pavilion, this was where the sultans would sneakily watch official processions opposite, especially the comings and goings outside the ornate Sublime Porte entrance (❺). In the case of Ibrahim I, sultan between 1640 and 1648 and nicknamed Ibrahim the Mad because of his eccentricities and excesses, rumor has it that the pavilion was a perfect vantage point to aim his crossbow from and threaten unsuspecting bystanders. These days, the building sports a smart yellow-and-white-painted facade with arched, barred windows. It is approached from inside the park via a sloping ramp the sultan once rode up. Today, with offices inside, it's off-limits to the public.

❺ ★ **Sublime Porte.** You might have passed this typically ornate rococo gateway when traveling up on the tram from Eminönü to Sultanahmet. On the right-hand side, its curvaceous roof dipping over the monogrammed marble gate of 1843 is hard to miss. Translated from the French to *Bab-i Ali*, this was the gateway to the political hub of the Ottoman Empire, its buildings containing the principal state departments, and later the official residence of the grand viziers (high-ranking political advisors, second only to the sultan). Today, the superb rococo gate, with armed police outside leads to the *vilayet,* the more pedestrian-sounding provincial government departments.

6 ★★ kids **Set Üstü Çay Bahçe.** Locals love to dwell here for samovars of tea, so it's especially busy on summer evenings and weekends. Perched high at the northeastern edge of the park overlooking Seraglio Point, with dramatic views of the Sea of Marmara, Bosphorus, and over to Asia, kids will love the grilled meatballs (*köfte*) or over-stuffed jacket potatoes (*kumpir;* 10 TL).

7 ★ **Statue of Aşık Veysel.** Although there are surprisingly few statues and monuments in such a historic park, one to look out for is

Crowds strolling through the park.

a charming sculpture of musician Aşık Veysel (1894–1973), playing the *saz* (traditional stringed instrument). His life was marked with drama and sadness. Born in a field near Sivas as his mother returned from milking the cows, he contracted smallpox and went blind as a child; his parents and his baby son died, and

Spring landscape in Gülhane Park.

Palatial Park Life

Perhaps it's no coincidence that Istanbul's primary parks had a strong connection with Ottoman court life. Gülhane Park, originally an area in the lower town of the ancient Greek city of Byzantium, was incorporated into Topkapı Palace as a rose garden for the sultans to stroll. Similarly, Yıldız Park (p 21), a forest in Byzantine times, was part of the Yıldız Palace complex and sultans' hunting ground—especially loved by Abdul Hamit II. The city's largest is the pine-filled Emirgan Park, near Sakıp Sabancı Museum (p 33) in the northern district of Emirgan, named after Persian prince Emir Gune Han. Although not attached to any Ottoman palace, this eventually belonged to Khedevi Ismail, who built noble wooden pavilions (köşk), used today for Istanbul's tea-drinking public.

later his wife ran off with his brother's servant. The superb *saz* player found his niche writing folk songs about the inevitability of death. Popular in Turkey as a poet and musician, he became the official state poet in 1965, died of leukemia in 1973, and is still revered today. New York rock musician Joe Satriani was so inspired by his *saz* playing on a trip to Istanbul that he dedicated to him the track "Aşık Veysel" on his 2008 album *Professor Satchafunkilus and the Musterion of Rock*.

Close by, and a world away, is Turkey's oldest **statue of Atatürk,** cast in bronze by Austrian sculptor Heinrich Krippel in 1928. ●

Samovars of tea at Set Üstü Çay Bahçe.

Dining Best Bets

The upscale Agatha restaurant. Previous page: The terrace at Mikla is one of Istanbul's most romantic settings.

Best **Contemporary Turkish**
★★★ Yeni Lokanta 66 Kumbaracı Yokuşu (p 109)

Best **Asian-Side Dining**
★★★ Çiya 43, 44, and 48B Güneşlibahçe Sok (p 102)

Best for a **Taste of the Caucasus**
★★ Fıccın 13/1 Kallavi Sok (p 103)

Best **Homely Atmosphere**
★ Datlı Maya 59/A Türkgücü Cad (p 102)

Best **Old City View**
★★★ Surplus 54 Ragıp Gümüş Pala Cad (p 108)

Best **Family-Run Meyhane**
★★ Sofyalı 9 9 Sofyalı Sok (p 107)

Best **Cozy Home-Cooking**
★★ Hala 26 Çukurlu Çeşme Sok (p 103)

Best **Sultanahmet Seafood**
★★★ Balıkçı Sabahattin 1 Cankurtaran Cad (p 101)

Best **Value Tünel Meal**
★★ Lokanta Helvetia 12 General Yazgan Sok (p 104)

Best **Dramatic Views**
★★★ Topaz 50 İnönü Cad (p 108)

Best for **Liver Lovers**
★★★ Canım Ciğerim 162 İstiklal Cad (p 102)

Best **Istanbul Photographs**
★★ Kafe Ara 8 Tosbağa Sok, off Yeniçarşı Cad (p 104)

Old City Dining

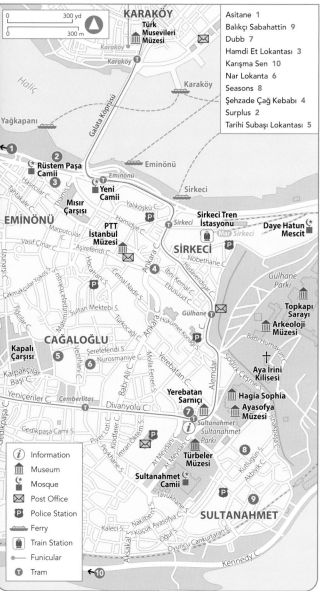

Asitane 1
Balıkçı Sabahattin 9
Dubb 7
Hamdi Et Lokantası 3
Karışma Sen 10
Nar Lokanta 6
Seasons 8
Şehzade Çağ Kebabı 4
Surplus 2
Tarihi Subaşı Lokantası 5

Beyoğlu Dining

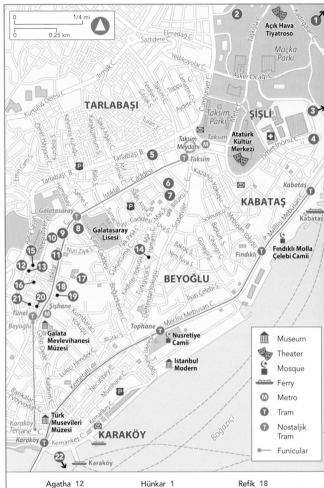

Agatha **12**
Borsa **2**
Canım Ciğerim **11**
Çiya **22**
Datlı Maya **14**
Enstitü **10**
Ficcın **9**
Gurme Boncuk **16**
Hala **7**

Hünkar **1**
Kafe Ara **8**
Leb-i Derya **18**
Lokanta Helvetia **21**
Mekan **17**
Melekler **6**
Meze by
  Lemon Tree **13**
Mikla **15**

Refik **18**
Sofyalı 9 **20**
Topaz **4**
Vogue **3**
Yeni Lokanta **19**
Zubeyir **5**

Bosphorus Dining

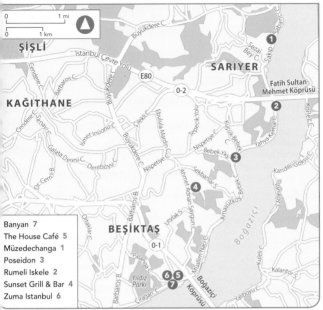

Banyan 7
The House Café 5
Müzedechanga 1
Poseidon 3
Rumeli Iskele 2
Sunset Grill & Bar 4
Zuma Istanbul 6

Istanbul Dining **A to Z**

★★ Agatha TEPEBAŞI *INTERNA-TIONAL* In the gorgeously reno-vated Pera Palace Hotel, this flagship fine-dining restaurant inter-twines cuisines from France, Italy, and Turkey—three of the countries on the fabled Orient Express route. Features an elegant dining room with the open kitchen on show. *52 Meşrutiyet Cad.* ☎ *0212/377-4000. www.jumeirah.com. Entrees 45–62 TL. AE, MC, V. Breakfast, lunch, and din-ner daily. Metro: Şişhane. Map p 100.*

★ Asitane EDIRNEKAPI *OTTO-MAN* Find out how the sultans dined with menus based on palace archives. Try their specialty, baked melon stuffed with lamb, veal, and pistachios, reflecting Arab and

Mediterranean fusion. Located next to the Kariye Museum (p 42), its garden is lovely in summer. *6 Kariye Camii Sok.* ☎ *0212/635-7997. www. asitanerestaurant.com. Entrees 26–42 TL. AE, MC, V. Lunch and dinner daily. Bus: 87. Map p 99.*

★★★ Balıkçı Sabahattin SULTANAHMET *SEAFOOD* This family-run restaurant in a tradi-tional house has dark wooden floors, *kilims*, and a fabulous fish menu popular with well-heeled Istanbullus. From octopus salad, move on to the fresh fish of the day. Tables spill out onto the peaceful courtyard in summer. Res-ervations recommended. *1 Cankur-taran Cad.* ☎ *0212/458-1824.*

www.balikcisabahattin.com. *Entrees 30–60 TL. MC, V. Lunch and dinner daily. Tram to Sultanahmet. Map p 99.*

★ **Banyan** ORTAKÖY *ASIAN FUSION* A huge open terrace overlooking the Bosphorus and a stylish dining room make Banyan especially popular in summer. Its fresh Asian fusion food includes sake-marinated filet mignon and king prawns with lemongrass risotto, plus fruity cocktails. Stylish and fun. *3 Salhane Sok, Muallim Naci Cad.* ☎ *0212/259-9060. www. banyanrestaurant.com. Entrees 30–85 TL. AE, MC, V. Lunch and dinner daily. Bus: Ortaköy. Map p 101.*

★ **Borsa** HARBIYE *TURKISH* Highly rated by wealthy Turks for its quality traditional dishes, this place is a real draw if you get a table on its huge open terrace. Handy for many hotels and adjoining the congress center, it's popular for business lunches. *Lütfi Kırdar Uluslararası Kongre ve Sergi Sarayı.* ☎ *0212/ 232-4201. www.borsarestaurants. com. Entrees 25–55 TL. MC, V. Lunch & dinner daily. Bus/Metro: Taksim. Map p 100.*

★★★ **Canım Ciğerim** BEYOĞLU *KEBABS* New, larger location, including a roof terrace, for this liver-lovers' favorite joint. Tiny cubes of liver, chicken, or lamb are skewered, barbecued, and served with mounds of fresh salad and flatbread. Friendly and cheap. *162 Istiklal Cad.* ☎ *0212/243-1005. Entrees 8–20 TL. MC, V. Lunch and dinner daily. Metro: Şişhane. Map p 100.*

★★★ **Çiya** KADIKÖY *TURKISH* A busy dining street on the Asian side has three branches of this wonderful restaurant. Their kebab restaurant is a bargain and always busy, serving a selection of fresh sizzling meats from around Turkey (maybe cooked with sour cherries and whole garlic cloves), plus a

The lovely garden at Asitane is located next to the Kariye Museum.

buffet for appetizers. Try all three to find your favorite. *43, 44, and 48B Güneşlibahçe Sok.* ☎ *0216/336-3013. www.ciya.com.tr. Entrees 10–20 TL. MC, V. Lunch and dinner daily. Boat: Kadıköy. Map p 100.*

★ **kids Datlı Maya** CIHANGIR *TURKISH* This cosy two-story restaurant may have only a few tables, but it has a truly unique character. It serves a range of stone-baked *lahmacun* (crispy dough topped with spiced ground meat) and other specialties from the southeast of Turkey. The ramshackle furniture lends it a homely feel. *59/A Türkgücü Cad.* ☎ *0212/292-9057. www. datlimaya.com. Entrees 10–22 TL. MC, V. Breakfast, lunch, and dinner daily. Metro/Bus: Taksim. Map p 100.*

★ **Dubb** SULTANAHMET *INDIAN* At one of the city's best Indian restaurants, feast on mixed kebabs, vegetarian dishes, and tandoori sea bream. Or taste several dishes on the set menu. Indian art lines the ochre walls, and the terrace overlooking Hagia Sophia is perfect for balmy summer evenings. *10 Incili*

Çavuş Sok, off Divan Yolu. ☎ 0212/
513-7308. www.dubbindian.com.
Entrees 16–40 TL, set meal 46 TL.
AE, MC, V. Lunch and dinner daily.
Tram: Sultanahmet. Map p 99.

★★ kids **Enstitü** TEPEBASI CON-
TEMPORARY TURKISH This stylish
apprentice-run restaurant recreates
Ottoman cuisine with a contemporary twist. A daily-changing lunch
menu might include zucchini fritters
with dill sauce and represents good
value. You can also take a cooking
workshop in the school upstairs. 59
Meşrutiyet Cad. ☎ 0212/251-2214.
www.istanbulculinary.com.tr. Entrees
16–28 TL. MC, V. Breakfast, lunch,
and dinner Mon–Sat. Bus: Tepebaşı.
Map p 100.

★★ kids **Ficcin** BEYOĞLU TURK-
ISH This restaurant serves up reliable local dishes along with some
more unusual varieties from the
Caucuses, such as Çerkez tavuğu
(chicken with walnuts and garlic)
and meat-filled pie. Its popularity is
such that it has expanded to four
different locations on the same
street. 13/1 Kallavi Sok, off Istiklal
Cad. ☎ 0212/293-3786. www.ficcin.
com. Entrees 6–14 TL. MC, V. Lunch
and dinner daily. Bus/Metro: Taksim.
Map p 100.

★★ **Gurme Boncuk**
ASMALIMESCIT ARMENIAN/TURK-
ISH One of many meyhanes (traditional restaurants) in bustling
Asmalımescit, this one has distinctive Armenian flavors as well as
favorite Turkish mezes. Perennially
popular, most locals get the fixed
menu, which includes a good range
of Turkish and Armenian dishes and
endless refills. 29 Asmalı Mescit Cad.
☎ 0212/245-3169. www.gurme
boncuk.com.tr. Entrees 18–30 TL, fixed
menu 95 TL. MC, V. Lunch and dinner
daily. Metro: Şişhane. Map p 100.

★★ kids **Hala** BEYOĞLU TURK-
ISH A good stop for a taste of

home cooking, this cozy and traditional Anatolian-style spot offers a
cheap, filling lunch or dinner on
gözleme (stuffed pancakes with
meat, spinach, or potatoes). Women
sit in the windows rolling thin yufka
dough, which is used to make mantı
(stuffed Turkish dumplings. 26 Çukurlu Çeşme Sok, off Büyük Parmakkapı
Sok. ☎ 0212/293-7531. Entrees 5–25
TL. MC, V. Lunch and dinner daily.
Bus/Metro: Taksim. Map p 100.

★★ **Hamdi Et Lokantası**
EMINÖNÜ TURKISH Spread over
four floors, Hamdi has a mouth-
watering selection of southeast
Turkish kebabs, including the house
specialty, fıstılı kebab (minced lamb
with pistachios). Book a table with
an unbeatable Bosphorus view.
17 Kalçin Sok, Tahmis Cad.
☎ 0212/528-0390. www.hamdi
restorant.com.tr. Entrees 23–30 TL.
MC, V. Lunch and dinner daily. Tram:
Eminönü. Map p 99.

★★ kids **The House Café**
ORTAKÖY BISTRO/EUROPEAN A
local chain with several branches
across the city, this is the most picturesque, with a chic, informal dining area and vast waterfront terrace.

Sizzling Sarımsak Kebabı at Ciya.

Think stylish comfort food (eggs Benedict), innovative pizzas, and a decent children's menu. Trendy locals love the after-work cocktails or detox smoothies. *1 Salhane Sok.* ☎ *0212/227-2699. www.thehouse cafe.com. Entrees 24–40 TL. AE, MC, V. Breakfast, lunch, and dinner daily. Bus/Boat: Ortaköy. Map p 101.*

★ **Hünkar** NIŞANTAŞI *TURKISH* This is where stylish Nişantaşı meets an earthy *lokanta* (traditional restaurant). Popular dishes include lamb shank with smoked eggplant puree, and *köfte* (meatballs); staff will happily advise. The large dining room spills out onto a tiny patio. *21 Mimar Kemal Öke Cad.* ☎ *0212/ 225-4665. www.hunkarlokantasi.com. Entrees 16–28 TL. MC, V. Lunch and dinner daily. Minibus: Nişantaşı. Map p 100.*

★★ **Karışma Sen** SULTANAH-MET *MEYHANE* This *meyhane* has been churning out tempting meze and freshly caught fish dishes for over 70 years. Just a short walk from Sultanahmet, this traditional restaurant is a long way from the touristy offerings of the historic peninsula and is a chance for an authentic Istanbul experience, with a view of the Marmara and the Asian side of the city. *28–30 Kennedy Cad.* ☎ *0212/458-0081. www. karismasen.com. Entrees 13–30TL. AE, MC, V. Lunch and dinner daily. Tram: Sultanahmet. Map p 99.*

★★ kids **Kafe Ara** GALATASA-RAY *BISTRO* A huge attraction are the photos by Istanbul's most famous photographer, Ara Güler, which adorn the walls. Buzzing with cultured locals dining on pasta and *köfte*, it's a great people-watching spot, especially from the patio. *8 Tosbağa Sok, off Yeniçarşı Cad.* ☎ *0212/245-4105. www.kafeara. com. Entrees 17–30 TL. MC, V. Breakfast, lunch, and dinner daily. Bus/Metro: Taksim. Map p 100.*

Trendy dining at Leb-i Derya.

★★ **Leb-i Derya (Richmond)** BEYOĞLU *TURKISH/INTERNA-TIONAL* On the sixth floor of a glass-fronted building, this stylish restaurant boasts panoramic views and is a great place to enjoy a fresh fruit cocktail with an unbeatable view of the city. Sister restaurant to the Leb-i Derya bar (p 117). *6/F Richmond Hotel, 227 Istiklal Cad.* ☎ *0212/243-4375. www.lebiderya. com. Entrees 25–60 TL. MC, V. Lunch and dinner daily. Map p 100.*

★★ kids **Lokanta Helvetia** TÜNEL *TURKISH* Cozy, with exposed brick walls and wooden tables, this place serves hearty, cheap homemade dishes. Vegetari-ans will love the delicious mixed hot and cold dishes such as potato with lentils or roast peppers in oil; carnivores can feast on chicken and lamb dishes. *12 General Yazgan Sok.* ☎ *0212/245-8780. Entrees 10–15 TL. No credit cards. Lunch and dinner daily. Tunnel: Tünel. Map p 100.*

★ **Mekan** BEYOĞLU *MEY-HANE* Mekan manages to be cozy and hip at the same time; a good-value restaurant with a charming brick-walled interior opening onto a small terrace. Service is friendly; cuisine is Turkish with Armenian influences, such as grilled vegetables with *halloumi* and chicken shish with tomatoes. *3 Eski Çiçekçi Sok, off Istiklal Cad.* ☎ *0212/252-6052. www. mekanrestaurant.com. Entrees 15–28 TL. MC, V. Lunch and dinner daily. Metro: Şişhane. Map p 100.*

★★★ kids **Melekler** TAKSIM *OCAKBAŞI* A no-frills barbecue joint with a few pavement tables where the Antakya-born owner cooks up fresh-grilled kebabs. Try spicy *Adana* or milder *Urfa* lamb kebab, or good old chicken wings, with piles of salad and fresh bread. *113 Ipek Sok, off Küçük Parmakkapı Sok.* ☎ *0212/243-0585. Entrees 5–15 TL. No credit cards. Lunch and dinner daily. Bus/Metro/funicular: Taksim. Map p 100.*

★★★ **Meze By Lemon Tree** TEPEBAŞI *CONTEMPORARY MEYHANE* If you want to experience a taste of contemporary Istanbul, head to this experimental restaurant. Here, the concept of a traditional Turkish tavern has been given a makeover, bringing it into the 21st century. The ambience is refined, the menu is seasonal yet creative, and the conversation flows as easily as the *rakı* that accompanies it. *83/B Meşrutiyet Cad.*

☎ *0212/252-8302. www.mezze.com. tr. Entrees 30–40 TL. AE, MC, V. Dinner daily. Metro: Şişhane. Map p 100.*

★★ **Mikla** TEPEBAŞI *TURKISH/ SCANDINAVIAN* On the top floor of the Marmara Pera hotel, the tiny terrace with Golden Horn views has to be one of Istanbul's most romantic, chic settings. Enjoy superb fusion cuisine, with meat dishes a specialty. End with after-dinner cocktails by the pool to the in-house DJ's chilled beats. The late-night bar is popular with wealthy 30-somethings on weekends. Reservations essential. *167 Meşrutiyet Cad.* ☎ *0212/293-5656. www. miklarestaurant.com. Entrees 35–60 TL. AE, MC, V. Dinner Mon–Sat. Bus: Tepebaşı. Map p 100.*

★★ **Müzedechanga** EMIRGAN *TURKISH/MEDITERRANEAN* Oozing style, with open kitchen and huge windows, the huge terrace is a major draw at this museum restaurant. Light lunchtime dishes, then it's all gourmet food for dinner (think grilled lamb loin with quince sauce) changing seasonally. It's been a hit since opening in 2005. A sister branch is in Cihangir. *Sakıp Sabancı Müzesi, Atlı Köşk, 22 Sakıp Sabancı Cad.* ☎ *0212/323-0901. www.changa-istanbul.com. Entrees*

Bookings are essential at the popular Meze.

Afiyet Olsun!

In recent years, Istanbul has improved its quality and quantity of world cuisines from Japanese to French in leaps and bounds. That said, you'll find that Turkish remains the cuisine of choice with the majority of locals. In *meyhanes* (Turkish-style taverns), meat and fish meals usually kick off with hot and cold meze appetizers: try *börek* (savory pastries), *patlıcan salatası* (smoked eggplant salad), *dolma* (stuffed vegetables), or *acı ezme* (spicy pepper dip). Often, a tray of meze options is brought to the table for you to select the most appealing. Fresh fish (waiters will advise on the freshest) is usually grilled or fried. Kebabs from around the country include *patlıcan kebap* (cubed meat layered with eggplant), *Iskender kebap* (lamb on pita bread with yogurt and tomato sauce), and many varieties of *köfte* (meatballs). There are plenty of options available for vegetarians such as *imam bayıldı* (stuffed eggplant with tomato and onions) and *zeytinyağlı* (seasonal vegetables cooked slowly in olive oil). Accompany with *rakı* (local aniseed spirit), and end with one of the many varieties of *helva* and fresh fruit. Most people will wish you *"afiyet olsun,"* the local equivalent of bon appétit.

28–58 TL. AE, DC, MC, V. Lunch and dinner Tues–Sun. Bus: Emirgan. Map p 101.

★★★ **Nar Lokanta** NURUOSMANIYE *TURKISH* The first restaurant venture of the Nar Gourmet produce brand, this restaurant offers regional Turkish tastes. The buffet starter section includes an ever-changing variety of seasonal vegetables braised in aromatic olive oil. The main course menu changes monthly but includes Turkish classics such as *hünkar beğendi* (chunks of slow-cooked lamb served on a bed of eggplant puree), and *mantı* (dumplings filled with spiced meat and served with garlic yogurt). *Armaggan, 65 Nuruosmaniye Cad.* ☎ *0212/522-2800. www.narlokantasi.com. Entrees 14–60 TL. MC, V. Lunch and dinner Mon–Sat. Tram: Beyazit. Map p 99.*

★ **kids Poseidon** BEBEK *FISH* Treat yourselves in one of Istanbul's poshest waterfront neighborhoods to fresh fish, either simply grilled or fried. Kick off with grilled calamari and go for anything in season; check for portion prices with the waiters. *58 Cevdetpaşa Cad.* ☎ *0212/287-9531. www.poseidonbebek.com. Entrees 38–60 TL. AE, DC, MC, V. Lunch and dinner daily. Bus: Bebek. Map p 101.*

★★ **Refik** ASMALIMESCIT *MEYHANE* There are a number of traditional Turkish *meyhanes* in the bustling nightlife district of Asmalımescit. This is one of the better ones, popular with local intellectuals and artists of all ages. Established in 1954, the walls are lined with old photographs that evoke memories of the Istanbul of yester-years. The mezes are a good quality, and the atmosphere gets livelier as the night gets later. *10–12 Sofyalı Sok.* ☎ *0212/243-2834. www.refikrestaurant.com. Entrees 15–35 TL. MC, V. Lunch and dinner Mon–Sat. Metro: Şişhane. Map p 100.*

★ **Rumeli Iskele** RUMELI HISARI *FISH* Fish is always pricey in Istanbul, good fish even more so. But this perennially popular restaurant is loved by well-heeled locals for rich mezes, simple fried fish, or hearty *buğulama* (fish stew). Book a waterfront table for a touch of romance. *1 Yahya Kemal Cad.* ☎ *0212/263-2997. Entrees 40–75 TL. AE, MC, V. Lunch and dinner daily. Bus: 25. Map p 101.*

★ kids **Seasons** SULTANAHMET *TURKISH/MEDITERRANEAN* Even if you can't afford a night at the Four Seasons, enjoy a romantic (but pricey) dinner in the garden's glass-walled gazebo. It might lack local atmosphere, but the quality of seasonal dishes is good. Typical choices include thyme-roast chicken or fresh seafood pasta; there's also a good children's menu. *1 Tevkifhane Sok.* ☎ *0212/402-3000. www.fourseasons. com/istanbul. Entrees 32–62 TL. AE, DC, MC, V. Breakfast, lunch, and dinner daily. Tram: Sultanahmet. Map p 99.*

★★ kids **Şehzade Cağ Kebabı** SIRKECI *KEBAB* While the rest of the city roasts its meat on vertical spits, this little restaurant takes a horizontal approach, serving up *cağ* kebab, a specialty of the eastern Anatolian city, Erzurum. The marinated lamb meat is cooked over a wood fire and served with homemade *lavaş* (thin flatbread). *3/A Hocapaşa Sok.* ☎ *0212/520-3361. www.sehzadecagkebap.com. Entrees 3–14 TL. MC, V. Lunch and dinner Mon–Sat. Tram: Sirkeci. Map p 99.*

★★ **Sofyalı 9** ASMALIMESCIT *MEYHANE* A much-loved

Chic decor at Mikla.

meyhane, this family-run place has a charming host and a mustard-walled interior. Always full in a busy nightlife area, enjoy mezes like *semizotu* (purslane in garlicky yogurt) and *dolma* (peppers stuffed with meat), washed down with local beer or aniseed *rakı*. *9 Sofyalı Sok, off Asmalımescit.* ☎ *0212/245-0362. www.sofyali.com.tr. Entrees 20–44 TL. MC, V. Lunch and dinner daily. Metro: Şişhane. Map p 100.*

★★ **Sunset Grill & Bar** ULUS *INTERNATIONAL* With a stunning hilltop location, Sunset is perennially popular, with superb dishes including sushi, sea bass, and T-bone steak. The menu caters to locals wanting modern European, as well as visitors preferring traditional Ottoman cuisine. The decked terrace is perfect on summer evenings; daytime meals see businesspeople shoulder to shoulder with ladies who lunch. *2 Yol Sok, Adnan Saygun Cad, Ulus Park.* ☎ *0212/ 287-0358. www.sunsetgrillbar.com. Entrees 50–80 TL. AE, DC, MC, V. Lunch Mon–Sat, dinner daily. Taxi. Map p 101.*

Sunset Grill & Bar.

★★★ **Surplus** EMINÖNÜ *CON-TEMPORARY TURKISH* Located on the top floor of a bright pink jewelry *han*, close to Galata Bridge, this elegant restaurant has panoramic views that take in Istanbul's best sights. Opened by Turkish food ambassador, Vedat Başaran, the menu aims to represent the cosmopolitan nature of the city in a thoroughly modern style. *Zindan Han, 54 Ragıp Gümüş Pala Cad.* ☎ *0212/520-1002. www.surplus. com.tr. Entrees 42–66 TL. AE, MC, V. Lunch and dinner daily. Tram: Eminönü. Map p 99.*

★ **kids Tarihi Subaşı Lokantası** BEYAZIT *TURKISH* A good example of a typical *esnaf* (tradesmen's) restaurant, located a stone's throw from the Grand Bazaar's Nuruosmaniye entrance. Established in 1959, this family business serves up a range of classic Turkish home-style cooking such as stuffed eggplant, vegetables braised in olive oil, and lamb stews. It's a little pricier than other similar restaurants, but the professional service and pressed tablecloths make it a more inviting place to linger. *48 Çarşıkapı Nuruosmaniye Cad.* ☎ *0212/522-4762. www.tarihisubasi.com. Entrees*

10–20 TL. MC, V. Lunch and dinner Mon–Sat. Tram: Beyazit. Map p 99.*

★★★ **Topaz** GÜMÜŞSUYU *MEDI-TERRANEAN* Opened in late 2007, this sleek, stylish restaurant has cuisine favoring contemporary Turkish/Mediterranean dishes and fantastic service. Splash out on the six-course Ottoman degustation menu, and book a table by the floor-to-ceiling windows for staggering Bosphorus views. *50 İnönü Cad.* ☎ *0212/249-1001. www.topaz istanbul.com. Entrees 34–62 TL, 6-course tasting menu 120–195 TL. AE, DC, MC, V. Lunch and dinner daily. Bus/Metro: Taksim. Map p 100.*

★★ **Vogue** AKARETLER *SUSHI/ INTERNATIONAL* With Bosphorus views from a rooftop terrace, this is where the beautiful people come to dine on top sushi. Settle on the terrace's soft white seats (indoors in winter) with contemporary cuisine, like braised zucchini rolls and hot chestnut cake. Sunday buffet brunch is a highlight. Reservations essential; open late. *13/F, 48 BJK Plaza, A-Blok, Spor Cad.* ☎ *0212/ 227-2545. www.voguerestaurant. com. Entrees 34–68 TL. AE, DC, MC, V. Lunch and dinner daily. Bus: Beşiktaş. Map p 100.*

ENGLISH		
Breakfast		
Lunch		
Dinner		
Beer		
Soft drinks		
Mineral water		
Starters (assor		
Red/white win		
Dessert		
Fish		
Eggplant		
Chicken		
Meat		
Meat-free		
Hot (spicy)		
Eggs	yumurta	yumurta
Beans	fasulye	fasul-yeh
Bread	ekmek	ekmek
White cheese	peynir	peynir
Anchovy	hamsi	hamsi
Fried	tava	tava
Grilled	izgara	izgara
Tomato	domates	do-mah-tes
Savory pastries	börek	burek
Meatballs	köfte	kerf-teh
Vegetables w/olive oil	zeytinyağlı	zeytin-yarluh
Turkish coffee	Türk kahvesi	Turk kar-veh-si
Tea	çay	chay
Fruit juice	meyve suyu	Mayveh su-yu
(Lentil) soup	(mercimek) çorba	(mer-ji-mek) chorba
Rice	pilav	pilav
Salad	salata	salata
The check, please.	Hesap, lütfen.	hesap, lutfen

★★★ Yeni Lokanta TÜNEL CONTEMPORARY TURKISH

This is the solo venture of chef Civan Er (former head chef at Changa), which opened in early 2013 and became an instant hit. The short menu changes with the seasons, the ingredients are sourced from Turkey's best regional producers, and the decor is an exercise in understated elegance. Cocktails are highly recommended, and meals begin with slices of warm sourdough served with smoked butter. Reservations essential. *66 Kumbaracı Yokuşu.* ☎ *0212/292-2550. www.lokantayeni.com. Entrees 38–59 TL. AE, MC, V. Lunch and dinner Mon–Sat. Metro: Şişhane. Map p 100.*

View the Bosphorus while dining at Topaz.

★★★ Zubeyir BEYOĞLU
OCAKBAŞI This kebab restaurant is a firm favorite with locals and visitors alike. This style of restaurant is known as an *ocakbaşı* and features a prominent grill, which guests can sit around for a unique experience. It specializes in perfectly good lamb and chicken kebabs, although they also serve an excellent range of fresh mezes. *28 Bekar Sok.* ☎ *0212/293-3951. Entrees 20–27 TL. AE, MC, V. Lunch and dinner daily. Bus/Metro: Taksim. Map p 100.*

★★ Zuma Istanbul ORTAKÖY
JAPANESE This top-notch restaurant imported from London fits well into Ortaköy's hip dining scene— this is one for a splurge. Try the tasting menu or special miso-marinated black cod. The first floor opens onto a terrace, with sushi bar and Japanese robata grill, and is all earthy wood tones and sleek sofas. Dress to impress; reservations essential. *7 Salhane Sok.* ☎ *0212/ 236-2296. www.zumarestaurant.com. Entrees 30–60 TL. AE, DC, MC, V. Lunch and dinner daily. Bus: Ortaköy. Map p 101.* ●

Nightlife Best Bets

Best Old City View
★★★ AYA Terrace *1 Tevkifhane Sok (p 114)*

Best Local Craft Beer
★★ Taps *119 Cevdet Paşa Cad (p 116)*

Best Leafy Courtyard
★★ Cezayir *16 Hayriye Cad (p 117)*

Best for a Wine & Cheese Evening
★★ Corvus Wine & Bite *5 Şair Nedim Cad (p 114)*

Best Long-Standing Gay Nightclub
★★ Tekyön *63 Sıraselviler Cad (p 120)*

Best for Electronic Music
★★★ Indigo *1–4 Arkasu Sok (p 118)*

Best Terrace for Cocktails
★★ 360Istanbul *9/F 163 Istiklal Cad (p 119)*

Best for High Society
★★ Anjelique *5 Salhane Sok (p 118)*

Best Vintage Decor
★★ 5.Kat *5/F 7 Soğancı Sok (p 115)*

Best for a No-Nonsense Beer
★★★ Arsen Lüpen *4/F 15 Mis Sok (p 114)*

Best for Old City Nargile
★ Café Meşale *45 Arasta Bazaar (p 116)*

Best for Hipster Spotting
★★ Unter *4 Kara Ali Kaptan Sok (p 117)*

Live gigs at Jolly Joker. Previous page: Night crowds stroll the streets and markets of Istanbul.

Beyoğlu Nightlife

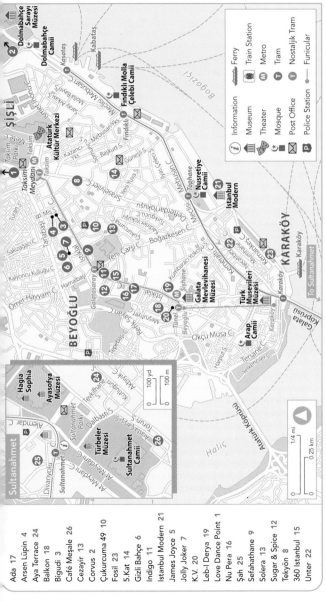

Ortaköy Nightlife

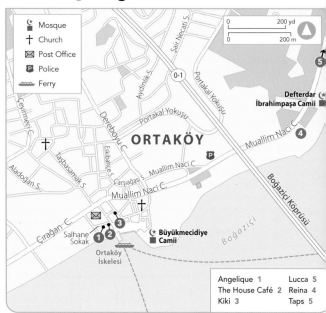

Ġ Mosque
† Church
✉ Post Office
🄱 Police
🚢 Ferry

Defterdar
İbrahimpaşa Camii

ORTAKÖY

Büyükmecidiye
Camii

Ortaköy
İskelesi

Boğaziçi Köprüsü

Angelique 1	Lucca 5
The House Café 2	Reina 4
Kiki 3	Taps 5

Istanbul Nightlife A to Z

Bars

★★★ Arsen Lüpen BEYOĞLU
This is a casual two-story bar,
accessed by taking the elevator
inside another restaurant (Address
Bab-ı Ali Café Bar). It arrives in a
large grungy space with a stage
that features live swing, Turkish, or
jazz music most nights. On the top
floor is a smoky terrace with
impressive views. *4/F 15 Mis Sok.*
☎ *0555/706-5999. Bus/Metro: Taksim. Map p 113.*

★★★ AYA Terrace SULTANAH-
MET This luxurious terrace is
located on top of the Four Seasons.
It has breathtaking views of the
Hagia Sophia and Blue Mosque

and is the ideal place to come for a
decadent glass of something cold.
*Four Seasons at Sultanahmet, 1
Tevkifhane Sok.* ☎ *0212/402-3000.
www.fourseasons.com. Tram: Sultanahmet. Map p 113.*

★★ Corvus Wine & Bite
AKARETLER Located on one of
Istanbul's most stylish streets (p 32),
come here for a mature evening of
fine Turkish wines. Owned by the
eponymous vineyard company, it
serves a civilized glass of their finest labels, accompanied by small
tapas plates and Turkish cheeses. *5
Şair Nedim Cad.* ☎ *0212/260-5470.
Bus: Beşiktaş. Map p 113.*

Cover Charges

Entry to nightclubs for DJs and live music varies greatly, depending on the day of the week and which live acts are performing.

★★ **5.Kat** CIHANGIR One of Istanbul's first venues to capitalize on its Bosphorus view, locals love Beşinci Kat's ("5th floor") terrace during summer. Inside, it's all deep red walls and chandeliers in an arty, gay-friendly bar, with actress-owner Yasemin Alkaya watching over the fun. Decent food served all day. Open until 3am at weekends. *5/F 7 Soğancı Sok.* ☎ *0212/293-3774. www.5kat.com. Bus/Metro: Taksim. Map p 113.*

★ **Gizli Bahçe** BEYOĞLU Not the place for a quiet drink after 9pm, when the music and roar of conversation reaches a deafening pitch, especially on weekends. Homely rather than chic, come for an early-evening beer and sink into a mismatched armchair on the terrace, before dining at a nearby *meyhane. 15 Nevizade Sok.* ☎ *0212/249-2192. Bus/Metro: Taksim. Map p 113.*

★ **James Joyce Irish Pub** BEYOĞLU If you're itching to watch a Manchester United match on TV, eat an Irish breakfast, and drink Guinness while being surrounded by "Oirish" paraphernalia, join young expats and locals at Istanbul's first Irish pub. The terrace is busy in summer, with nightly live music in winter. *26 Balo Sok, off Istiklal Cad.* ☎ *0212/244-7970. www.irishpubthejamesjoyce.com. Metro/bus: Taksim. Map p 113.*

★★ **K.V.** TÜNEL In an ornate 19th-century courtyard, K.V. (pronounced "keh-veh") has outdoor tables among plants and fairy lights for a romantic touch. When chilly, step into the tiny high-ceilinged restaurant with huge chandeliers and pink neon lighting. It's popular, so getting a table on weekends can be difficult, especially when there's live jazz. *10 Tünel Geçidi, off General Yazgan Sok.* ☎ *0212/251-4338. www.kv.com.tr. Tunnel: Tünel. Map p 113.*

★ **Şah** SULTANAHMET One of the Old City's few authentic bars, it's a gathering place in summer with a mixture of tourists and locals. There are separate stone-walled partitions with rugs and stools off the courtyard, plus adjacent cafe and restaurant. DJs play European hits nightly. *9 İncili Çavuş Çıkmaz Sok, off Divan Yolu.* ☎ *0212/519-5807. www.sahbar.com. Tram: Sultanahmet. Map p 113.*

A selection of wines at the cozy Solera Winery.

No Smoking?

Most Turks smoke like chimneys, so a trip to a bar, cafe, or club usually comes with cigarette fumes. So what changed when the smoking ban hit Turkey in 2009? Nothing much! Some venues adhere strictly, but many turn a blind eye and—allegedly—know the right people to pay off. Controversially, even *nargile* (tobacco waterpipe) smoking was banned indoors. Instead, it is enjoyed at outdoor tables with tea and backgammon, but not generally with alcohol. Your best bets for this are along Fuat Uzkinay Sokak, off Istiklal Caddesi, and near Istanbul Modern (p 30), behind Tophane mosque.

★ **Sefahathane** BEYOĞLU
Tucked away down Atlas Pasaj by the cinema, this tiny bar-cafe has rock music, photos on the walls, and a laidback bohemian atmosphere that is refreshingly unpretentious. Come for beers or fancy cocktails. *Atlas Pasajı, Istiklal Cad.* ☎ *0212/251-2245. www.sefahathane.com.tr. Bus/Metro: Taksim. Map p 113.*

★★★ **Solera Winery** GALATASARY   This cozy bar is just a 5-minute walk from Istiklal Caddisi. Its small size means that it fills up quickly and is the place for a good chat rather than a big party. It stocks over 1,000 Turkish and international wines, and its knowledgeable owner, Süleyman Er, can help you choose the right bottle. Also serves simple meze and sharing plates. *44 Yeniçarşı Cad.* ☎ *0212/252-2719. Bus/Metro: Taksim. Map p 113.*

★★ **Taps** BEBEK   Istanbul's first brewpub, this little gem is still one of the only places in Istanbul to drink craft beer. Despite being located in one of the plushest neighborhoods, the simple decor gives it a casual feel. What really makes it special is the view of the Bosphorus, across the road. 119

Cevdet Paşa Cad. ☎ *0212/263-8700. www.tapsbebek.com. Bus: Bebek. Map p 114.*

Cafe-Bars & Restaurant Bars

★ **Ada** BEYOĞLU   Inside this huge bookstore, the cavernous cafe covers most of the first floor. Good for an early-evening glass of wine while listening to excellent music from around the world, or a coffee while browsing through books. Open until about 10pm every evening. *158A Istiklal Cad.* ☎ *0212/251-6682. www.adakitapcafe.com. Bus/Metro: Taksim. Map p 113.*

★★ **Balkon** ASMALIMESCIT
Occupying the top two floors of a building a couple of doors down from Babylon (p 127), this bar attracts for its staggering view. It serves an extensive menu of international and Turkish foods and tends to get pretty lively with a young local crowd on weekend nights. *5 Sehbender Sok.* ☎ *0212/293-2052. Metro: Şişhane. Map p 113.*

★ **Café Meşale** SULTANAHMET
It might be a tourist trap, but this sunken courtyard can be a pleasure in the evenings, when it fills up with locals and tourists who smoke

sheesha and enjoy live entertainment. No alcohol is on offer but you can do as the locals do and enjoy a tea and game of backgammon. *45 Arasta Bazaar.* ☎ *0212/518-9562. Tram: Sultanahmet. Map p 113.*

★★ Cezayir GALATASARAY

This restaurant is loved for its garden terrace in summer and its plant-filled indoor bar and stylish upstairs. It's a real hit with Istanbul's 30-something nightbirds, especially for its weekend DJs. *16 Hayriye Cad.* ☎ *0212/245-9980. www.cezayir-istanbul.com. Bus/Metro: Taksim and walk. Map p 113.*

★★★ Çukurcuma 49 CIHANGIR

This cool and cozy cafe bar is in Istanbul's most bohemian quarter. Here, local artists, writers, and musicians rub shoulders with clued-up expats. They specialize in pizza using Turkish produce and wines from the Aegean island of Bozcaada. *49/A Turnacıbaşı Sok.* ☎ *0212/249-0048. Bus/Metro: Taksim. Map p 113.*

★★ The House Café ORTAKÖY

A popular restaurant (p 103), the outdoor deck comes alive on summer evenings. Bar staff create fruity cocktails, or you can sip a cold beer while watching the colored lights on the bridge. The wooden-floored interior is also inviting. *1 Salhane Sok.* ☎ *0212/227-2699. www.thehousecafe.com. AE, MC, V. Bus/boat: Ortaköy. Map p 114.*

★★ Istanbul Modern Café & Restaurant TOPHANE

Attached to the museum (p 30) with a tiny Bosphorus-facing terrace, this is a restaurant by day and popular bar in the evenings. Very stylish. *4 Antrepo, Liman Işletmeleri Sahasi, Meclis-i Mebusan Cad.* ☎ *0212/292-2612. www.istanbulmodern.org. Tram: Tophane. Map p 113.*

★★ Leb-i Derya GALATASARAY

Also a restaurant, and little brother to Leb-i Derya (Richmond) (p 104), its tiny rooftop terrace attracts young, well-heeled professionals. Find a seat outside and drink in the staggering view as you take in lounge music, liqueur-laced tea, and carefully concocted cocktails. *7/F 57 Kumbaracı Yokuşu.* ☎ *0212/293-4989. www.lebiderya.com. Metro: Şişhane. Map p 113.*

★ Lucca BEBEK

This bistro bar is favored by hip Bebek locals, who love its brasserie-style cuisine and contemporary art gallery. It's one for people-watching and checking out the beautiful people dancing to the DJ's house music. *51 Cevdetpaşa Cad.* ☎ *0212/257-1255. www.luccastyle.com. Bus: Bebek. Map p 114.*

★★ Unter KARAKÖY

This uber cool hotspot is popular with the local youth who go out to see and be seen in the city's most rapidly developing neighborhood. There's a Turkish/international menu that attracts the crowds during the day and a well-stocked bar for the evenings. On weekend nights, local

Riverside views at The House Café.

Making Friends?

DJs get them on their feet. *4 Kara Ali Kaptan Sok.* ☎ *0212/244-5151. www.unter.com.tr. Tram: Tophane. Map p 113.*

Clubs & DJ Bars

★★ **Anjelique** ORTAKÖY   One of Istanbul's best-loved summer clubs with a Bosphorus-facing terrace. Dress to impress if you want to fit in with the high society partying to DJs' beats. International cuisine

The fireplace at Anjelique.

including sushi is on the club's restaurant menu. *5 Salhane Sok, Muallim Naci Cad.* ☎ *0212/327-2844. www. anjelique.com.tr. Bus/boat: Ortaköy. Map p 114.*

★★ **Fosil** KARAKÖY   Opened in 2013, this local favorite is a much-needed addition to Karaköy's nightlife scene. This bar/club is immensely popular on weekends for its diverse music policy (with an indie slant) and its floor-to-ceiling windows, which look out onto the Bosphorus. *34C Kemankeş Cad.* ☎ *0507/812-8531. www.fosil.com.tr. Tram: Karaköy. Map p 113.*

★★★ **Indigo** GALATASARAY The world's finest electronic techno acts and DJs regularly perform in this club, loved for its great lighting, sound system, and laser shows. Serious clubbers seek solace in the vast, dark space. Buy advance tickets for popular acts. *1–4 Arkasu Sok, off Istiklal Cad.* ☎ *0212/244-8567. www.indigo-istanbul.com. Cover charge. Bus: Taksim. Map p 113.*

★★ **Jolly Joker Balans** BEYOĞLU This popular venue has a bit of everything: snack food, cold beer, and live soccer on the TV. Local (and occasionally international) bands play to a young crowd. *22 Balo Sok, off Istiklal Cad. ☎ 0212/293-5690. www.jjistan bul.com. Metro: Taksim. Map p 113.*

★★ **Kiki** ORTAKÖY This bar, formerly popular but cramped bar in Cihangir, has expanded to a three-story building overlooking the Bosphorus in affluent Ortaköy. Here, revelers spread out over three floors and an open-air terrace while local and international DJs spin the tunes. *8 Osmanzade Sok. ☎ 0212/ 258-5524. www.kiki.com.tr. Bus: Ortaköy. Map p 114.*

★ **Nu Pera** TEPEBAŞI. This multifaceted complex has two restaurants and a backroom bar/club called Pop. However, in the summer months, the party moves upstairs to NuTeras where local DJs play to the in-crowd. *149/1 Meşrutiyet Cad. ☎ 0212/245-6070. www.nupera.com.tr. Bus: Tepebaşı. Map p 113.*

★ **Reina** ORTAKÖY Local celebs (and wannabes) flock to be seen at this vast entertainment and restaurant complex. You might get in early in the week—after making reservations—for drinks and music on the terrace bar. Black-suited doormen are choosy; think brash clothing rather than tasteful glamour. During winter, the terrace is heated. Steep cover charge (varies) and drinks are pricey. *44 Muallim Naci Cad. ☎ 0212/259-5919. www. reina.com.tr. Boat/bus: Ortaköy. Map p 114.*

★★ **360Istanbul** BEYOĞLU At the top of Mısır Apartmenı (p 31), this terrace bar-club-restaurant is a real hit with *fashionistas.* Glass walls mean enjoying the views even when it's too chilly for the terrace. On weekends, house DJs fill the dance floor into the small hours. Line your stomach with international cuisine before sampling top cocktails. *9/F 163 Istiklal Cad. ☎ 0212/251-1042. www. 360istanbul.com. Bus/Metro: Taksim. Map p 113.*

Gay Nightlife

★★ **Bigudi** TAKSIM Istanbul's first lesbian bar has changed venues several times since opening in 2007, and is opened only on weekends. A women-only terrace club, plus a cafe-bar downstairs open to all, things get busy after midnight. *5 Mis Sok, off Istiklal Cad. ☎ 0535/509-0922. Bus: Taksim. Map p 113.*

Ambience at 360Istanbul.

Pricey Tipple

Istanbul is now recognized as a world-class city for nightlife, on a par with London and New York. Unfortunately, it's matched by similar prices for alcohol, thanks to excessive government taxation. Gone are the days when a beer cost a dollar! Costs can be reduced by sticking to local drinks; Efes and Bomonti and reliable local beers (bottled or draught) and Turkish wines have improved enormously over recent years—try an Angora or Kavaklidere. Avoid domestic vodka and gin, and *rakı* (the famous aniseed liquor) should be treated with caution: stick to drinking it mixed with water at dinner.

★★ **Love Dance Point** HARBIYE With the slogan, "love is here, where are you?" and scantily clad male dancers, this large, glitzy club has become one of Istanbul's most popular gay nightlife destinations. *349/1 Cumhurriyet Cad.* ☎ *0212/232-5683. www.lovedp.net. Metro: Osmanbey. Map p 113.*

★ **Sugar & Spice** BEYOĞLU This is a good daytime spot to get up-to-date info from local gay guys about Istanbul's nightlife. A simple cafe and bar, most locals know it by its former name, the Sugarclub Café. It has DJs on summer weekends with crowds spilling out onto the courtyard. *3 Saka Salim Çıkmazı, off Istiklal Cad.* ☎ *0212/245-0096. www.sugar-cafe.com. Bus/Metro: Taksim. Map p 113.*

★★ **Tekyön** BEYOĞLU Istanbul's most popular gay club, previously for local "bears," now attracts a mixed crowd; gay and straight women are welcome, but perhaps not on weekends when things get busy. Loud Turkish and Euro pop is the norm, with plenty of space for a chat upstairs, until everyone packs

Drinks at Fosil.

onto the dance floor. Don't arrive before midnight! *63 Sıraselviler Cad.* ☎ *0535/233-0654. www.clubtekyon.com. Bus: Taksim. Map p 113.* ●

Arts & Entertainment Best Bets

Riders at the start of a race at Veliefendi Racecourse. Previous page: Crowds at the parking lot basement at garajistanbul.

Best for **Eclectic DJs & Fusion Bands**
★★★ Babylon 3 *Şeybender Sok* (p 127)

Best **Venue for an Orchestra**
★★ Hagia Eirene *Topkapı Sarayı* (p 126)

Best **Experimental Theater**
★★ garajistanbul 11A *Kaymakam Reşat Bey Sok* (p 126)

Best for a **Cozy Jazz Night**
★★ Nardis 14 *Galata Kulesi Sok* (p 128)

Best **Goal Celebrations**
★★★ Beşiktaş FC *Vodafone Arena* (p 129)

Best **Music for a Summer Night**
★★ Cemil Topuzlu Açıkhava Tiyatrosu *Harbiye* (p 125)

Best **Place to Bet on the Ponies**
★ Veliefendi *Veliefendi Hipodromu* (p 129)

Best for **Avant-Garde Bands**
★★ Salon IKSV 5 *Sadi Konuralp Cad* (p 128)

Best **Spiritual Experience**
★★★ Whirling Dervish Ceremony, Galata Mevlevihanesi 15 *Galip Dede Cad* (p 127)

Best **Night at the Opera**
★★ Süreyya Opera House 29 *Bahariye Cad* (p 126)

Best **Big Productions**
★★★ Zorlu Center PSM *Zincirlikuyu* (p 127)

Best for **Local Chamber Music**
★★ Akbank Sanat 8 *Istiklal Cad* (p 125)

Best for **Stretching the Legs**
★★★ Cycling on the Princes' Islands (p 129)

Beyoğlu A&E

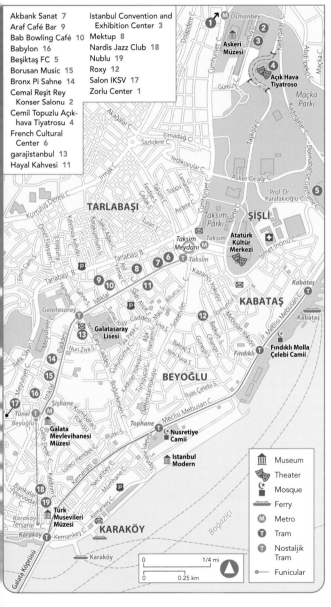

Greater Istanbul A&E

GAZİOSMANPAŞA

ŞİŞLİ AYAZAĞA

SARİYER

KAĞITHANE

BEŞİKTAŞ

ŞİŞLİ

EYÜP

BEYOĞLU

BAYRAMPAŞA

KARAKÖY

FATİH

ÜSKÜDAR

EMİNÖNÜ

ZEYTİNBURNU

KADIKÖY

Marmara Denizi

Fenerbahçe FC 6
Galatasaray FC 1
Hagia Eirene 5
Süreyya Opera House 7
Veliefendi 3
Whirling Dervish Ceremony 4
Zorlu Center 2

| 0 | | 2 mi |
| 0 | 2 km | |

Arts & Entertainment A to Z

Dance, Music & Theater

★★ Akbank Sanat BEYOĞLU
This privately sponsored cultural center has a small theater, cinema, and even its own chamber orchestra (a good example of the benefits of banks sponsoring the arts). Hosting regular local dance groups, concerts, and films, and a prominent venue in the city's arts festivals (p 160). *8 Istiklal Cad.* ☎ *0212/252-3500. www.akbanksanat.com. Tickets from 20 TL. Bus/Metro: Taksim. Map p 123.*

★ Borusan Muzik Evi BEYOĞLU
Established in 2009, this newly renovated six-story building houses many forms of the arts. It boasts contemporary art galleries, a concert hall, modern dance performances, and rehearsal space for the Borusan Istanbul Philharmonic Orchestra. *Orhan Adli Apaydın Sok, off Istiklal Cad.* ☎ *0212/336-3280. www.borusanmuzikevi.com. Tickets from 20 TL. Bus: Taksim. Map p 123.*

★★ Cemal Reşit Rey Konser Salonu HARBIYE
This huge theater is home to its own symphony orchestra, with a regular and varied program including classical, jazz, and world music, plus occasional traveling ballet and modern dance companies. Closed during summer. *Darülbedayi Cad, Harbiye.* ☎ *0212/232-9830. www.crrkonsersalonu.org. Bus: Harbiye. Map p 123.*

★★ Cemil Topuzlu Açıkhava Tiyatrosu (Cemil Topuzlu Open Air Theater) HARBIYE
This fantastic contemporary amphitheater is loved in summer, when it hosts a diverse range of performances from Balkan genius Goran Bregović to the *House* star, Hugh Laurie, and everything in between. Most concerts are mid-July to early August. *Taşkışla Cad. Harbiye. www.biletix.com. Box office* ☎ *0212/296-2404. Tickets from 20 TL. Metro: Osmanbey. Map p 123.*

★ French Cultural Center
TAKSIM   Located inside the gorgeous grounds of the French consulate, this small theater is a venue for Istanbul's theater and film festivals, as well as hosting its own exhibitions and events. *Istiklal Cad.*

Try to experience a concert at Hagia Eirene.

Ticket Prices

Where entry prices are not given, this is because prices vary according to the event. At some venues, entry can be free (generally early in the week), whereas major acts can command high ticket prices. Please check for individual events.

☎ 0212/393-8111. www.infist.org. Tickets from 15 TL. Bus/Metro: Taksim. Map p 123.

★★ **garajistanbul** GALATASARAY A venue for contemporary performing arts, this space was created in a parking lot basement—an unlikely venue for such a vibrant arts group. Launched by a group of local artists in 2007, it quickly made a name for itself, hosting performances from visiting avant-garde dance and theater troupes, and producing works by in-house writers through their production company GarajistanbulPro. English surtitles if the performance is in

Catch the Whirling Dervish sema ceremony.

Turkish. *11A Kaymakam Reşat Bey Sok, off Yeni Çarşı Cad.* ☎ *0212/244-4499. www.garajistanbul.org. Tickets approx 30–50 TL. Bus: Taksim. Map p 123.*

★★ **Hagia Eirene** SULTANAHMET The famous Byzantine church within the grounds of Topkapı Palace (p 24) hosts occasional concerts, especially during June's Istanbul Music Festival. If you're lucky enough to be visiting during that time, make sure to book well in advance. *Topkapı Sarayı. www.iksv.org. Tickets from 40 TL. Tram: Gülhane. Map p 124.*

★★ **Istanbul Convention & Exhibition Centre** HARBIYE One of the city's premier spots for watching ballet, along with traditional Turkish and classical music, with regular concerts by the Borusan Istanbul Philharmonic Orchestra. Also hosts the phenomenal Contemporary Istanbul art fair each November and features a branch of the respected Turkish restaurant, Borsa. *4 Gümüş Cad.* ☎ *0212/373-1100. www.icec.org. Metro: Osmanbey. Map p 123.*

★★ **Süreyya Opera House** KADIKÖY One of the main venues for regular Istanbul State Opera and Ballet performances. Built in the 1920s on the model of the great European theaters, with Art Deco influences, it underwent a huge renovation in 2006. *29 Bahariye Cad.* ☎ *0216/346-1531.*

www.sureyyaoperasi.org. *Tickets from 20 TL. Boat: Kadıköy. Map p 124.*

★★★ Whirling Dervish Ceremony TÜNEL Galata Mevlevihanesi

hosts *sema* ceremonies performed for visitors by the Dervishes, on the second and last Sunday of each month. After closing for major refurbishment, it reopened in June 2011; please check gate for performances, prices, dates, and times (p 51). *15 Galip Dede Cad.* ☎ *0212/245-4141. www.galata mevlevihanesimuzesi.gov.tr. Bus/ funicular: Taksim. Tunnel: Tünel. Map p 124.*

★★★ Zorlu Center PSM ZINCIRLIKUYU

Located inside a luxury shopping and dining center, this state-of-the-art performing arts center is the largest in Turkey. Currently, it's the only place to catch Broadway shows, and it also hosts a range of both Turkish and international music stars from across the genres. *Zorlu Center, Zincirlikuyu.* ☎ *0212/336-9160. www.zorlu centerpsm.com. Metro: Gayrettepe. Tickets from 40 TL. Map p 124.*

Rock & Jazz

★ Araf Café Bar BEYOĞLU

Slightly down-market and popular with English teachers and students, this lively bar has an eclectic selection of live "alternative world music" and DJ sets most nights, usually with no cover charge. *32 Balo Sok, off Istiklal Cad.* ☎ *0212/ 244-8301. www.araf.com.tr. Bus: Taksim. Map p 123.*

★★★ Babylon ASMALIMESCIT

One of the best music venues in the city, this relatively small venue started out as more of a club, but found its niche as a great live music venue. Most of the acts are international, incorporating a range of music genres from nu-jazz and Latin to Balkan gypsy-techno fusion. On

Live music at Babylon.

weekends, guest international DJs give the place a more "clubby" feel. For popular acts, buy tickets in advance from the box office or online. *3 Şeybender Sok, off Asmalımescit.* ☎ *0212/292-7368. www.babylon.com.tr. Tickets from 25 TL. Metro: Şişhane. Map p 123.*

★★ Bronx Pi TÜNEL

A local favorite, hidden away in the buzzing Asmalımescit area of Istiklal Caddesi, at the end of a passage overflowing with cheap clothing stores. It's a good option for watching alternative names from the local rock and pop scene, but on occasion also hosts international acts. *8 Terkoz Çıkmazı. off Istiklal Cad.* ☎ *0531/384-8080. www.istanbul bronx.com. Tickets from 20 TL. Metro: Şişhane. Map p 123.*

★★ Hayal Kahvesi BEYOĞLU

A real local favorite, this venue has live bands most nights, usually Turkish rock and pop acts. The atmosphere is laid-back and grungy, rather than anything too flashy. *11C Büyükparmıkkapi Sok.* ☎ *0212/244-2558. www.hayal kahvesibeyoglu.com. Tickets from 30 TL. Metro/bus: Taksim. Map p 123.*

What's On?

Listings of theater, dance, movies, concerts, and sporting events appear in the bi-monthly magazine, *The Guide Istanbul* (www.theguideistanbul.com) and the monthly English edition of *Time Out Istanbul* (www.timeoutistanbul.com). The English-language daily newspaper *Hürriyet Daily News* (www.hurriyetdailynews.com) also has basic listings. Buy advance tickets for concerts, plays, or sports events at **www.biletix.com**. The website has good day-to-day listings of what's on. Most cultural festivals (p 160) are organized by the excellent **Istanbul Kültür Sanat Vakfi** (Istanbul Foundation for Culture and Arts); check **www.iksv.org** for dates and listings. Look out for flyers appearing on the walls of Istiklal Caddesi advertising concerts. **Movie halls,** especially around Istiklal Caddesi and at multiplexes in shopping malls, show recent Hollywood releases. Check whether they are subtitled into Turkish, rather than dubbed (ask "*Orijinal dilde mi?*").

★ **Mektup** BEYOĞLU Among the many bars in the backstreets of Beyoğlu, the quality of the Türkü music on offer here stands out. Featuring nightly performances by both emerging and established artists, it's a popular choice, so it's wise to book ahead on weekends. *20 Imam Adnan Sok.* ☎ *0212/251-0110. www.mektupbar.com. Tickets from 10 TL. Bus/Metro: Taksim. Map p 123.*

★★ **Nardis Jazz Club** GALATA Live music from Turkish and international acts every night in this stone-walled cozy den draws in the jazz fans. The venue was created for local musicians and their friends by husband-and-wife owners Önder (musician) and Zuhal Focan. Food and drink are pricey; talking during acts is not allowed. *14 Galata Kulesi Sok.* ☎ *0212/244-6327. www.nardisjazz.com. Tickets from 40 TL. Metro: Şişhane. Map p 123.*

★★ **Nublu** KARAKÖY This cozy bar has moved from a previous location to the basement of the Gradiva Hotel. It's a relaxed and intimate jazz club, with live music from local and overseas bands, jam sessions, DJs, and occasional after-parties. *2 Bankalar Cad.* ☎ *0212/249-7712. www.nubluistanbul.net. Closed Mon and Tues. Tram: Karaköy. Tickes from 20 TL. Map p 123.*

★ **Roxy** CIHANGIR This popular club and music venue, with a cavernous interior, features live rock and pop concerts every Wednesday night. On weekends, either live music or local DJs keep the (barely) 20-something local crowd on their feet until the early hours. *5 Aslanyatağı Sok, Siraselviler Cad.* ☎ *0212/249-1283. www.roxy.com.tr. Tickets from 35 TL. Bus/Metro: Taksim. Map p 123.*

★★ **Salon IKSV** ŞIŞHANE Located on the ground floor of Istanbul's leading arts and culture organization, this venue hosts mostly alternative international names from rock, pop, and jazz, in a stylish if rather soulless venue that closes earlier than most of

Istanbul's other music venues. *5 Sadi Konuralp Cad.* ☎ *0212/334-0700. www.saloniksv.com. Metro: Şişhane. Tickets from 25 TL. Map p 123.*

Cycling
★★★ kids Rent-A-Bike
PRINCES' ISLANDS If you feel like stretching your legs or just getting away from the madness of the city, head to one of the Princes' Islands in the Marmara Sea. Just an hour away by public ferry, these are car-free oases that make for a fun day out. You can take a horse-drawn carriage or use pedal-power and rent a bicycle for the day to explore. *Bike hire approx 15 TL per day. www.adalar.bel.tr. Ferries leave from Kabataş.*

Horse Racing
★ kids Veliefendi BAKIRKÖY
This historic racecourse is head-quarters of the Turkish Jockey Club. Although Atatürk promoted this noble sport, most people are more interested in the betting than any particular equine finesse (thankfully, rules at betting counters are pretty easy to understand). There's usually one weekend and one midweek race meeting. International jockeys and horses participate in the most

lucrative race meeting of the year, the Topkapı Trophy in September. There's a decent selection of cafes and bars, as well as a picnic area. Check the website or the *Hürriyet Daily News* for race schedules. Female visitors should be prepared to be the only women there. *Türkiye Jokey Kulübü, Veliefendi Hipodromu, Bakırköy.* ☎ *0212/444-0855. www.tjk.org. Entry 2–10 TL. Tram to Zeytinburnu, then minibus or taxi. Map p 124.*

Soccer (Football) Clubs
★★★ Beşiktaş FC GÜMÜŞSUYU
The most accessible ground—a 10-minute downhill walk from Taksim Square—the old stadium was demolished in 2013 and the new Vodafone arena rebuilt in the same location in 2014. Beşiktaş's last league title came in 2003, and the club has yet to make inroads into European trophies. You will find a healthy number of women and families in the crowd. *Vodafone Arena.* ☎ *0212/310-1000. www.bjk.com.tr. Tickets from 30 TL. Bus/Metro: Taksim. Map p 123.*

★ Fenerbahçe FC KADIKÖY
Over on the Asian side, this spectacular stadium, one of Europe's finest, is home to the

Getting a jazz funk on at the cosy Nardis Jazz Club.

Soccer—a National Obsession

Between late August and early May, it's hard to avoid the soccer season, especially as the usual top three teams in the Super Lig—Turkey's top league—are all from Istanbul: Beşiktaş, Fenerbahçe, and Galatasaray. If you're a sports fan, attending a match is a recommended experience, although given the intense passion and rivalry of supporters, it's advisable to avoid a match between two local teams. Alternatively, you can join the boisterous crowds watching the games in the many bars that line the streets around Nevizade Sokak, off Istiklal Caddesi.

Canaries, Turkey's most successful club—domestically, at least. Their kit shops are modestly called Feneriums. *Şükrü Saraçoğlu Stadium, Kızıltoprak.* ☎ *0216/449-5667. www.fenerbahce.org. Tickets from 35 TL. Ferry: Kadıköy. Map p 124.*

★ **Galatasaray FC** SEYRANTEPE Turkey's most famous (and arguably most supported) team, "Cim Bom" has won the domestic league numerous times, plus the UEFA Cup in 2000. The notorious Ali Sami Yen stadium (famed for the banner "Welcome to hell") was replaced by the immense, multipurpose Türk Telecom Arena stadium, which opened in early 2011. It soon broke official world records for the noisiest crowd, in its match against archrival Fenerbahçe. *Turk Telekom Arena, Seyrantepe.* ☎ *0212/273-2850. www.galatasaray.org. Tickets from 30 TL. Bus: Seyrantepe. Map p 124.* ●

Fenerbahçe FC fans having some fun, pre-match.

Lodging **Best Bets**

Best **Location for Grand Bazaar**
★★★ Hotel Niles *19 Dibekli Cami Sok (p 138)*

Best **Secret Garden**
★★★ Hotel Empress Zoe *4 Akbıyık Cad (p 137)*

Best for **Famous Guests**
★★★ Pera Palace *52 Meşrutiyet Cad (p 140)*

Best **Sympathetic Period Conversion**
★★ House Hotel Galatasaray *19 Bostanbaşı Cad (p 139)*

Best **Use for an Old Distillery**
★★★ Sumahan on the Water *51 Kuleli Cad (p 141)*

Best **Contemporary Style**
★★ Witt Istanbul Suites *26 Defterdar Yokuşu (p 142)*

Most **Affordable Jacuzzi**
★★ Tan Hotel *20 Doktor Eminpaşa Sok (p 141)*

Best for **Secluded Romance**
★★ A'jia *27 Çubuklu Cad (p 135)*

Best **Sultanahmet Cheapie**
★★ Peninsula *6 Adliye Sok (p 140)*

Best **Ultra Chic Lobby**
★★★ W Hotel *22 Süleyman Seba Cad (p 142)*

Best **Circular Bed**
★★ Eklektik Guest House *4 Kadribey Çikması (p 137)*

Best **Value in Beyoğlu**
★ Büyük Londra *53 Meşrutiyet Cad (p 136)*

Best for **Making the Most of an Ex-Nunnery**
★★ Tom Tom Suites *Boğazkesen Cad (p 142)*

Best **Guest Relations Staff**
★★★ Sirkeci Konak Hotel *5 Taya Hatun Sok (p 141)*

Best for **Business Travelers**
★★ Mövenpick *4 Büyükdere Cad (p 139)* and ★★ Ansen 130 *70 Meşrutiyet Cad (p 135)*

Most **Unusual Exterior**
★★★ Four Seasons Hotel *1 Tevkifhane Sok (p 137)*

Businesslike elegance at Mövenpick Hotel. Previous page: Ottoman-era elegance at the Dersaadet.

Old City Lodging

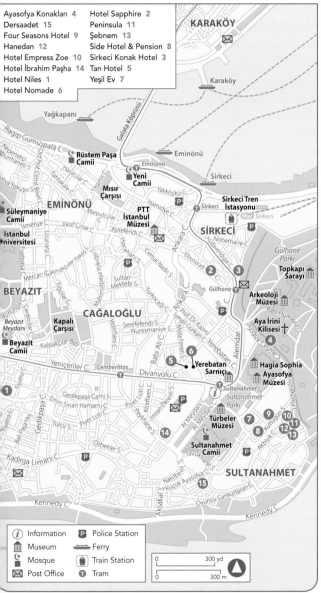

Ayasofya Konakları 4
Dersaadet 15
Four Seasons Hotel 9
Hanedan 12
Hotel Empress Zoe 10
Hotel İbrahim Paşa 14
Hotel Niles 1
Hotel Nomade 6
Hotel Sapphire 2
Peninsula 11
Şebnem 13
Side Hotel & Pension 8
Sirkeci Konak Hotel 3
Tan Hotel 5
Yeşil Ev 7

_(i)_ Information
🏛 Museum
☪ Mosque
✉ Post Office
🚓 Police Station
⛴ Ferry
🚉 Train Station
Ⓣ Tram

0   300 yd
0   300 m

Beyoğlu Lodging

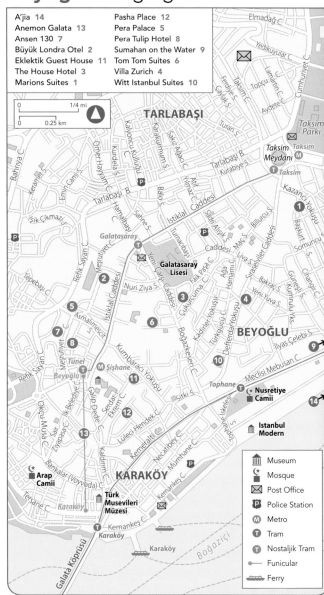

A'jia 14
Anemon Galata 13
Ansen 130 7
Büyük Londra Otel 2
Eklektik Guest House 11
The House Hotel 3
Marions Suites 1

Pasha Place 12
Pera Palace 5
Pera Tulip Hotel 8
Sumahan on the Water 9
Tom Tom Suites 6
Villa Zurich 4
Witt Istanbul Suites 10

TARLABAŞI

Taksim Parkı

Taksim Meydanı

Taksim

Galatasaray

Galatasaray Lisesi

BEYOĞLU

Nusretiye Camii

Tünel

Beyoğlu

Şişhane

Istanbul Modern

Arap Camii

KARAKÖY

Türk Musevileri Müzesi

Karaköy

Karaköy

Boğaziçi

🏛 Museum
⛪ Mosque
✉ Post Office
🅿 Police Station
Ⓜ Metro
🚊 Tram
🚋 Nostaljik Tram
● Funicular
⛴ Ferry

Galata Köprüsü

Bosphorus Lodging

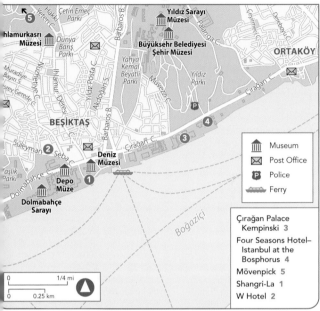

🏛	Museum
⊠	Post Office
🅿	Police
⛴	Ferry

Çırağan Palace Kempinski 3

Four Seasons Hotel–Istanbul at the Bosphorus 4

Mövenpick 5

Shangri-La 1

W Hotel 2

Istanbul Lodging **A to Z**

★★ **A'jia** KANLICA Far from the city center, this restored Ottoman waterfront mansion perches on the Asian side of the Bosphorus in the pleasant suburb of Kanlıca. Rooms have stunning sea views, some with a private balcony, and an uncluttered feel with wooden floors and contemporary art. Great dining on the terrace. *Ahmet Rasim Pasha Mansion, 27 Çubuklu Cad.* ☎ *0216/413-9300. www.ajiahotel.com. 16 units. Doubles from 300€. AE, MC, V. Taxi to Kanlıca. Map p 134.*

★★ **Anemon Galata** GALATA Part of a reliable chain, this "special" hotel, housed in a building of significant historic interest, has comfortable rooms with period furniture and sparkling white linens.

It's right next to the famous tower, with perfect views from the terrace, and has the recommended Pitti restaurant. *Büyükhendek Cad.* ☎ *0212/293-2343. www.anemonhotels.com. 30 units. Doubles from 115€. MC, V. Taxi from Taksim. Map p 134.*

★★ **kids Ansen 130** TEPEBAŞI Housed in a restored century-old building, these good-value chic Zen rooms have a kitchenette, sofa, and writing desk. Rooms are spacious, each with a huge plasma TV, Wi-Fi, and power shower, all in contemporary, minimalist style. Check for good online deals. *70 Meşrutiyet Cad.* ☎ *0212/245-8808. www.ansen suites.com. 10 units. Doubles from 150€. AE, MC, V. All buses from Taksim. Map p 134.*

Where to Stay?

Hotels cluster around Sultanahmet and Beyoğlu, poles apart in ambience and amenities, so your choice depends on priorities. If you prefer views of the Blue Mosque and proximity to historical monuments, Sultanahmet is for you. Bring earplugs for neighboring mosques' dawn call to prayer, and be prepared for carpet touts and never-ending souvenir shops. If good restaurants, bars, and clubs are important, stay in Beyoğlu, where Istiklal Caddesi and Tünel buzz most of the night—although noise from all these entertainment venues can be a problem. Work on this logic: It's easier to travel to Sultanahmet during the day than to travel back there after a night out in Beyoğlu.

★ **Ayasofya Konakları** SULTA-NAHMET These nine wooden houses are part of a clever rebuilding project on a cobbled pedestrian street (Soğukçeşme Sok; p 67) behind Hagia Sophia. The 64 rooms have tasteful 19th-century-style decor, including a small Turkish bath in the Pasha Suite. Most rooms are without TV. Breakfast is served on quaint terraces. *Soğukçeşme Sokağı.* ☎ *0212/513-3660. www.ayasofyakonaklari.com. 64 units. Doubles from 170€. MC, V. Tram: Sultanahmet. Map p 133.*

★ **Büyük Londra** TEPEBAŞI The entrance in this century-old mansion oozes faded decadence, and the lobby bar is all Victoriana and a caged parrot. Guest rooms vary from the simple to downright basic, but it's the best-value period hotel in the city—and perfectly located for Beyoğlu's nightlife. *53 Meşrutiyet Cad.* ☎ *0212/245-0670. www.londrahotel.net. 54 units. Doubles from 50€. AE, MC, V. Bus: Tepebaşı. Map p 134.*

★★ **Çirağan Palace Kempinski** BEŞIKTAŞ Splurge on a room in this former Ottoman palace, with outstanding top-notch (and

top-dollar) features including the outdoor "infinity" pool (heated in winter) and spa. Lottery winners could try the multi-roomed Grand Sultan Suite (30,000€). *32 Çirağan Cad.* ☎ *0212/326-4646. www.kempinski-istanbul.com. 314 units. Doubles from 420€. AE, DC, MC, V. Bus: Beşiktaş to Ortaköy. Map p 135.*

★★ **kids** **Dersaadet** SULTANAH-MET This family-run Ottoman-era house in a quiet neighborhood has

Ayasofya Konakları's recreated tradition.

well-kept rooms and great service. Some rooms have Bosphorus views—one double has its own *hamam*—and the penthouse suite boasts 180-degree views and Jacuzzi. Breakfast is served on the flower-filled roof terrace. *5 Kapıağası Sok, off Küçük Ayasofya Cad.* ☎ *0212/458-0760. www. hoteldersaadet.com. 17 units. Doubles from 95€. AE, MC, V. Tram: Sultanahmet. Map p 133.*

★★ Eklektik Guest House

GALATA Hidden away down a quiet street, this gay-friendly guesthouse has seven unique rooms in a converted Ottoman house. Choose from contemporary style in the Black Room, marble shower in the Sultan's Room, or the Red Room's circular bed—pure camp. Breakfast is served at a communal table. *4 Kadribey Çıkmazı, off Serdar-i Ekrem Cad.* ☎ *0212/243-7446. www.eklek tikgalata.com. 7 units. Doubles from 90 €. No credit cards. Tunnel: Tünel. Map p 134.*

★★★ Four Seasons Hotel SUL-

TANAHMET An Istanbul favorite, this is Sultanahmet's most luxurious hotel, with world-class service. Converted from the neo-classic Sultanahmet Prison in 1986, it has a distinctive ochre watchtower (and prisoners' graffiti in the basement); its high-ceilinged rooms are spacious and luxurious. The hotel also houses the Seasons restaurant (p 107). *1 Tevkifhane Sok.* ☎ *0212/ 638-8200. www.fourseasons.com/ istanbul. 65 units. Doubles from 560€. AE, DC, MC, V. Tram: Sultanahmet. Map p 133.*

★★ Four Seasons Hotel—Istanbul at the Bosphorus

BEŞİKTAŞ Making a huge impact since opening in 2008, Istanbul's second Four Seasons is in a refurbished 19th-century Ottoman palace overlooking the water. The

Seaview terrace at Dersaadet.

contemporary feel is enhanced with mahogany furnishings and hand-painted motifs on the ceilings, plus luxury spa and indoor and outdoor pools. *28 Çirağan Cad.* ☎ *0212/ 381-4000. www.fourseasons.com/ bosphorus. 166 units. Doubles from 320€. AE, DC, MC, V. Bus: Beşiktaş. Map p 135.*

★★ Hanedan SULTANAHMET

A friendly little guesthouse in a quiet street where no-frills rooms mean bare floorboards with simple furniture and fantastic terrace views of the Sea of Marmara with your buffet breakfast. For a little extra, some large rooms have a sea view. *Adliye Sok, off Akbıyık Cad.* ☎ *0212/516-4869. www.hanedanhotel.com. 10 units. Doubles from 70€. MC, V. Tram: Sultanahmet. Map p 133.*

★★★ Hotel Empress Zoe SUL-

TANAHMET Converted from three townhouses, this American-owned hotel has a vast selection of rooms, from standard double to duplex with two bedrooms and kitchen. Cleverly combines original features with mod-cons. The tiny garden is a peaceful hideaway for

One of seven unique rooms at the Eklektik Guest House.

breakfast. *4 Akbıyık Cad.* ☎ *0212/518-2504. www.emzoe.com. 25 units. Doubles from 140€. MC, V. Tram: Sultanahmet. Map p 133.*

★★ Hotel Ibrahim Paşa SULTANAHMET

A stone's throw from the Hippodrome, this charming boutique hotel has been lovingly fashioned from a pair of elegant 19th-century townhouses. Rooms are on the small side but tastefully decorated to combine the best of period and contemporary design.

There's a roof terrace with expansive Old City and sea views and a lovely little breakfast room. *14 Çayıoğlu Sok.* ☎ *0212/518-9595. www.ibrahimpasha.com. 24 units. Doubles from 195€. AE, MC, V. Tram: Sultanahmet. Map p 133.*

★★★ kids Hotel Niles BEYAZIT

Downhill from the Grand Bazaar, this gem of a hotel, loved for its friendly service, has simple rooms with tasteful faux-Ottoman decor. Rooms range from small to spacious suites and a duplex—ideal for families—some with private *hamam*. All standard doubles were refurbished in 2013. Buffet breakfast is served on the roof terrace. *19 Dibekli Cami Sok, off Ordu Cad.* ☎ *0212/517-3239. www.hotelniles.com. 39 units. Doubles from 100€. MC, V. Tram: Beyazit. Map p 133.*

★★ Hotel Nomade SULTANAHMET

This small boutique hotel in a converted early-20th-century townhouse is right in the heart of the sightseeing and Old City eating action. Rooms are on the petite side, and the trendy white furniture is getting a little tired, but this is an atmospheric and ultra-convenient place to stay—not least because of the great roof terrace, with breakfast or a sundown drink overlooking

An elegant room at the Hotel Ibrahim Paşa.

How Much?

Prices listed are the online rate for high season (roughly mid-Mar–late Oct), including breakfast and tax, often 10 to 20% less in low season. Top hotels often have good deals on their websites or through online booking agencies, and can be quieter in August, with fewer business visitors. You can also try phoning the hotel direct to ask for any special rates, especially out of season; some offer discounts for cash payments. Hotels book up quickly and prices usually increase for Şeker Bayram (the festival after Ramazan), Christmas, and major local events.

the mighty Hagia Sophia. *15 Divan Yolu Cad.* ☎ *0212/513-8172. 16 units. www.hotelnomade.com. Doubles from 70€. Tram: Sultanahmet. Map p 133.*

★★ **Hotel Sapphire** SIRKECI Fantastic value in a convenient part of town, away from Sultanahmet's carpet shops but near enough to the sights. Simple, light rooms have ornate touches, minibar, and small baths. There are also family-friendly large triple rooms, a large ornate lobby, and friendly and efficient staff. *14 Ibnikemal Cad.* ☎ *0212/520-5686. www.hotelsapphire.com. 55 units. Doubles from 90€. MC, V. Tram: Sirkeci. Map p 133.*

★★ **The House Hotel** GALATASARAY Part of the House Café chain, this 19th-century four-story mansion underwent a stylish renovation and opened as a hotel in 2010. Its 20 suites all retain the original architectural qualities, including graceful high ceilings, Italianate marble, and parquet floors. Hilly neighborhood. *19 Bostanbaşı Cad.* ☎ *0212/252-0422. www.thehousehotel.com. 20 units. Doubles from 165€. MC, V. Bus: Taksim. Map p 134.*

★ **Marions Suite** CIHANGIR Formerly known as Suite Home Cihangir, this is tucked away in a central residential neighborhood. Contemporary suites come in different styles and sizes; huge sofas and kitchenettes are a real bonus, with separate living room and balcony in the larger suites. Long-stay business travelers love the small meeting rooms and spa. *12 Pürtelaş Sok.* ☎ *0212/243-2424. www.themarionssuite.com. 14 units. Doubles from 95€. MC, V. Metro/bus: Taksim. Map p 134.*

★★ **Mövenpick** LEVENT A good chain choice for business guests in the heart of the banking district. Contemporary rooms have extra-large desks, Wi-Fi, and the Skyline Club Lounge for all executive-floor guests. The hotel also houses business and banqueting rooms, a sauna, and a pool. *4 Büyükdere Cad.* ☎ *0212/319-2929. www.moevenpick-hotels.com. 249 units. Doubles from 255€. AE, DC, MC, V. Metro: 4. Levent. Map p 135.*

★★★ **Pasha Place** GALATA Beautifully restored apartment in a turn-of-the-19th-century townhouse on a quiet (for this buzzing neighborhood) cobbled street. There are great views across rooftops to the Old City and Bosphorus from two of the bedrooms and the elegant

Hotel Niles in busy Beyazit.

sitting room. Waxed wood floors or original tiles, high ceilings, neutral tones, and chic furnishings make for a great stay. There are 15 similar apartments dotted around the area. Sleeps 6. *Serdar-ı Ekrem Cad* ☎ *+44/7729-251676. www.istanbul place.com. Apartment 300€ per night. Metro: Şişhane. Map p 134.*

★★ kids **Peninsula** SULTANAH-MET Converted from an old townhouse on a traffic-free street, rooms are simple, although there's no TV. Standard rooms are small, the basement rooms cheaper, with two interconnecting rooms suitable for families and a good-value larger double. Friendly staff, with superb buffet breakfast on the terrace. A good budget option. *6 Adliye Sok, Akbıyık Cad.* ☎ *0212/458-6850. www.hotelpeninsula.com. 12 units. Doubles from 40€. MC, V. Tram: Sultanahmet. Map p 133.*

★★★ **Pera Palace** TEPEBAŞI Istanbul's first-ever hotel, built for Orient Express passengers, reopened in late 2010 after a major renovation. This luxury hotel, whose guests have included Agatha Christie, Atatürk, and Queen Elizabeth II, combines

original 19th-century features with an elegant high-tech edge. *52 Meşrutiyet Cad.* ☎ *0212/377-4000. www.jumeirah.com. 115 units. Doubles from 228€. AE, DC, MC, V. Bus: Tepebaşı. Map p 134.*

★★ kids **Pera Tulip Hotel** TEPEBAŞI This compact, friendly hotel enjoys a great Beyoğlu location, and extras include a small business center, meeting rooms, a *hamam,* and an indoor pool. Chic rooms have lovely touches such as bold-patterned cushions and strong colors. Larger executive rooms are worth the extra cost. *103 Meşrutiyet Cad.* ☎ *0212/243-8500. www.pera tulip.com. 84 units. Doubles from 120€. AE, DC, MC, V. Bus: All buses from Taksim. Map p 134.*

★ kids **Şebnem** SULTANAHMET Rooms are simply done with white walls and dark-wood floors, but at the pricey end for guesthouses in this area. Rooms with a tiny garden are worth the extra. Breakfast is served on the flower-filled terrace. Free Wi-Fi and use of laptops are on offer from the obliging staff. *1 Adliye Sok, off Akbıyık Cad.*

The opulent lobby at the Pera Palace.

Special Hotels

Of all the cities in all the world, Istanbul surely boasts some of the most astounding variety of accommodation, from sleek apart-hotels the size of small houses to restored Ottoman mansions with original furnishings. I've avoided listing too many international chain hotels, as I think it's important to enjoy the city's independent hotels with their own character. However, there are two exceptions: The **Four Seasons** (Sultanahmet) is famously housed in a former prison. Another great chain addition is **Shangri-La,** joining a cluster of Bosphorus-lining luxury hotels; this one is built in a former tobacco factory and claims to the city's first seven-star hotel.

☎ 0212/517-6623. www.sebnem hotel.net. 15 units. Doubles from 100€. MC, V. Tram: Sultanahmet. Map p 133.

★★★ kids Shangri-la Hotel
BEŞIKTAŞ This luxurious hotel is situated, aptly, on the Bosphorus close to an older Istanbul symbol of opulence, the Dolmabahçe Palace. Housed in a 1920s tobacco factory, the subtly decorated but very spa-cious rooms have private balconies, the pricier ones with superb Bos-phorus views, and facilities include everything from babysitting to a sleek business center. *Hayrettin Iskelesi Sok* ☎ 0800/028-3337. www.shangri-la.com. 186 units. Dou-bles from 360€. AE, MC, V. Bus: Beşiktaş. Map p 135.

★ kids Side Hotel & Pension
SULTANAHMET The beauty of Side (pronounced *see-deh*) is the choice of accommodation, from a simple pension room with shared bathroom (great if you're on a bud-get) to a small self-catering apart-ment with a Jacuzzi, all very reasonable, especially for families. *20 Utangac Sok.* ☎ 0212/458-5870. www.sidehotel.com. Doubles from 50€, 2-bedroom apartments from 100€. MC, V. Tram: Sultanahmet. Map p 133.

★★★ kids Sirkeci Konak Hotel
SIRKECI This luxury boutique hotel has wonderful guest relations and a great location next to the outer walls of the Topkapı Palace. Tastefully furnished rooms have dark-wood floors and a writing desk, some have a balcony, and there's a private Jacuzzi in the triple deluxe suite. Guests enjoy free afternoon tea in the bar and use of the small pool and *hamam. 5 Taya Hatun Sok.* ☎ 0212/528-4344. www. sirkecimansion.com. 52 units. Dou-bles from 184€. AE, MC, V. Tram: Sirkeci. Map p 133

★★★ Sumahan on the Water
ÇENGELKÖY A village on the Asian side of the Bosphorus is per-fect for a romantic hideaway in this boutique hotel renovated from an Ottoman distillery. Rooms are effortlessly elegant and minimalist in light woods, each with huge win-dows and unbeatable views. Duplex suites have their own ter-race; many rooms have a *hamam. 51 Kuleli Cad.* ☎ 0216/422-8000. www.sumahan.com. 27 units. Dou-bles from 295€. AE, MC, V. Boat/bus: Çengelköy. Map p 134.

★★ kids Tan Hotel SULTANAH-
MET A cut above other hotels in this price bracket, this new hotel in

a quiet side-street has large modern rooms, all with fridge, large sofa, and Jacuzzi. Grand suites (with fluffy bathrobes) have a sofa bed and sleep three people. Rooms on higher floors have decent views. *20 Doktor Eminpaşa Sok, Çatalçeşme Meydanı.* ☎ *0212/520-9130. www.tanhotel.com. 20 units. Doubles from 110€. MC, V. Tram: Sultanahmet. Map p 133.*

★★ Tom Tom Suites BEYOĞLU

Situated opposite the Italian consulate in an oasis of 19th-century peace just off Istiklal Caddesi, the tasteful suite rooms of this handsome period building were once home to Franciscan nuns. Bathrooms are very luxurious and even standard suites feature king-size beds. *Boğazkesen Cad.* ☎ *0212/ 292-4949. www.tomtomsuites.com. 20 units. Doubles from 190€. AE, MC, V. Metro/bus: Taksim. Map p 134.*

★★ Villa Zurich CIHANGIR

This friendly hotel in an up-market, vaguely bohemian neighborhood much favored by ex-pats has well-appointed rooms in tasteful pale blues and creams, many with bath and Jacuzzi. Front-facing rooms have small balconies. The decent Doğa

Gorgeous fountain at Hotel Yeşil Ev.

Balık restaurant is on the roof terrace. *36 Akarsu Yokuşu Cad.* ☎ *0212/293-0604. www.hotelvillazurich.com. 45 units. Doubles from 99€. MC, V. Bus/ Metro: Taksim. Map p 134.*

★★★ W Hotel AKARETLER

Mirrored tables, purple neon, and silver drapes—and that's just the welcome area. Housed in the former Dolmabahçe Palace kitchens, this hotel, firmly aimed at affluent hipsters, has rooms with a contemporary twist on classic Ottoman style, including marble sinks. There's a hip bar on site and a glance at the flashy website will soon reveal whether this is your kind of hotel. *22 Süleyman Seba Cad.* ☎ *0212/381-2121. www.wistanbul.com.tr. 134 units. Doubles from 298€. AE, DC, MC, V. Bus: Beşiktaş. Map p 135.*

★★ Witt Istanbul Suites

BEŞIKTAŞ This exquisitely designed boutique hotel has modish suites with a luxury apartment feel. Each 60 sq. m (645 sq. ft.) suite has a kitchenette and huge bathroom, with an elegant floral motif on walls and furnishings. Sweeping views from the top floor's fitness studio deter any inclination to laziness. *26 Defterdar Yokuşu.* ☎ *0212/393-7900. www.witt istanbul.com. 17 units. Doubles from 250€. AE, MC, V. Bus: Beşiktaş. Map p 134.*

★ Yeşil Ev SULTANAHMET

Rebuilt from an existing Ottoman wooden house, this popular guest-house has brass beds and antique furniture, although its steep prices mean value for money is debatable. The standard double room is tiny and the bathroom minuscule. Still, its green wooden exterior and garden are charming, and service is good. *5 Kabasakal Cad.* ☎ *0212/517-6786. www.yesilev.com.tr. 19 units. Doubles from 200€. AE, MC, V. Tram: Sultanahmet. Map p 133.* ●

Princes' Islands

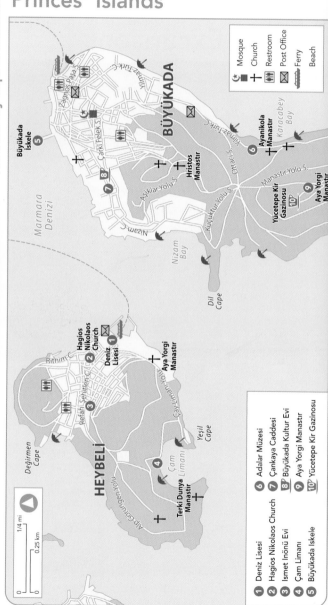

Legend:
- ☪ Mosque
- ■ Church
- ⊞ Restroom
- ⊠ Post Office
- Ferry
- Beach

BÜYÜKADA
- Büyükada İskele ⑤
- Ayanikola Manastır ⑥
- Hristos Manastır
- Yücetepe Kir Gazinosu ⑩
- Aya Yorgi Manastır ⑨
- Marmara Denizi
- Nizam Bay
- Dil Cape
- Karacabey Bay

HEYBELİ
- Hagios Nikolaos Church ②
- Deniz Lisesi ①
- Aya Yorgi Manastır
- Rithim C.
- Değirmen Cape
- Yeşil Cape
- Çam Limanı ④
- Terki Dunya Manastır

1. Deniz Lisesi
2. Hagios Nikolaos Church
3. İsmet İnönü Evi
4. Çam Limanı
5. Büyükada İskele
6. Adalar Müzesi
7. Çankaya Caddesi
8. Büyükada Kultur Evi
9. Aya Yorgi Manastır
10. Yücetepe Kir Gazinosu

0 1/4 mi
0 0.25 km

Previous page: Eski Cami, Erdine.

The jewel-like cluster of nine islands off Istanbul has a color-ful history: Summer houses for the elite; a haven for Jewish, Greek, and Armenian minorities; and exile for "White Russians"—today, they're a traffic-free escape for locals. You can't visit every island in one day, so head to Heybeliada and Büyükada to walk, cycle, or hire a *phaeton* (horse and carriage). Stick to weekdays to avoid the crowds. START: **Heybeliada ferry pier.**

1 ★ Deniz Lisesi (Naval High School). You can't miss the huge waterfront naval school from the ferry pier on Heybeliada (literally, "Saddlebag Island" due to its shape). Originally, the Naval War Academy was set up in 1852. It's been a high school since 1985, and the white facade makes a striking sight. It's closed to the public, and uniformed cadets on patrol will pre-vent you from taking photographs close up. *Heybeliada Iskele.*

2 ★ Hagios Nikolaos Church. Dominating the village's main square, this Greek Orthodox church, dedicated to St. Nikolaos, patron saint of mariners, celebrated 150 years in 2007. It's usually locked except during Sunday services, attended by around 30 locals. The interior is adorned with gold, chan-deliers, and frescoes. Opposite, in the square, are several **bicycle hire** shops. If you prefer to travel by **phaeton,** head back to rent one by the ferry pier. *Belediye Meydanı, Ayyıldız Cad. Service: Sun 9–11am.*

3 ★★ Ismet Inönü Evi. A 15-minute walk along **Refah Şehitleri Caddesi** brings you to this historic wooden mansion. Now a house museum, this was once a part-time residence of Ismet Inönü, president of the new Republic of Turkey (1938–50). The house is per-fectly preserved, from his book-filled office to his daughter's cartoon stickers on her closet. Pho-tos on the walls include vacation snaps of the family in bathing suits

Dramatic approach to Princes' Islands.

enjoying Heybeliada's beaches.
🕐 *45 min. 59 Refah Şehitleri Cad.* 📞 *0216/351-8449. Free admission. Tues–Sun 10am–5pm (closed Nov–Mar).*

4 ★ Çam Limanı (Pine Bay). Depending on how far you want to walk, cycle, or ride, continue along **Refah Şehitleri Caddesi** until you descend to the small bay of Çam Limanı, a beautiful, almost 1-hour walk with woods, fields, and occa-sional glimpses of the sea. (If in doubt, follow the road that the *phaetons* take.) The bay is a good spot to rest on sun loungers or swim off the wooden pier. From here, go back along **Gemici**

Büyükada passenger port.

Kaynağı Sokak until you pass **Deniz Lisesi** (①) on your right and the **ferry pier,** from where you sail to Büyükada.

⑤ ★ Büyükada Iskele (Büyükada Quay). After a 15-minute journey, ferries arrive at **Büyükada's** (Big Island) striking quay, with ornate tiles on the upper front facade of the terminal. Built in 1914, this replaced the wooden quay built in 1899, and was used as the first movie hall on the island in 1950–51. Pick up a map of the island from the tourist office. If you

Take a phaeton on Princes' Island.

want to explore on two wheels, head to the bicycle-hire shops on **Çınar Caddesi.**

⑥ ★ Adalar Müzesi (Museum of the Princes' Islands). Opened in late 2010, this little museum shows, through exhibits, locals' accounts, and photographs, how the islands were such a phenomenon; to be home to so many different ethnic communities— Armenians, Jews, Greeks, and Russians co-existing in such harmony—was quite an achievement. History, local geology, day-to-day living, and political developments provide fascinating insight. ⏱ *45 min. Adalar Müzesi Hangar, Aya Nikola Mevkii.* ☎ *0216/382-6430. www.adalar muzesi.org. Admission 5 TL. Tues– Sun 10am–5pm.*

⑦ ★ Çankaya Caddesi. If you're walking up to **Aya Yorgi Manastır** (St. George's Monastery)—a long but rewarding hour's walk—take the longer, more picturesque route along Çankaya Caddesi, which is lined with grandiose wooden mansions, previous residents of which included Ottoman diplomats, painters, princes, and lawyers. Leon Trotsky lived in a brick-built villa at the bottom of Hamlacı Sokak.

Practical Matters

Ferries and sea-buses leave from Kabataş (p 165), with more frequent service during the summer (mid-June–mid-Sept). Fast ferries take 50 minutes to reach Büyükada, then 10 minutes onward to Heybeliada (9 TL with a *jeton* (token); 7.10 TL with your Istanbulkart). Slow ferries take 90 minutes between Kabataş and Büyükada. Ferries have some seating outside (check for sun direction before finding a spot), with simple refreshments served on board. Buy a *jeton* before boarding for 5 TL, or use your Istanbulkart (3.5 TL; p 164). It's advisable to avoid the last ferry of the day on weekends, or arrive with time to spare at the pier; they're usually very overcrowded. Check at the pier for times or look online (fast ferries: www.ido.com.tr/en; slower ferries: www.sehirhatlari.com.tr/en.

8 ★ **Büyükada Kültür Evi.** With a 50-year-old phaeton in the garden, this mansion has been converted into a cultural center, housing exhibitions and summer concerts. Build up your strength with tea, beer, and snacks on the terrace. *21 Çankaya Cad.* ☎ *0216/382-8620. Coffee and snacks from 10 TL.*

Enjoying the beach at Princes' Islands.

9 ★★ **Aya Yorgi Manastır (St. George Monastery).** You might opt for a *phaeton*, or bargain for a donkey ride for this long uphill cobbled path, although the walk is highly recommended. On the left you'll see pieces of fabric tied onto the bushes, each representing a prayer—usually from women wishing for a child. The bell tower is your first glimpse of the monastery. Pass through the tiny courtyard—women should cover their head and legs—into the 6th-century monastery's silent interior. On the right is a large glass container filled with prayer notes, written by people of all religions who believe that St. George performs miracles. ⏱ *1 hr. Yüce Tepe. Free admission. Daily 9:30am–6pm.*

10 ★★★ **Yücetepe Kir Gazinosu.** This simple restaurant adjacent to the monastery is perfect for its terrace with panoramas of the islands. There's little else but meatballs and perhaps eggplant with yogurt, but add a cool beer and the views and it's unbeatable. *Yüce Tepe.* ☎ *0216/382-1333. Meatballs 10 TL.*

Bursa

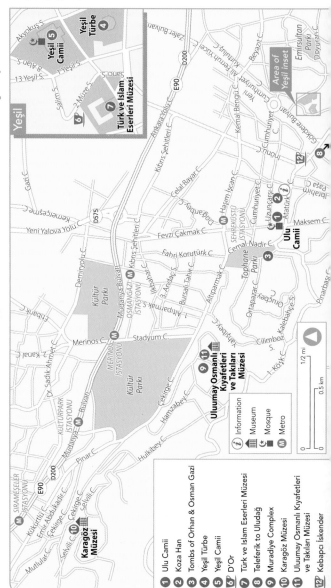

Yeşil

Yeşil Türbe 4

Yeşil Camii 5

Türk ve Islam Eserleri Müzesi 7

Area of Yeşil inset

Ulu Camii

Uluumay Osmanlı Kıyafetleri ve Takıları Müzesi

Karagöz Müzesi

- Information
- Museum
- Mosque
- Metro

0 — 1/2 mi
0 — 0.5 km

1 Ulu Camii
2 Koza Han
3 Tombs of Orhan & Osman Gazi
4 Yeşil Türbe
5 Yeşil Camii
6 D'Or
7 Türk ve Islam Eserleri Müzesi
8 Teleferik to Uludağ
9 Muradiye Complex
10 Karagöz Müzesi
11 Uluumay Osmanlı Kıyafetleri ve Takıları Müzesi
12 Kebapçı Iskender

Silk, mineral spas, ski slopes, and mausoleums: The Ottoman Empire's first capital, Bursa, nestles at the foot of Mount Uludağ. A packed day gives you time to savor ancient and modern delights, from bejeweled sultans' tombs to traditional puppet shows, ending with Bursa's famous *Iskender kebap*. START: **Bus to Ulu Cami.**

❶ ★★ Ulu Cami (Great Mosque). The largest Ottoman mosque, built before the conquest of Istanbul, is typical of early Seljuk Turkish architecture. Built in 1400 by Ali Naccar, its interior is beautifully decorated with bold, black calligraphic designs, outstanding against plain cream walls. Especially beautiful is the 16-sided white marble *şadırvan* (fountain for ritual ablutions), which, unusually, lies inside. Uniquely, the mosque has 20 arches—four rows of five—supported by 12 arches. This is said to originate from Sultan Bayezid I's vow to build 20 mosques after winning the Battle of Nicopolis in 1396. But perhaps realizing the rashness of his promise, he adapted it so that each single dome could "represent" a mosque. ⏱ *30 min. Atatürk Cad. Open daily dawn–dusk.*

Bursa's Great Mosque.

❷ ★★ Koza Han. Literally meaning "Cocoon Inn," this *caravanserai* is the centerpiece of **Kapalı Çarşısı** (Grand Bazaar). An international trading center since the 15th century, the silk market was the location of healthy trade between merchants when Bursa was the final stop on the Silk Road from China. Even today, tiny stores surrounding the cafe-filled courtyard do a thriving business in multicolored silk scarves and clothing (although much is now imported). Enjoy a glass of tea in the courtyard peppered with ancient plane trees and watch the world go by. The cocoon auction takes place late June/early July, bringing silk-breeders from around the world to sell their valuable wares. ⏱ *1 hr.*

❸ ★★ Tombs of Orhan & Osman Gazi. The tombs of the Ottoman state's original founders are located inside the tiny **Tophane Park**. After conquering Bursa, Osman Gazi (Osman I) was the founder and first sultan of the empire that was finally established in 1326. It is thought that his deathbed wish, made to his son Orhan, was to be buried "under that silver dome—Bursa will be the city where our throne stands." Almost 7 centuries later, it's fascinating to remember those words when gazing at their ornate tombs. Osman's tomb dazzles with mother-of-pearl casing and embroidered cover and stands on a subtly colored mosaic floor, Byzantine remnants from the Monastery of Prophet Elijah. A few meters away, inside a separate structure, is the tomb of his son.

Both tombs were constructed in 1863 by Sultan Abdülaziz, replacing earlier ones destroyed by fire and an earthquake. The park's most noticeable landmark is the 35m-high (115 ft.) five-floor clock tower, built as a fire watchtower in 1905. Outside the park, pastel-colored restored Ottoman houses lie around Kale Sokak, near the hisar (castle) entrance. ⏱ *30 min. Tophane Park.*

④ ★★ Yeşil Türbe (Green Tomb). It's a pleasant walk east from the bazaar area over the Gök Dere river to the Yeşil neighborhood. Marking a change in the architectural style (from Seljuk to Ottoman), the hexagonal mausoleum of Sultan Mehmed I (1382–1421) was built by Hacı Ivaz Paşa (who also designed the mosque, **⑤**). Its distinctive appearance is thanks to the green-blue tiles cladding the exterior, which were added to the tiles from Kütahya after the 1855 earthquake. Enter through the carved wooden doors to the richly tiled interior, with scriptures and brightly colored flower designs echoing the mosque's interior. Of the eight tombs, Mehmed's, on a raised

central platform, is of course the most magnificent. Restored in 2008, the building is a distinctive sight, especially among the pretty cypress trees. ⏱ *15 min. Daily 9am–5pm.*

⑤ ★★ Yeşil Cami (Green Mosque). Lying opposite Yeşil Türbe, this is one of the jewels in Bursa's crown. One of many important buildings damaged in the devastating 1855 earthquake, its central doorway is surrounded by intricate carved marble stonework, a typical Timurid feature. For such a famous mosque (one of the finest Ottoman creations), it's surprisingly small, but what incredible detail. Look out for the colorful glazed tiles, the densely decorated *mihrab* (niche pointing to Mecca), and the squinches supporting the dome. ⏱ *15 min.*

⑥ ★ kids D'Or. Opened in early 2011, this slick little cafe serves homemade organic dishes, from hearty breakfasts to fried eggplant and delicious homemade baklava. It also sells organic honey, herbs, olive oil, and teas from all over Turkey. *4 Müze Sok.* ☎ *0224/327-9098. Turkish breakfast 14 TL.*

The intricate carved marble of Yeşil Camii.

Healing Waters

Since Roman times, Bursa has been a magnet for those seeking the curative waters of its thermal springs. Today, the Çekirge neighborhood on Bursa's western side has luxury hotels with their own spas, making the most of the warm mineral-rich spring mountain waters flowing from Uludağ. Alternatively, head to a traditional *hamam* such as **Eski Kaplıca, Yeni Kaplıca,** or **Kukurtlu Kaplıca**— believed to cure everything from leprosy to syphilis and obesity.

❼ ★ Türk ve Islam Eserleri Müzesi (Museum of Turkish and Islamic Arts). Housed in the original *medrese* (religious school) in the mosque complex, the museum's tiny rooms surround the courtyard. You'll see the first coins produced by the Bursa mint after Orhan Gazi's conquest of Bursa in 1477, as well as 13th-century ceramics. The calligraphy room, with an enormous, highly decorated 14th-century Qur'an, has accoutrements such as the original ink sets. ⏱ *40 min. Free admission. Tues–Sun 9:30am–5pm.*

❽ ★ kids Teleferik to Uludağ. Depending on the weather, take a cable-car trip up the mountain, either for skiing and snowboarding (Dec–Apr) or, in the warmer months, for gorgeous walks in Uludağ National Park. The ski center has decent facilities for a brief stay, or just a day trip, with equipment hire, ski trainers, and hotels. *Cable car departs approx every 30 min 8am–10pm with halfway stop at Kadıyayla; 15 TL return.*

❾ ★★ Muradiye Complex. This peaceful courtyard complex, built by Murat II (the "Muradiye") in 1426, the last Ottoman Sultan reigning in the city, is one of our favorite Bursa sites. Inside there's a mosque, *medrese*, hospice, *hamam*, and tombs built for him

and his relatives. Inside Murat II's tomb, look up to the hole in the dome allowing rain to fall on his tomb, as he had wished. One of the most striking tombs is that of Şezahde Mustafa and Cem Sultan, with fine, early Iznik tiles. ⏱ *1 hr.*

❿ ★★ kids Karagöz Müzesi. Traditional shadow puppetry, for which Bursa is famed, is honored in this new museum. According to legend, Karagöz dates back to two construction workers, Karagöz and Hacivat, building the Orhan Gazi mosque in 1396. They entertained their workmates with comedy

The Muradiye Complex in Bursa.

Getting There & Around

The best way to Bursa is by fast ferry from Yenikapı to Güzelyalı (80 min.; 9–27 TL single depending on ticket type and ferry time), then it's a bus ride to the start of the Metro (30 min.; 3 TL and a Metro ride to the center (30 min.; 3 TL). The best way to get around is by *dolmuş*, a comfortable white shared taxi with the *dolmuş* sign on the roof. Routes are fixed, with journeys costing 3 TL; make sure you're on the correct road and then flag down a cab and call out your destination to the driver. For an overnight stay, try the quaint **Safran Otel** (Arka Sok 4, off

Try a massage at Marigold Thermal & Spa Hotel.

Ortapazar Cad; ☎ 0224/224-7216) in a restored Ottoman house. To submerge in warm mineral pools in the Çekirge district, the five-star **Marigold Thermal & Spa Hotel** (1 Murat Cad 47; ☎ 090/444-4000; www.marigold.com.tr) has luxury facilities.

routines, causing hilarity—and also time-wasting, which led the enraged sultan to order the beheading of the two men. Two centuries later, the two formed the basis of puppetry "soap opera," humorous stories performed with hand-painted flat puppets typically in mosques and public spaces during the Ramazan fasting month. At the museum, characters from these stories are explained, accompanied by modern-day wooden models. The second exhibition room has 200-year-old hand-painted puppets made with camel skin and traditional musical instruments used in performances. Kids love the puppet shows performed downstairs in the little theater; even though the narration is in Turkish, you can get the

gist of its comic value (on weekdays, most of the audience is made up of giggling local primary school kids). Across the road, don't miss the huge **Karagöz and Haciabat Monumental Grave.** *Tip:* If you want to buy puppets to take home, visit one of Bursa's most famous Karagöz "practitioners": Şinasi Çelikkol at his antique shop in the covered market (12 Eski Aynalı Çarşı). ⏱ *1 hr. Çekirge Cad.* ☎ *0224/233-8429. Admission 5 TL. Tues–Sun 9am–5:30pm.*

⓫ ★ kids **Uluumay Osmanlı Kıyafetleri ve Takıları Müzesi (Ottoman Folk Costumes and Jewelry Museum).** A real labor of love, local septuagenarian Esat Uluumay, once a prize-winning folk

Traditional shadow puppets at the Karagöz Müzesi.

dancer, displays his personal collection of Ottoman traditional costume from countries including Iraq and Yemen. Kitschly mounted on rotating pedestals, there's enormous variety in the 400-odd displays. They include silk religious garb from the Armenian Catholic church, an Ottoman judge's outfit, 19th-century bridalwear from Skopje, and folk-dancing outfits from 19th-century Kosovo. His collection of jewelry is astounding—look out for chains that (apparently) inspired Madonna's stylist for her 1992 tour,

as well as filigree headdresses. ⏱ *1 hr. Il Murat Cad, Şair Ahmetpaşa Medresesi.* ☎ *0224/222-7575. Admission 5 TL. Daily 9am–6pm (Mon 1–6pm).*

12 ★★ **kids Kebapçı Iskender.** This is the most famous place to taste Bursa's specialty *kebap*, from the direct descendants of its creator: Sliced lamb served on tomato sauce on bread, slathered with browned butter. Delicious! *Atatürk Cad 60.* ☎ *0224/221-4615.* Iskender kebap *18 TL.*

Edirne

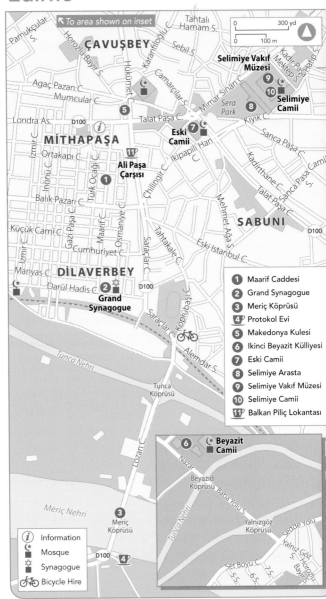

↖ To area shown on inset

ÇAVUŞBEY

MİTHAPAŞA

Ali Paşa Çarşısı

Eski Camii

Selimiye Vakıf Müzesi

Selimiye Camii

Sera Park

SABUNI

DİLAVERBEY

Grand Synagogue

Tunca Nehri

Meriç Nehri

Meriç Köprüsü

Tunca Köprüsü

1 Maarif Caddesi
2 Grand Synagogue
3 Meriç Köprüsü
4 Protokol Evi
5 Makedonya Kulesi
6 Ikinci Beyazit Külliyesi
7 Eski Camii
8 Selimiye Arasta
9 Selimiye Vakıf Müzesi
10 Selimiye Camii
11 Balkan Piliç Lokantası

Beyazit Camii

Beyazıd Köprüsü

Yalnızgöz Köprüsü

ℹ Information
✹ Mosque
✡ Synagogue
🚲 Bicycle Hire

0 ___ 300 yd
0 ___ 100 m

Once the capital of the Ottoman Empire, Edirne sits strategically near the Greek and Bulgarian borders; today, it's best known for the Selimiye Mosque and the Kırkpınar oil-wrestling festival. It's an attractive city, smaller and more relaxed than Istanbul, with most places of interest clustered in the center. START: **Hürriyet Meydanı.**

1 ★ **kids** **Maarif Caddesi.** In the street running south from Hürriyet Meydanı, there's a charming collection of traditional *Türkevi* (Turkish wooden houses). Head down to **Kırkpınar Evi** on the right, a restored house-museum exhibiting the history of Edirne's traditional oil wrestling (p 158). Inside are lovely exhibits of this traditional sporting event, though opening hours are erratic. ⏱ *45 min (if open).*

2 ★ **Grand Synagogue.** Edirne's only synagogue is at the southern end of Maarif Caddesi, once populated with Jews who worked in the bazaar. During Edirne's huge fire in 1905, 13 synagogues were destroyed and replaced by this one, but no Jewish community exists today. Repairs to this grand building were ongoing at the time of writing, due to be completed sometime in 2014. ⏱ *10 min. Maarif Cad.*

3 ★ **Meriç Köprüsü (Meriç Bridge).** From the synagogue, it's a 15-minute walk down Karaağaç

Yolu to the pretty bridge over the Maritza River. Completed in 1847, the 263m-long (863 ft.) stone bridge with 12 pointed arches has drainage ports to prevent the floods that destroyed the previous wooden bridge. After your tea break (**4**), look out for a minibus to the city center.

4 ★★ **kids** **Protokol Evi.** Once the police station, this restored house over the bridge is now a charming cafe. Take a table at the terrace's edge for a perfect view of Selimiye Mosque with a glass of tea. *Lozan Cad.* ☎ *0284/223-3282.*

5 ★★★ **kids** **Makedonya Kulesi.** Also known as Saat Kulesi (clock tower), this landmark, built in 1894, is now part of an "archeological park" excavated in 2003. The park's main external wall is a mix of Roman, Byzantine, and Ottoman construction, with remains of a 10th-century Byzantine church and fresco, plus late-Roman pottery

Walk over the 19th-century Meriç Köprüsü.

ovens. Spot fragments of Ottoman human bones embedded in the foliage-covered southern wall, once the cemetery. If the gate is locked, ask in the cafe opposite for a key. ⏱ *45 min. Mumcular Sok. Free admission. Daily 8:30am–6pm.*

⑥ ★★★ Ikinci Beyazit Külliyesi (Beyazit II Complex).

It's a little far to walk, so pick up a minibus from opposite the tourist office. North of the city, this *külliye* (mosque complex), comprising originally a mosque, kitchens, a hospital, and a school, is a real treasure. The highlight is the award-winning **Museum of Health,** in the former psychiatric hospital. Its superb displays reveal the hospital's groundbreaking treatment of its patients, with care and empathy from top-rated doctors. It used progressive therapies such as musicians playing on a stage and a fountain providing soothing sounds. Most interesting is the hospital's revolutionary design, an octagonal ward for high efficiency with few staff and a sloping floor to catch the fountain's overflow. Check out the exhibition on eye-watering 16th-century Ottoman medical procedures. ⏱ *90 min. Admission 10 TL, free for kids 7 and under. Daily 9am–5pm.*

⑦ ★★ Eski Cami (Old Mosque).

With room for 3,000 worshippers, Edirne's oldest Ottoman monument, completed in 1414 under Mehmet I, has a striking interior dominated by the huge Arabic calligraphy of ALLAH and MOHAMMED on its walls. Built in a perfect square, each of its nine domes—in the style of Ulu Cami in Bursa (p 149)—is 13m (43 ft.) in diameter. Look out for the small piece of stone from Mecca encased in glass, on the wall near the *minbar* (pulpit). Outside on the left is a statue of *pehlivans* (wrestlers), an Edirne

emblem. ⏱ *30 min. Corner of Talatpaşa Aşfaltı and Londra Aşfaltı. Open daily dawn–dusk.*

⑧ ★ Selimiye Arasta.

Like many markets of this era, this was founded as a charitable establishment for the Selimiye Mosque. Its 73-arch layout dates back over 5 centuries—its fruit-shaped soap and fridge magnets less than that. The piles of cheap shoes are a reminder that part of this market was the "ready-made Shoe-Makers' Bazaar," as recorded by Evliya Çelebi, the prolific Ottoman writer and traveler (1611–82). Merchants in past centuries swore an oath in the mosque that their transactions would be honest. *Selimiye Camii complex. Free admission. Open daily 9am–dusk.*

⑨ ★★ kids Selimiye Vakıf Müzesi (Selimiye Foundation Museum).

Opened in 2007, this smart museum occupies the Dar'ul Kurra *medrese* adjacent to **Selimiye Camii,** built by Sinan in 1575. It's laid out around a square garden, using individual classrooms for different themes. Most displays specialize in Ottoman crafts such as calligraphy and ornate brassware, and if you're a fan of inlaid wood, you'll love the 18th-century wooden Qur'an stands and tables inlaid with

Eski Cami.

Practical Matters

Speedy, comfortable buses run from Istanbul's Esenler bus station to Edirne, the 250km (155 miles) taking 2½ hours. Allow extra time for the *servis*, the free shuttle minibus service collecting passengers from various points to the *otogar*; the ticket office will inform you where and when. On arrival at Edirne, jump on a minibus to Hürriyet Meydanı or Selimiye Camii. For a full-day trip, try to depart around 7am, and buy your return ticket to leave late evening. The **Edirne Tourist Office,** 17 Hürriyet Meydanı (☎ 0284/213-9208) has helpful staff and maps. For bicycle hire, try **Diramalilar Motorsiklet & Bisiklet** behind the sports stadium (☎ 0543/294-5868).

---

mother-of-pearl. ⏱ *1 hr. Selimiye Külliyesi, Sarul Kurra Medresi.* ☎ *0284/212-1133. Free admission. Tues–Sun 8am–5pm.*

🔟 **★★★ Selimiye Camii (Selimiye Mosque).** Why not save the best till last? Wonder-architect Mimar Sinan did, completing this at age 80 in 1575. He regarded it as his finest creation and symbol of the Ottoman state. (It's also been nominated for UNESCO World Heritage Status.) Through the main entrance, you pass the impressive statue of the architect, indicating the reverence Edirne held for him. The four pencil-slim minarets are dazzling, each 71m (233 ft.) high with three ornate balconies. In the middle of the courtyard lies the 16-sided *şadırvan* (ablutions fountain, where men wash before praying). Inside, the plain walls mean that your eyes are drawn up to the 40m-high (131 ft.) dome, covered with intricate painted designs in blue and deep red. With this dome, 31.5 m (103 ft.) in diameter, Sinan finally achieved his ambition to exceed in size the dome of the Byzantine cathedral of Aya Sofya in Istanbul. Take a close look at the ornately carved marble *minbar* with tiled top, plus the gold, exquisite Iznik tiles, and

mother-of-pearl used throughout. ⏱ *1 hr. Mimar Sinan Cad. Open daily dawn–dusk; no entry at prayer time.*

🍽 **★ Balkan Piliç Lokantası.** This no-nonsense eatery is handily placed in Edirne's center on a pleasant pedestrianized street. It serves tasty chicken dishes and hearty soups. *Saraçlar Cad 14.* ☎ *0284/225-2155. Entrees 15 TL.*

Sinan's masterpiece: Selimiye Camii.

Slippery Sport

Statues of wrestlers dot the city, a nod to Edirne's ancient tradition of the Kırkpınar *yağli güreş* (oil wrestling) competition, every year in late June/early July. With roots dating back to the 14th century, when Ottoman troops returned from conquest, modern-day wrestlers compete in heavy leather breeches, their bodies covered in olive oil. The 3-day tournament takes place a few miles outside the center, with traditional music, excitable crowds, and a spirit of tradition and ceremony. The winner of each level, determined by weight, wins cash prizes, with the heavyweight (*başpehlivan*) also winning a golden belt. The festival is popular, so if you're planning to attend, book your hotel and bus tickets in plenty of time.

Wrestlers, competing in the Sile Annual Oil Wrestling Event, acknowledge a sport dating back to the 14th century.

The Savvy Traveler

Before You Go

Government Tourist Offices

In the U.S.: 821 UN Plaza, New York, NY 10017 (☎ 212/687-2194); 2525 Massachusetts Avenue, Washington, DC 20008 (☎ 202/612-6800); 5055 Wilshire Boulevard Suite 850, Los Angeles, CA 90036 ☎ 323/937-8066; www.tourism turkey.org). **In the U.K.:** 4/F 29–30 St. James's St., London SW1A 1HB (☎ 020/7839-7778; www.goto turkey.co.uk).

The Best Times to Go

May to June and **September to October** have a comfortable temperature (daytime 16°–25°C/61°–77°F) and many events. During humid August, some hotels offer discounts due to fewer business visitors. Many Istanbullus head to the coast for holidays.

Business and opening hours alter during **Ramazan** (the month-long fasting from dawn to dusk). The Islamic lunar calendar is used, so its date moves approximately 11 days annually. Ramazan for 2015 begins June 18 (estimated). During this month, avoid eating, drinking, or smoking in the street out of respect for those fasting. Smaller restaurants, especially in conservative neighborhoods, may close all day; all places are generally busy for *iftar* (meal to break the fast). During the two biggest religious festivals, **Şeker Bayram** (3-day festival marking the end of Ramazan) and **Kurban Bayram** (Feast of Sacrifice, 10 weeks later), many attractions and shops close for 2 days. Hotels and flights fill up in advance and are more expensive. Many people travel to, and from, Istanbul to visit family.

Previous page: Istanbul sign posts.

Festivals & Special Events

Most art and cultural festivals are organized by the **Istanbul Kültür Sanat Vakfı** (Istanbul Foundation for Culture and Arts; ☎ 0212/334-0700; www.iksv.org). **Pozitif** (☎ 0212/334-0100; www.pozitiflive. com) organizes funky music events in the city. Most events, including music, festivals, and sports, can be booked at **Biletix** (various outlets including Istiklal Kitabevi, 55 Istiklal Cad, www.biletix.com.tr).

SPRING. The cultural year kicks off with the **Istanbul International Film Festival** for 2 weeks in April, with Turkish and international films (with English subtitles) plus awards to honor top Turkish films and directors. Screened in six cinemas, mainly in Beyoğlu, tickets sell out fast. Also in April is the **Tulip Festival,** when the nearly 15 million bulbs planted across the city come into bloom, best seen in Gülhane and Emirgan parks. May's 3-week **International Istanbul Theater Festival** is a mix of overseas theater and dance companies, plus new productions from around Turkey. Performances take place at venues ranging from the Hagia Eirene to tiny stages at museums. In May, music lovers flock to the **Chill Out Festival** (www.chilloutfest.com) organized by Lounge 102 FM at the Kemer Golf & Country Club, a 12-hour fest with genres from jazz and funk to soul and hip-hop.

SUMMER. The **International Istanbul Music Festival** (3 weeks in June; www.iksv.org/muzik) showcases over 500 artists, with over 20 performances from symphony orchestras and baroque music ensembles. **Istanbul Pride Week** in late June incorporates LGBT cultural events and meetings in various venues, culminating in the march, growing in numbers since the first in 2003. The prestigious **International Istanbul Jazz Festival** (2 weeks in June; www.iksv.org/caz) has seen the likes of Herbie Hancock and Al Jarreau gracing the stages of jazz clubs and parks. **Rock 'n' Coke** (www.rockncoke.com) is Turkey's largest open-air music festival, attracting 50,000 with major acts (2013 saw Arctic Monkeys and Prodigy) at the Hezarfen Airfield, outside the city.

FALL. Istanbul goes arty with Turkey's largest contemporary art show, the **International Istanbul Bienal** (www.iksv.org/bienal), lasting 3 months from September (next one scheduled for 2015). Run by international guest curators, the city exhibits works by about 100 international artists in various venues. October sees runners compete in the **Istanbul Eurasia Marathon** (www.istanbulmarathon.org), the course passing over the first Bosphorus suspension bridge, making entrants trans-continental runners. In October or November, **Contemporary Istanbul** (☎ 0212/244-7175; www.contemporaryistanbul.com), a selling fair at the Istanbul Convention and Exhibition Center, incorporates all arts from local and international galleries. Going since 1993, the **Akbank Jazz Festival** (www.akbanksanat.com) favors fusion events at hip venues, with Brazilian or Middle Eastern beats, and plenty of Turkish musicians. Everything stops—including pedestrians and traffic—when the siren sounds on November 10 at 9:05am to mark the **anniversary of Atatürk's death.**

WINTER. A **blues festival** (www.pozitiflive.com), known as the Efes Pilsen Blues Festival until

controversial changes in the laws governing the sale of alcohol came into force in 2012, warms up chilly November evenings, with international blues artists performing with local artists.

The Weather

Spring and fall are usually dry and sunny; summers (July–Aug) can be hot and humid, not much fun on crowded transport but good to enjoy Bosphorus-front evenings in cafes, restaurants, and nightclubs. Some up-market terrace clubs and restaurants close in winter (mid-Oct–mid-May) or switch to indoor venues. December to February can be cold and wet with occasional snow.

Useful Websites

- **www.mymerhaba.com**: Covers all Turkey with practical information, although the What's On section isn't very up to date.

- **www.todayszaman.com**: Online version of *Today's Zaman*, an English-language daily paper with some listings for Istanbul.

- **www.hurriyetdailynews.com**: Online version of the English-language daily newspaper.

- **www.theguideistanbul.com**: Online version of a glossy listings and features magazine devoted to the city's arts, cultural, and culinary life.

- **www.timeoutistanbul.com**: The latest listings and features from the worldwide *What's On* magazine.

- **www.biletix.com**: Online booking agent for tickets for concerts, sporting events, and shows, plus details of their outlets.

- **www.iksv.org**: Organizers of the majority of Istanbul's culture and music festivals.

The Savvy Traveler

AVERAGE TEMPERATURE & RAINFALL IN ISTANBUL					
	°C (LOW)	°C (HIGH)	°F (LOW)	°F (HIGH)	RAINFALL (CM)
Jan	3	8	37	46	10.9
Feb	3	9	36	48	9.2
Mar	3	11	37	52	7.2
Apr	7	16	45	61	4.6
May	9	22	48	54	3.8
June	16	25	61	77	3.4
July	18	28	64	82	3.4
Aug	19	29	66	84	3.0
Sept	16	24	61	75	5.8
Oct	13	20	55	68	8.1
Nov	9	15	48	59	10.3
Dec	5	11	41	52	11.9

- **www.muze.gov.tr**: Official state museum site, useful for latest visiting hours, entry prices, etc.

- **www.kultur.gov.tr**: Official website of the Turkish Ministry of Culture and Tourism.

- **www.tourismturkey.org**: Official Turkish tourism site in the U.S.

- **www.gototurkey.co.uk**: Official Turkish tourism site in the U.K.

- **www.pozitiflive.com**: Listings of (mainly) contemporary music events.

- **www.istanbululasim.com/en**: Official site for Istanbul's metro, tram, and funicular system.

- **www.iett.gov.tr**: Covers the city's bus network.

- **www.turkeytravelplanner.com**: Guide to the country written by U.S. travel writer Tom Brosnahan.

Cellphones (Mobiles)

Most U.K. phones can send and receive calls/SMS, and most tri-band cellphones from the U.S. work here—although roaming charges are expensive. The Turkish government has restricted visitors buying local SIM cards on phones brought from overseas. If it's your first time in Turkey, you can buy a SIM card (approximately 50 TL) and have instant access, though your phone will be blocked after 10 days. The alternative is to register your phone, which can take several days and costs 150 TL. For longer stays, buy a cheap handset in Istanbul and a pay-as-you-go SIM card. The main Turkish networks are Turkcell (www.turkcell.com.tr), Türk Telekom (www.turktelekom.com.tr), Avea (www.avea.com.tr), and Vodafone (www.vodafone.com.tr); all companies have branches around the city.

Car Rental

Driving in Istanbul is *really* not advisable; traffic jams are a nightmare, drivers are aggressive, fuel is expensive, and public transport and taxis are relatively cheap. Major car-hire companies have counters at the airport terminals, plus offices around Taksim, although it's cheaper to book online in advance. Try **Avis** (www.avis.com), **Budget** (www.budget.com), **Hertz** (www.hertz.com), and **National** (www.nationalcar.com); prices can vary wildly. Drivers must be 21 or over. Check the website of **Turkish Touring and Automobile Club** (www.turing.org.tr) for information on driving licenses and permits.

Getting There

By Plane

Atatürk International Airport is the main international airport, in Yeşilköy (☎ 0212/463-3000; www.ataturkairport.com). Major **airlines** flying into Istanbul from the U.S. and U.K. include Turkish Airlines, Delta Airlines, and British Airways. Another option is Turkish carrier AtlasJet (www.atlasjet.com) from London Luton. Other U.S. airlines require changing in London or other major European cities. The airport is located 28 km (17 miles) west of the city center.

The **Havataş** (www.havatas.com) airport bus departs from outside the arrivals hall, approximately every 30 minutes between 4am and 1am, ending in Taksim (Cumhuriyet Caddesi), and stopping in Aksaray (for Sultanahmet) and Tepebaşı (inform the driver before you board). Tickets cost 10 TL (single). The journey takes around 40 minutes. Traveling to the airport, the bus leaves Taksim half-hourly (on the hour and half-hour) from 4am to 1am. Regular private minibuses go from Sultanahmet and the Old City (ask at your hotel).

Yellow **taxis** queue outside arrivals; check that the meter is switched on (p 165). Fares are approximately 50 TL to Taksim (40 min) and 40 TL to Sultanahmet (30 min).

The cheapest option is by the M1 **metro,** changing at Zeytinburnu onto the T1 tram (total 6 TL), taking around 50 minutes. The metro runs daily, approximately 6am to midnight.

Istanbul's second airport, **Sabiha Gökçen International Airport** (☎ 0216/585-5000; www.sgairport.com), is in Pendik on the Asian side. You'll land here from London with budget airlines **easy-Jet** (www.easyjet.com) and Turkish

airline **Pegasus** (www.flypgs.com). Located 50km (31 miles) east of the city center, a half-hourly **Havataş** bus service (13 TL) takes approximately 1½ hours to Taksim. The bus leaves the Taksim office every half-hour from 4am to 1am.

By Train

Turkey's train system (www.tcdd.gov.tr) has dramatically improved in recent years, with high-speed links between Istanbul and Ankara and fast connections between some other cities. Many services remain much slower and less regular, though cheaper. There are daily overnight services to Sofia (15 hr.) and other European cities, including Bucharest and Budapest. See www.seat61.com for the latest and best information. The partial opening of the Marmaray metro system in late 2013 means that as of 2014, trains are likely to run from Halkalı, 28km (17 miles) west of Istanbul, rather than the old terminus of the Orient Express at **Sirkeci** station. Trains to cities on the Asian side, including Ankara (express taking 5½ hr.), Kayseri, Gaziantep, and Van, plus daily to Iran, have also been affected by the Marmaray project. Trains no longer run to **Haydarpaşa** station, near Kadıköy on the Asian side. When the Marmaray project is complete (scheduled for 2014 but likely to be delayed), trains should run from Pendik, an Istanbul suburb in Asia.

By Bus

Comfortable coaches are the preferred way to travel long distance to other Turkish and European cities. The main bus station (*otogar*) is in Esenler, but you can book tickets in offices located on İnönü Caddesi in Gümüşsuyu, Sultanahmet, and

Beşiktaş, from where private shuttle buses (servis) take you to the otogar. If you arrive in Istanbul by bus, ask the driver for the servis, or take the metro to Aksaray and change to the T1 tram for Sultanahmet or Kabataş/Taksim. As well as national routes, international services include Sofia (8 hr.), Thessaloniki (12 hr.), and many other European cities. Welcoming extras on board include complimentary refreshments, personal TV/radio screens, and Wi-Fi, and there are regular rest/food stops.

Reputable companies include **Varan** (19B Inönü Cad; ☎ 0212/251-7474; www.varan.com.tr), **Ulusoy** (59 Inönü Cad; ☎ 444/1-888; www.ulusoy.com.tr), and **Kamil Koç** (29 Inönü Cad; ☎ 444/0-562; www.kamilkoc.com.tr).

By Car
The highways leading into and out of Istanbul are fast, new, and reasonably traffic-free. Most highways operate with a toll fee of a few liras, not payable in cash; buy a prepaid card in advance. The downside is that once you get into the city, major traffic snarls are inevitable and route-finding a nightmare. Worse, fuel in Turkey is the second most expensive in the world, and the roads here are considered some of Europe's most dangerous. The speed limit is 120km/h (75 mph) on highways. If you bring your own car into Turkey, ensure that you have an international driving license, car registration documents, and an international green card. (Check www.turing.org.tr for details.)

By Boat
Fast ferries operated by IDO (www.ido.com.tr) run across the Sea of Marmara from Yenikapı to Yalova (for Iznik), Mudanya (for Bursa), and Bandırma (for Çanakkale/Troy).

Getting Around

By Public Transport
Istanbul's public transport system, is rapidly improving. An Istanbulkart ("smart card") is recommended; buy a new one for a 6 TL deposit, then top up with cash and "bleep" in as you board the bus, tram, ferry, or metro. Look out for the white booths labeled AKBIL SATIŞ NOKTASI (note that the pre-Istanbulkart travel pass system is known as Akbil, and still runs in parallel with the new system) at transport hubs including Taksim Square and Eminönü. At 1.95 TL for each single journey, it is cheaper and far more convenient than the alternative; buying a jeton (token) from a Jetonmatik machine for 3 TL. The Istanbulkart also gives a further discount (1.25 TL as opposed to 1.95 TL) for connecting services taken within 90 minutes. Cash is not an option on the city's public transport system.

By Tram
The sleek T1 tram (www.istanbululasim.com.tr/en) from Kabataş to Zeytinburnu is one of the best ways to get around the Old City, with stops including Eminönü (Spice Market), Sirkeci (train/metro station), Sultanahmet (Blue Mosque), and Beyazit (Grand Bazaar). It crosses Galata Bridge and ends at Kabataş, from where the underground **funicular** goes up to Taksim, connecting with the M2 **metro** (below), and ferries depart for the Princes' Islands.

In contrast, the **Nostaljik Tramvay** is a revival of Istanbul's historic tram system, running from Taksim Square to Tünel. The 1.6-km (1-mile) journey down Istiklal Caddesi (8am–10pm) takes up to 15 minutes. Pay by *Istanbulkart* or an electronic ticket (4 TL) purchased from a kiosk at Tünel. This connects with the historic **Tünel,** one of the world's oldest underground routes, traveling 573m (1,879 ft.) between Karaköy and Tünel's main square (saving the steep uphill hike) between 7am–10pm (4 TL for an electronic ticket, cheaper multi-passes available; 1.95 TL with the *Istanbulkart*).

By Taxi

You'll find yellow metered taxis all over Istanbul. If a driver attempts to fix a price in advance, or says the meter isn't working, don't take the ride. Ensure that the meter is switched on as your journey starts. Most taxi drivers are decent, although some will try to take the longer, "scenic" route. Tipping is not required, although rounding up a couple of liras is appreciated. Avoid handing over large bills. Take your hotel card for address details; few drivers speak English.

By Metro

The Marmaray metro line partially opened in late 2013. This line links the Old City on the European side of the Bosphorus with the Asian side of the city via the Bosphorus tunnel. Get on at Sirkeci in the Old City to be whizzed under the Bosphorus to Üsküdar in Asia. A bridge across the Golden Horn, opened in early 2014, links the Marmaray line with the M2 metro line, which now runs from Yenikapı in the Old City, via Taksim, to Hacıosman. The M1 light metro (partially underground) runs from Aksaray to Esenler Otogar (main bus station) and Atatürk Havalimanı (airport).

By Bus

Most buses are green single-deckers, run by IETT, with hubs including Taksim Square, Eminönü, Beyazit, and Kabataş. There's a journey planner on their website (http://harita.iett.gov.tr). Most services run between 6:30am and 11:30pm. Buy a *jeton* for 3 TL or use your *Istanbulkart*.

By Boat

The network of fast catamarans, slow passenger ferries, and full-day excursions form an integral part of Istanbul, with routes crisscrossing the Bosphorus, the Golden Horn, and Marmara. From quick trips between Üsküdar and Beşiktaş to an evening sail up the Bosphorus, ferryboats are the most pleasant way to get around. The main departure points are Eminönü, Karaköy, Beşiktaş, and Kabataş on the European side, and Üsküdar and Kadıköy on the Asian. Pay for your journey by *Istanbulkart* or *jeton,* except for private day trips on the Bosphorus. Catamarans run to the Princes' Islands, operated by IDO (www.ido.com.tr), but most visitors use the slower ferries to cross to Asia or head up the Golden Horn. These are operated by Sehir Hatları (www.sehirhatlari.com.tr).

By Dolmuş & Minibus

Yellow *dolmuş* (meaning "stuffed") minibuses operate like shared taxis on fixed routes, departing when full. Start and end points are fixed, but you can get off at any point, shouting "*inecek var*" to the driver to stop. You can flag the bus down anywhere on the route. Banned from the Old City, the only vaguely useful routes for most visitors are up and down the Asian side of the Bosphorus and from Taksim Square to Yedikule, near the land walls. Fares are payable to the driver—you can't use the *Istanbulkart*.

On Foot

Istanbul is best seen on foot, especially around the Old City and Beyoğlu. Watch out for the traffic, as Istanbul drivers have scant regard for crosswalks (zebra crossings), often make turns without looking out for pedestrians, and never use their indicators.

Fast Facts

ACCOMMODATION Istanbul is geared to both tourists and business travelers, so the city has plenty of beds, from Ottoman-style traditional guesthouses to high-end international hotel chains. The number of suite hotels (almost self-contained apartments) and contemporary boutique hotels has shot up. Prices have increased substantially in recent years and are now on a par with many European cities. For longer stays, look for good deals on apartments and suites. For short-term rentals, try **Istanbul Holiday Apartments** (☎ 0212/251-8530; www.istanbulholidayapartments.com; from U.S. and Canada, ☎ 800/753-2877). Longer-term rental is available at **Istanbul Rentals** (☎ 0212/638-1215; www.istanbulrentals.com) or from private renters at **www.airbnb.com**. Don't arrange hotels on arrival at the airport as you're likely to get ripped off.

ATMS/EXCHANGE Maestro, Cirrus, MasterCard, and Visa are accepted at **ATMs,** although some machines deal only with Turkish banks. Major banks may deal with American Express. Commission-free *döviz* (exchange bureaus) accept all major international currencies and are dotted around Istiklal Caddesi, Divanyolu in Sultanahmet up to Beyazit, and the Grand Bazaar. Count the notes out in front of the cashier to prevent "errors." Banks usually charge a small commission to change money, often a bureaucratic process. Traveler's checks are exchanged at banks, with commission.

BANKS Banks open Monday to Friday 9am to 5pm; some close 12:30 to 1:30pm.

BUSINESS HOURS Most stores open daily 10am to 7pm, with many around Istiklal Caddesi open until 9pm; some small, independent stores close on Sundays. Most galleries and museums close on Mondays. Offices generally operate Monday to Friday, 9am to 5pm.

CLOTHING Men and women should avoid wearing shorts above the knee and singlets (tank tops). For mosque visits in tourist areas, women will be given gowns to cover up if their clothing is revealing; carry a light wrap suitable to cover the hair and upper arms when visiting off-the-beaten-track mosques. Women wearing skimpy clothes are more likely to get unwanted attention, especially in the Old City.

CONSULATES & EMBASSIES **U.S. Consulate,** 2 Uçşehitler Sokaği, Istiniye, ☎ 0212/335-9000, http://istanbul.usconsulate.gov. **Canadian Consulate,** 16/F Tekfen Tower, 209 Büyükdere Cad, Levent 4, ☎ 0212/385-9700, http://turkey.gc.ca. **U.K. Consulate,** 34 Meşrutiyet Cad, Tepebaşı, ☎ 0212/334-6400, http://ukin turkey.fco.gov.uk. **Irish Consulate,** 417 Meridyen Iş Merkezi, Ali Riza Gurcan Cad, Merter, ☎ 0212/482-2434, www.dfa.ie. **Australian Consulate,** 16/F Suzer Plaza, 15 Elmadağ Askerocaği Cad, Şişli, ☎ 0212/243-1333, www.dfat.gov.au. **New**

Zealand Consulate, 48 Inönü Cad, Taksim, ☎ 0212/244-0272, www. nzembassy.com.

CREDIT CARDS Withdraw cash in Turkish liras from all ATMs with credit or Visa debit cards, usually with a commission of 2 to 4% (depending on your bank's rates). All hotels and restaurants (except the most basic) accept credit cards, especially Visa and MasterCard; fewer take American Express or Diners Club.

A PIN is required when using credit cards at all outlets. To report **lost or stolen** cards from Turkey **for U.S. cardholders:** American Express ☎ 001-715/343-7977; Visa ☎ 00-800/13-535-0900; Master-Card ☎ 00-800/13-887-0903. For **U.K. cardholders:** Visa ☎ 00-800/13-535-0900.

CUSTOMS It is forbidden to export genuine antiquities from Turkey. Bear this in mind if buying older goods (such as a carpet) and ask the dealer for a certificate of authenticity (and get a receipt for items over $100). Check www. gumruk.gov.tr for details. It is officially forbidden to import any electronic items not for personal use.

DENTIST The American Hospital and the German Hospital (see "Hospitals") both have dental clinics.

DRUGS Possessing, buying, or selling any illegal drugs (including cannabis) is a serious offense, with high penalties and harsh police treatment.

ELECTRICITY The current is 220 AC, 50Hz, with standard European-style two-pin plugs. Adapters can be bought locally, or bring a multipurpose traveling adapter from home. U.S. visitors may need a voltage converter for laptops.

EMERGENCIES For ambulance ☎ 112; Police ☎ 155; Fire ☎ 110; Traffic Police ☎ 154.

GAY & LESBIAN TRAVELERS Istanbul is home to gay (and gay-friendly) bars and clubs (p 119), with increasingly liberal attitudes. Homosexuality is actually legal in Turkey, although generally not tolerated in this conservative country. In mid-2008, local courts shut down the human-rights organization **Lambdaistanbul** (LGBT Solidarity Association), organizers of Gay Pride, but it was reinstated after an appeal (Tel Sok 28/5; off Istiklal Cad; ☎ 0212/245-7068; www.lambda istanbul.org). **Sugar & Spice** (p 120) is a good meeting and information point for gay and lesbian visitors. The Gay Pride march culminates in a week of activities, usually held in June.

HEALTH Even the locals don't drink tap water, so stick to bottled or filtered water. No inoculations are necessary for Istanbul, but mosquitoes can be a nuisance in summer. If you have an upset stomach, stick to yogurt, plain rice, and black tea with sugar. If things get worse, visit the *eczane* (pharmacy; see "Pharmacies").

HOLIDAYS Public holidays: January 1 (New Year's Day), April 23 (National Sovereignty and Children's Day), May 19 (Atatürk Commemoration and Youth Sports Day), August 30 (Victory Day), October 29 (Republic Day). In addition, first 2 days of Şeker Bayram (from July 17 in 2015 and July 5 in 2016) and Kurban Bayram (from Sept 22 in 2015 and Sept 12 in 2016).

HOSPITALS For advice, call the Hospital Information Hotline (☎ 0212/444-0911). Some of the best private hospitals, with English-speaking staff, include the **American Hospital,** Güzelbahçe Sok, Nişantaşı (☎ 0212/444-3777; www. americanhospitalistanbul.org) and the **German Hospital,** 119 Sıraselviler Cad, Taksim (☎ 0212/293-2150). Bring your credit card; payment is required at the time of treatment, with reimbursement through your insurance company.

INSURANCE Check your existing policies before you buy travel insurance to cover trip cancellation, lost luggage, theft, and medical expenses. Recommended U.S. insurers include **Access America** (☎ 800/284-8300; www.access america.com), **Travel Assistance International** (☎ 866/884-3556; www.allianztravelinsurance.com), and for medical insurance, **MEDEX Assistance** (☎ 800/732-5309; www. medexassist.com). Other travelers should shop around for the best deal from back home, and remember that **EHIC** cards for subsidized or free hospital treatment are not valid in Turkey, which is outside the E.U. Bring ID and credit cards in case you need emergency medical treatment.

INTERNET Most hotel rooms have Wi-Fi or cable Internet. Basic Internet cafes dot Beyoğlu, and there are a few more in Sultanahmet (approx 2 TL per hour), many with Skype facilities; look for the INTERNET sign often in a window on the third or fourth floor. Watch out for the different keyboard with Turkish characters (ç, ş, ı, etc.) when typing in Web addresses and passwords.

LOST PROPERTY If your credit cards are stolen, call your card company immediately and file a report with the police. If anything is lost or stolen, including your passport, go to the Tourist Police (see "Police"), who will help you fill out the necessary forms.

MAIL & POSTAGE Post offices—PTT—have prominent yellow-and-black signs, usually open Monday to Friday 9am to 5pm; the main office at Sirkeci (*Büyük Posthane Cad*) is open daily. Other useful branches are 90 Istiklal Caddesi,

Beyoğlu, and 2 Cumhuriyet Cad, Taksim. PTT branches are the only places to buy postage stamps.

MONEY The currency of Turkey is the **Türk lirası** (Turkish lira) or TL. Banknotes come in denominations of 5, 10, 20, 50, 100, and 200 TL. The lira is divided into 100 kuruş; coins come in 1, 5, 10, 25, 50 kuruş, and 1 TL. At the time of writing, $1 = 2.3 TL, £1 = 3.6 TL, and 1€ = 3.0 TL.

NEWSPAPERS & MAGAZINES English-language newspapers include *Hürriyet Daily News* (www.hurriyet dailynews.com) and *Today's Zaman* (www.todayszaman.com). The monthly magazine *Time Out Istanbul* has arts and entertainment listings, available in larger bookstores and newsstands. *The Guide* (www. theguideistanbul.com) is a bi-monthly, mini-directory of restaurants, nightlife, and shops.

PASSPORTS It is compulsory to carry ID in Turkey at all times; for tourists, this means passports. Police carry out occasional spot checks, especially in bars. If you don't have ID, you may be taken to the police station. Leave a photocopy of your passport photo page and Turkish visa (see "Visas") in your hotel. Contact your consulate (see "Consulates & Embassies") if you lose your passport.

PHARMACIES There are pharmacies (*eczane*) around the city, especially near the hospitals in Taksim (see "Hospitals"). Local pharmacies take turns to provide 24-hour service (*nobetçi*), the address of which is posted on the windows. Some close on Sundays. Pharmacists provide basic medical services and sell some medication without prescription. Those in Beyoğlu and Sultanahmet probably speak some English.

POLICE For emergencies ☎ 155; Traffic police ☎ 154; Tourist police: Yerebatan Caddesi,

opposite Yerebatan Sarnıçı
☎ 0212/527-4503.

SAFETY Violent crime is rare in Istanbul, but minor, opportunistic crime exists. Watch your bags at all times, and be wary of pickpockets in crowded major sights and on public transport. You often see young solvent-sniffers asking for money on quiet Beyoğlu streets at night—walk briskly past. Avoid walking along unlit streets at night alone.

SMOKING The smoking ban hit Turkey in July 2009, when all bars, restaurants, shops, and taxis were made smoke-free. Although this law is adhered to in most major hotels and restaurants, things are more lax in many bars and clubs (p 116).

TAXES Turkish value-added tax (KDV) is 18% on most goods—8% on food—and included in the price. Foreign visitors can reclaim tax on all goods costing over 100 TL at shops with the TAX FREE SHOPPING sign; ask for a full VAT receipt. This can be processed at the airport and a refund made in cash (Turkish liras) or to your credit card, with a small deduction. For more information, contact Global Refund Turkey, 29 Ferah Sokak, Teşvikiye (☎ 0212/232-1121; www.globalrefund.com).

TELEPHONES For national telephone enquiries ☎ 118; international operator ☎ 115. The local code for Istanbul is ☎ 0212 for the European side and ☎ 0216 for the Asian side. Include the local code for all calls made within Istanbul. To dial Istanbul from overseas: ☎ 001 (or 00 from UK) + 90 (Turkey code) + 212 (or 216) + 7-digit local number. Public telephones only take cards; for local calls use a regular **telefon kartı,** which is inserted into the phone; for cheaper mobile and international calls buy a prepaid discount calling card, scratch off the PIN and dial the access phone number. Use these in your hotel room to minimize extortionate phone charges, especially for overseas calls. Kiosks by public phones sell all types of cards, or buy from *bakkal* (grocery stores).

TIME ZONE Turkey is 2 hours ahead of GMT, and 3 hours ahead between the last weekend of March and the last weekend of October.

TIPPING Top restaurants usually include service charge (*servis dahil*) on your check, especially at hotels, but if service is good, add an extra 5%, especially as many waiting staff survive on tips. If not included, leave a tip of around 10% at bars that give table service. It's not necessary to tip cab drivers, just round up to the nearest lira. Pay tour guides about 10% if they are good, caretakers at mosques a few liras.

TOILETS (RESTROOMS) Most toilets (*tuvalet*) in restaurants and bars are clean. Public lavatories usually have an attendant and charge around 1 TL. The most basic (in parks and mosques) are squat toilets. A pack of tissues and wet wipes is always handy to carry around. All mosques have basic toilets.

TOURIST INFORMATION Atatürk International Airport arrivals hall; Sirkeci station (to the left of the main entrance) ☎ 0212/511-5888; Sultanahmet Meydanı (square) ☎ 0212/518-1802; opposite the Hilton Hotel (Elmadağ) ☎ 0212/233-0592; Merkez Caddesi, 1/F, no 6 (opposite Atatürk Kültür Merkezi, Taksim Square) ☎ 0212/246-5313). Unfortunately, the service and knowledge is poor at most offices, but at least you can pick up a free city map.

TRAVELERS WITH DISABILITIES With so many steep, cobbled, and narrow streets, Istanbul is difficult to get around in a wheelchair. There are lifts at all metro stations and easy access onto trams and some buses. Most hotels have elevators and disabled access rooms, although some "boutique" Ottoman and traditional hotels do not; check before booking.

VISAS As of April 2014, most visitors to Turkey, including EU and US citizens, are required to purchase an e-visa in advance of arrival; visas are not issued at immigration entry points. To obtain your e-visa go to www.evisa.gov.tr and follow the online instructions. Payment is by MasterCard or Visa credit/debit card. Print out and show the e-visa at immigration. At the time of writing, a visa for both British and U.S. passport holders was $20, valid for 90 days within 180 days.

WOMEN Turkish men are renowned Romeos, so tread carefully. Traveling alone or in women-only groups can attract more attention, some of it unwanted. If you wish to discourage it, say you're married, and be firm but polite if hassling gets too much. Aksaray has pockets of red-light districts and "girlie bars" and can lead to hisses and too-close proximity; avoid eye contact and give these guys a wide berth. Long blonde hair attracts attention—if it all gets to be too much, tie it back or cover it up with a scarf or hat. Making a scene and getting the attention of locals will usually do the trick of chasing them away.

Istanbul: **A Brief History**

7TH CENTURY B.C. First settlement of Istanbul when Megarians flee the Dorian occupation of Greece.

680 B.C. Megarians cross the Marmara and settle in Chalcedon, today's Kadıköy.

660 B.C. Megarian commander, Byzas, starts a new settlement on the European side of the Bosphorus, today's Sarayburnu. He names it Byzantium.

318 B.C. Byzantium taken over by Antigonus, commander of Alexander the Great.

A.D. 324 Constantine becomes head of the Roman Empire, making Byzantium the capital, and becomes the first Roman ruler to adopt Christianity.

330 Constantine I moves capital of the Roman Empire to Byzantium, renaming it Constantinople.

381 Constantinople becomes the seat of the Patriarch, nominal head of the Orthodox Church.

412 Theodosius II builds the city walls, enlarging the city.

532 Thousands killed and much of the city burnt in Nika insurrection. Emperor Justinian I rebuilds the city, including Hagia Sophia.

1071 Byzantine army defeated by Seljuk Turks in the Battle of Manzikert and most of Anatolia is lost.

1082 Venetians allotted quarters in the city with special trading privileges, later joined by the Genoese.

1204 Constantinople captured in the Fourth Crusade, forcing the emperor into exile. Venetians take control of the church. Crusaders rule until 1261.

1299 The reign of Osman I (Osman Gazi), founder of the Ottoman Empire, begins.

1422 Ottoman Sultan Murad II fails in his attempted siege of Constantinople.

1452 Mehmet II builds Rumeli Hisarı (fortress) to blockade the Bosphorus.

1453 Mehmet II captures Constantinople after a 53-day siege. The last Byzantine Emperor, Constantine XI, is killed in battle.

1455 Kapalı Çarşısı (Grand Bazaar) is built.

1457 Capital of the Ottoman Empire is transferred from Adrianople (Edirne) to Istanbul.

1459 Mısır Çarşısı (Spice Market) is built.

1520–66 Reign of Süleyman I (Süleyman the Magnificent)—conqueror, lawmaker, and commissioner of many magnificent mosques.

1839 Tanzimat reforms begin to modernize and revive Ottoman Empire, influenced by Europe, including secular schooling system and attempted equality.

1854 Crimean War sees Ottoman Turks side with British and French against the Russians. Florence Nightingale in charge of military hospitals in Selimiye Army barracks, near Üsküdar.

1914 Ottoman Empire sides with the Central Powers during World War I. A year later, Mustafa Kemal thwarts the Allies' attempt to take the Dardanelles.

1918 Ottoman Empire finishes on the losing side in World War I; it is divided up between European powers.

1919 British and French occupy Istanbul; the empire is in terminal crisis. Anatolia is under Greek occupation.

1920 Mustafa Kemal leads the Turkish War of Independence, leading to the abolition of the Ottoman Empire.

1923 Founding of the Republic of Turkey with Mustafa Kemal, now known as Atatürk, its leader; capital moves from Istanbul to Ankara.

1925 Gregorian calendar officially replaces the Islamic (lunar) calendar; the fez is prohibited.

1928 Turkey officially becomes secular when the clause retaining Islam as the state religion is removed from the constitution.

1934 Women are given the vote. Atatürk proclaims Ayasofya, previously Hagia Sophia, a national museum.

1938 Atatürk dies on November 10 at 9:05am; the anniversary and exact time is marked every year.

1945 Turkey declares war on Germany and Japan, having remained neutral during most of World War II. Turkey joins the UN.

1955 Istanbul riots, forcing many Greeks to leave the city.

1960 Military coup against the ruling Democratic Party.

1965 Süleyman Demirel becomes prime minister, the first of seven terms of office.

1970s Large increase in Istanbul's population with migrants from rural Anatolia.

1971 Army forces Demirel's resignation following political violence.

1973 First bridge crossing the Bosphorus is completed, linking Istanbul's European and Asian sides.

1974 Turkish troops invade Northern Cyprus.

1980 Military coup follows political deadlock and imposes martial law. Curfew in Istanbul between 2 and 5am.

1982 Military coup and curfew ends; new constitution creates 7-year presidency.

1987 Turkey applies for full E.E.C. membership.

1993 Tansu Çiller becomes Turkey's first (and so far only) woman prime minister.

1999 PKK leader Abdullah Öcalan captured in Kenya; receives death sentence, later commuted to life imprisonment. August 17, huge earthquake reaching 6.7 on the Richter scale hits greater Istanbul, killing more than 23,000 people.

2002 Women given full legal equality with men. Turkey reaches the semifinals of the soccer World Cup.

2003 Truck bombs kill 53 people and wound 700 in attacks on Neve Shalom synagogue (Nov 15) and British Consulate (Nov 17). Al Qaeda claims responsibility.

2004 State TV broadcasts its first Kurdish-language program, previously banned in Turkey.

2005 New Turkish lira (TL) introduced, knocking off six zeros from the old lira. Negotiations for Turkey to join the EU officially launched.

2006 Istanbul author Orhan Pamuk wins Nobel Prize in Literature.

2007 Armenian community leader and newspaper editor of *Agos*, Hrant Dink, is assassinated outside his office in Istanbul by an ultra-nationalist. AK Party, led by PM Recep Tayyip Erdoğan, wins parliamentary election.

2008 Turkish Parliament votes to lift the ban on women students wearing Islamic headscarves at university, provoking huge protests.

2009 Smoking ban comes into force in Turkey on July 1. State broadcaster TRT introduces its first Kurdish-language TV channel.

2010 Istanbul, for the most part successfully, is the European Capital of Culture.

2011 Turkey enjoys a buoyant economic 2010, as GDP grows to 7.3%, one of Europe's highest. Recep Tayyip Erdoğan's AK Party wins a third term of office in the general election.

2012 In controversial circumstances, the chief of the Turkish armed forces, Ilker Başbuğ, is put on trial for treason, part of ongoing "deep state" conspiracy trials known as Balyoz and Ergenekon.

2013 Plans to redevelop iconic Taksim Square and destroy Gezi Park spark mass demonstrations and are the first real challenge to the pro-Islamic AK Party government.

Art & Architecture Highlights

Byzantine Empire (330–1453)
This was the city's most significant period for art. It began when Emperor Constantine built his new capital, inaugurated in A.D. 330. Many architects came from Rome to take part, but it took a couple of centuries for a distinctive "Christian" style of architecture to develop. Justinian (483–565) was the most influential Byzantine emperor, rebuilding the battered city after the Nika Revolt in A.D. 532, creating present-day Istanbul's

best-known landmarks, with Hagia Sophia (p 7) serving as a superb example of "Christian" architecture. For the Byzantines, exteriors were unimportant, as attention went to the all-important interior, which glittered with religious art, mosaics, and frescoes—also seen in the Kariye Museum (p 20).

Most Byzantine churches followed a standard pattern of iconography. The central dome was adorned with a mosaic of *Christ Pantocrator;* below that came angels, archangels, and biblical figures. Lower still came figures of saints. The Virgin Mary was often portrayed in the apse. Figures were static with flat areas of color, frontal pose, and characteristic use of gold background.

Justinian also constructed aqueducts and underground cisterns, enlarging Emperor Constantine's Yerebatan Sarnıcı (Basilica Cistern) in A.D. 532 (p 16).

Ottoman Empire (1453–1920s)

After the conquest of the city in 1453, many churches were converted into mosques. Figurative art is forbidden in Islam, so mosaics and frescoes were covered over. The Ottoman Empire,was renowned for its mosques, influenced by Seljuk, Byzantine, and Arabic design. The concept of the *külliye* (mosque complex; also a charitable foundation) flourished under Süleyman I (1494–1566), typically with the mosque in a walled courtyard, and outside a *medrese* (religious school), soup kitchens, an orphanage, travelers' lodgings, a hospital, and a *hamam* (bath). Under Süleyman I, **calligraphic art** flourished, especially the elaborate writing of Qur'ans, where Arabic script was written in highly decorative form. Later sultans developed their *tuğra,* a stylized personal monogram.

Mimar Sinan's mosques (p 9) typically had cascading domes. His Süleymaniye mosque complex (built 1550–57; p 8) is a masterpiece; a *külliye* built on one of the city's seven hills, using the vast central dome as its key feature, plus distinctive slender minarets, typically Ottoman. They usually had a vast inner space, huge central dome, plus semi-domes, vaults, and columns, creating space and serenity.

Sinan's *hamams*—best seen at Çemberlitaş Hamam (p 22) or Roxelana's baths (p 67)—also made full use of glorious domes.

Best seen in Rüstem Paşa mosque (p 9) and Sultanahmet (Blue) Mosque (p 16) are decorative, non-figurative, **tiles,** especially from the city of Iznik, usually stylized trees and flowers.

Turkish Baroque

The early 18th century marked a gradual Westernization of Ottoman art, using curves, floral patterns, and motifs best seen at the fountain of Ahmet III (1728), near Topkapı Palace's entrance. Such fountains usually had a large square block with wall fountains at the center of each facade, with the marble surfaces of the kiosk carved with floral patterns and decorated with calligraphic panels. The roof projected outward, forming large eaves to shade the walls.

Late Ottomans & the Tanzimat Declaration

Under Abdülmecit I (1823–61), the Tanzimat Declaration (1839) was a series of modernizing reforms introduced to enable the Ottoman Empire to compete with Europe. Foreign and non-Muslim artists and architects gained importance, most significantly the Armenian-born **Balyan** family—a five-generation dynasty of Ottoman imperial architects (around 1700–1894)—who built in a Western European style, changing the architectural face of the country. Their mosques moved from spiritual ambience to the ornamental, as seen at Ortaköy mosque of 1854 (p 21), combining baroque, Romantic, and Oriental architecture. Other significant Balyan creations include the Dolmabahçe (1856; p 20) and Beylerbeyı palaces (1865; p 63).

This period also saw Orientalist painters and the first "proper" professional artists. Previously, Ottoman painting was restricted to portraiture of the sultans by Renaissance painters. From the 19th century, Istanbul was visited by European diplomats and merchants, as well as painters who depicted everyday Ottoman life. The late 19th century saw the first Ottoman painters travel to Paris to study, including Osman Hamdi Bey (1842–1910) and Şeker Ahmet Paşa (1847–1907), ironically under the French Orientalist painters. They returned to Istanbul to establish the first art academies.

Turkish Republic

Art Nouveau influenced the early 20th century; Italian architect Raimondo d'Aronco created modern structures using elements of Islamic architecture. Motifs from stonework, wood, wrought iron, and glass were a statement of social standing and modernization, especially in Beyoğlu (known as Pera pre-1923), then the epitome of modern living. Today's Istiklal Caddesi (p 47) has superb facades from this era. Once Atatürk formed the Turkish republic in 1923 and shifted the capital to Ankara, modern architectural development stalled. The late 20th and early 21st centuries, however, have seen fine contemporary additions, especially Kanyon and the city's tallest skyscraper, Istanbul Sapphire.

Useful Phrases

Most people working in hotels and restaurants speak a smattering of English, but don't bank on it elsewhere. A few letters are pronounced differently in Turkish, but once you learn these you will find that the language is totally phonetic and so easy to read. If in doubt, put equal emphasis on each syllable and pronounce every letter—for example don't fall into the trap of pronouncing "ph" like an "f." The main letters to look out for are **ç** (pronounced "ch"), **ş** ("sh"), **c** ("j"), **ö** ("or," as in "work"), **ğ** (silent, just elongate the vowel following it), and **ı** ("e" as in "the"). Menu terms are in the Dining chapter (p 109).

Everyday Phrases

ENGLISH	TURKISH	PRONUNCIATION
Hello	merhaba	merhaba
How are you?	nasılsınız?	Nasiulsunuz?
Goodbye	güle güle	gul-eh gul-eh
Thank you (very much)	teşekkür (ederim)	teshekur erderim

ENGLISH	TURKISH	PRONUNCIATION
Please	lütfen	lutfen
I don't know.	bilmiyorum	bilmiyorum
Yes/No	evet/hayır	evet/hayur
How much?	Ne kadar/kaç lira?	ne kadar/kach lira?
I don't understand.	anlamıyorum	anlamuh-yorum
I can't speak Turkish.	Türkçe bilmiyorum	Turk-cheh bilmiyorum
Do you speak English?	Ingilizce biliyor musunuz?	Ingiliz-jeh biliyor musunuz?
Where is the toilet?	Tuvalet nerede?	Tuvalet neh-reh-deh?
Can you write it down?	Yazar mısınız?	Yazar musunuz?
left/right	sol/sağ	sol/saah
Ladies	bayan	bay-an
Gents	bey	bey
mosque	cami	jar-mi
museum	müze	muh-zey
church	kilise	kili-seh
OK, fine	tamam	tamam
Do you have any rooms?	Boş odanız var mı?	bosh odanuz var muh?
for one night	bir gece için	beer geh-jeh ichin
with shower	duşlu	dush-lu
Can I see the room?	Odayı görebilir miyim?	odayu gure-bilir miyim?
Do you have any . . .?	. . . var mı?	. . . var muh?
The room is . . . too hot/cold/small.	Oda . . . cok sicak/soguk/küçük	oda . . . chok suhjak/so-uk/kuchuk
The check please	Hesap lütfen	hesap lut-fen
My name is . . .	Ismim . . .	ismim . . .
I don't feel well.	Iyi hissetmiyorum	Iyi hisset-miyorum
I need a doctor (who speaks English).	(Ingilizce bilen) doktor lazım	(Ingiliz-jeh bilen) doktor laz-um
When does it . . .	Ne zaman . . .	Neh zaman . . .
. . . open?	açilir?	aji-lir?
. . . close?	kapanır?	kapan-ur?
What time is it?	Saat kaç?	Saat kach?
It's 10 o'clock.	Saat on	Saat on
It's 2:30.	Saat iki buçuk	Saat iki buchuk
At what time?	Saat kaçta?	Saat kach-ta?

Numbers

NUMBER	TURKISH	PRONUNCIATION
1	bir	beer
2	iki	iki
3	üç	uch
4	dört	durt
5	beş	besh
6	altı	alt-uh
7	yedi	yedi

NUMBER	TURKISH	PRONUNCIATION
8	sekiz	sekiz
9	dokuz	dokuz
10	on	on
11	on bir	on beer
12	on iki	on iki
20	yirmi	yirmi
21	yirmi bir	yirmi beer
30	otuz	otuz
40	kırk	kurk
50	elli	el-li
60	altmış	alt-mush
70	yetmiş	yetmish
80	seksen	seksen
90	doksan	doksan
100	yüz	yewz
200	iki yüz	iki yewz
210	iki yüz on	iki yewz on

Days of the Week

ENGLISH	TURKISH	PRONUNCIATION
Monday	pazartesi	pazartesi
Tuesday	salı	sar-luh
Wednesday	çarşamba	char-shamba
Thursday	perşembe	per-shembeh
Friday	cuma	jumah
Saturday	cumartesi	jumar-tesi
Sunday	pazar	pazar

Index

See also Accommodations and Restaurant indexes, below.

Photo **Credits**

Notes